The Negro Project:

Margaret Sanger's Diabolical, Duplicitous, Dangerous, Disastrous and Deadly Plan for Black America

by

Bruce Fleury

Foreword by Ron Edwards

DORRANCE
PUBLISHING CO
EST. 1920
PITTSBURGH, PENNSYLVANIA 15238

Dorrance Publishing Co
585 Alpha Drive
Suite 103
Pittsburgh, PA 15238
Visit our website at *www.dorrancebookstore.com*

ISBN: 978-1-4809-1862-7
eISBN: 978-1-4809-1839-9

Dedication

To all who have suffered over the decades, to all who have perished in the pursuit of the warped utopian dream of a "Heaven on Earth," to all who have been denied their most basic, fundamental, unalienable right in the name of "choice," and to generations lost to sterility, euthanasia, and abortion, I humbly and solemnly dedicate this work. You will not be forgotten.

I further dedicate these pages to those who labor so tirelessly, so selflessly, and so compassionately with no thought of reward, to end once and for all the madness that now engulfs us. You are legion, and you too will not be forgotten. May God Bless and keep you all.

Contents

Foreword

"Bruce Fleury is one of the truly great American patriots and thinkers of our time. His fearless foray into the abysmal history of eugenics and the vile, racially-motivated mission of abortion is both stunning and oh, so revealing.

Bruce's unbridled written effort to intellectually stem the tide of senseless murder of more than sixty million of our sovereign American citizens will more than challenge the racist democrat Margaret Sanger's mission to wipe out those whom she dubbed "human weeds."

I do believe this stupendous book is going to first, mightily challenge the murderous abortion industry to cease and desist. Then it will encourage America to once again promote life, liberty, and the pursuit of happiness.

Finally, we have someone with the courage and the insight to expose and confront with grace, impeccable evidence and truth, an evil, dark practice that will diminish due to the blinding light of utter reality that is so eloquently written in this most worthy of publications.

Bruce has done in one book what government schools have either refused to or been totally incapable of. His labor of love educates, stimulates, and encourages us to stand up for the God-given gift of LIFE. He totally gets that LIFE is meant for all who are conceived. Thank you, Bruce."

Ron Edwards, host of *The Edwards Notebook*,
an award-winning radio commentary,
public orator, and writer

Acknowledgments

This book is the end result of nearly a year and a half of hard work. It has been, in a word, a journey, a journey which led me into territory I never thought I would enter, a journey which left me at times angry, ashamed, and appalled at Man's inhumanity to man. But, at the same time, it has been a gratifying journey as well, as I encountered some very special people who have helped restore my faith in what Ronald Reagan once described as "the better angels of our nature."

And as with any book, this volume is the culmination of the efforts of more than just a single author, a single writer. While the research that contributed to these pages was largely my own (and there was a *lot* of it!), no less important was the input and support of so many other great Americans who believed in the importance of what I was doing. The way I look at it, these individuals were the ones who enabled me to tell a story that has rarely, if ever, been presented in this way. I can safely say that, after all is said and done, if it had not been for them, you might not be reading this right now.

And so, with grateful heart and undying thanks, it is my sincere pleasure to now acknowledge the contributions of the following individuals for making this book what it is. First, I want to thank Pastor Levon R. Yuille of the National Black Pro-Life Congress, the Bible Church in Ypsilanti, Michigan, and the host of the *Joshua's Trail* radio program. Brother Lee, your dedication and commitment to the truth has served as an inspiration to me from the day I heard your voice over the air for the first time. Your references to the Negro Project sparked me to begin this journey, and your gracious consent to an interview lent a very special something to these pages. To Ron Edwards, who wrote the foreword to *The Negro Project,* thank you for your kind words of encouragement and support. You are a great American patriot, a wonderful friend, and a dynamite interview!

To Dr. Ellis Washington, thanks for your input, as well, and thank you especially for the simple, yet great words of advice: the key to writing is to write, even if it's only one paragraph per day. To Dr. Alveda King and the Reverends Johnny L. Hunter, Walter B. Hoye, and Jesse Lee Peterson, thanks so much to each of you for giving of your time so freely and graciously. Your input and observations are appreciated far more than you will ever know, and I felt, after talking to each of you, that I had made a new friend as a result. To Brian Beleski, the producer of the *Joshua's Trail* broadcast, thank you for the support and encouragement you showed me from the moment I announced my intention to write this book. You're a great American and one of my biggest boosters. I'll never forget it, I can assure you.

And I would be completely remiss if I did not mention the support and encouragement of two other great Americans, Milt Harris and Charles McCollough, who have faithfully assisted Pastor Yuille each Saturday morning on the *Joshua's Trail* radio broadcast.

I would also like to thank my brother, John Fleury, for serving as my proofreader on this project. His keen eye has saved me on more than one occasion from the effects of what I call "fat finger syndrome." Thanks so much, Jack. And finally, last but most certainly not least, I want to thank my beautiful wife, Janette, for being so patient with me during the course of this project. I couldn't have done any of this without her love, patience, and support.

Bruce Fleury

Introduction

This book seeks to tell a story that is in many ways lost to history and which affects the lives of a specific racial demographic group, namely Americans of black descent. It is a story of evil and ugly prejudice, and it examines the unholy alliance that was forged between the American eugenicist Margaret Sanger and a handful of duplicitous black people from all walks of life, but particularly those ministers who became unwitting dupes in one of the most monstrous plots ever conceived.

In the following pages, we will examine the alliance between the founder of the organization we know today as Planned Parenthood and these individuals, an alliance that was called the Negro Project, the purpose of which was nothing less than the *self-imposed* extermination of an entire group of Americans based on one reason and one reason alone: the color of their skin, a scheme which would take place with the unwitting participation of those who, in the case of these "men of the cloth," held such sway and influence over their own flocks.

To be honest, I had never heard of the Negro Project. Like most Americans, I knew something about Margaret Sanger, for example, that she was the founder of the modern birth-control movement and the founder of Planned Parenthood. However, it was not until I began to listen to a weekly radio show called *Joshua's Trail* that I became aware of just what this scheme was and what it involved. Pastor Levon R. Yuille, the host of the show, and his colleagues Ron Edwards, Charles McCollough, Milt Harris, and Ellis Washington, would refer quite often to this enterprise and its deliberate attempt to rid the world of blacks and other minorities. Sanger herself referred to them as "human weeds" that were in need of eradication lest their progeny continue to hold back what she would call human "progress." It was at this point that

I decided to look into the matter for myself. What I found was disturbing to say the least, and I soon discovered why she harbored such ideas.

Not only was Sanger the founder of the birth-control movement and of Planned Parenthood, the nation's largest abortion provider. This was bad enough in itself, but as I looked more closely into her life, I discovered something that was far more unsettling. Sanger was out-and-out racist and religious bigot who was also deeply involved in the eugenics movement of the early to mid-twentieth century. But that's not all I discovered. Her work in eugenics, or attempts to improve the human race through "selective breeding," led her to categorize the disabled (either physically or mentally), members of other races or cultures, or any other negative aspect she could attribute to them, as being somehow "unfit" to continue to live. And, where black Americans were concerned, her Negro Project would be the vehicle by which this eradication would be carried out.

Moreover, Margaret Sanger did not act alone. She had plenty of help with her scheme and legions of followers to help her bring it off, as the reader will soon discover. And her ideas were not unique to this country. Rather, they were readily accepted and became official state policy in nations like Germany, where Hitler's race-obsessed *Reichsfuhrer-SS* Heinrich Himmler referred to those who did not fit in either racially or genetically as "useless eaters." Sanger's theories on eugenics had a direct connection to Nazi atrocities like the infamous *Aktion T-4* forced euthanasia program and, eventually, the Holocaust.

Among the chapters included herein are a short biography of Margaret Sanger herself and a brief history of the American eugenics movement, along with its effects beyond these shores. We will also go to the heart of the most urgent moral and social issue facing America today, the fact that more than one-third of the 1.5 million abortions that take place here annually are performed on black women, and that Planned Parenthood, which claims to be a "women's health" organization, is actually the nation's largest abortion provider, performing more than 300,000 of these procedures a year, overwhelmingly at the expense of the American taxpayer. And to top it off, we will see how and why this group places the great majority of its "clinics" in America's black inner cities, an occurrence that can by no means be called a coincidence.

Sanger herself had stated publicly that she was opposed to abortion, but when the group she founded, the American Birth Control League, became the Planned Parenthood Federation of America, abortion became and remains to this day the vehicle of choice in achieving its founder's dream of ridding the world or what she called "human weeds." In light of this, we will leave it to the reader to judge the sincerity of her public statements on this subject.

As we go along, we will examine some of the useful idiots and willing adherents from the pulpits to academia to the popular culture who to this day have carried on the evil work of a woman who arguably did more than anyone other than Dr. Alfred Kinsey to damage the social fabric of this great nation in the twentieth century. And we will also see how her ideas are an integral part of the United Nations' *Agenda 21,* a world-wide power-grab masquerading as something called "sustainable development."

Nevertheless, through it all, there is hope. This book will also delve into the courageous efforts of pro-life advocates across the nation in bringing to light the almost completely-forgotten horrors of the Negro Project, as well as their dire warnings of the extinction-level event that will befall black America if the eugenicists and their fellow-travelers in the "pro-choice" movement ever come to hold complete sway. Finally, we will learn how individual, everyday Americans can make a difference in bringing an end to this madness, once and for all.

The Negro Project: Margaret Sanger's Diabolical, Duplicitous, Dangerous, Disastrous, and Deadly Plan for Black America is not a book for the faint of heart. It is not meant to be. It covers a touchy and uncomfortable subject that demands recognition and resolution from a reluctant nation too often distracted by everyday concerns. So be it. As America's Founding Fathers stated in the *Declaration of Independence,* "let facts be submitted to a candid world" to bolster the case that is about to be made herein.

The great philosopher George Santayana reminds us that those who forget their history "are doomed to repeat it." And so, let us here and now remember this sordid and evil event, the Negro Project. Let us revisit it, bring it into the cold, harsh light of truth, and learn from it so that nothing like it ever happens again, to anyone. For no one, regardless of race, economic or social standing, or physical or mental condition, deserves what befell our black brothers and sisters under this evil endeavor. This is how, this is why, the book you are about to read came to be.

Chapter 1:

A Short Biography of Margaret Sanger

> *"We should hire three or four colored ministers, preferably with social service backgrounds, and with engaging personalities. The most successful educational approach to the Negro is through a religious appeal. We don't want the word to go out that we want to exterminate the Negro population, and the minister is the man who can straighten out that idea if it ever occurs to any of their more rebellious members."* — Margaret Sanger to Clarence J. Gamble, December 10, 1939

In order to comprehend what brought such a monstrous undertaking as the Negro Project about, it is important for us first to understand Margaret Sanger herself. Just as important to this understanding are the people, events, and circumstances that surrounded her upbringing and which influenced her work in women's health, "family planning," and, later on, in eugenics. Only then can we begin to get an idea of what drove this woman to ultimately advocate the nightmarish agenda she embraced, one that caused such human suffering and misery, and one that had such far-reaching consequences for humanity.

The woman who in later years would establish Planned Parenthood, Margaret Sanger was born Margaret Higgins on September 18, 1879, in Corning, New York, one of 11 children of Anne Purcell Higgins and Michael Hennessy Higgins. The family could have been much larger, but Sanger's mother lost eight other children over a 22-year period, eventually succumbing to cervical cancer and tuberculosis at the age of 49. Margaret's father was an Irish immigrant who came to America when he was 14 to escape the potato famine that was then ravaging his native land. He arrived in the U.S. in time to take up arms in the Civil War, though he had to wait a year to enlist in the Army, where he served as a drummer in the 12th New York Volunteer Cavalry.

According to *Wikipedia's* online article on Sanger, Michael studied medicine and phrenology after leaving the Army, but opted instead to become a stonecutter, "making stone angels, saints, and tombstones." [1] This may have been influenced by the fact that he was a devout Catholic who later became an atheist and activist for women's suffrage and free public education.

The sixth of eleven surviving children in the Higgins family, the young Margaret spent much of her time as most girls of her day did, assisting with chores and looking after her younger brothers and sisters. When the time came for Margaret to go away to college in 1897, her sisters paid her two-year tuition to Claverack College, a boarding school in Claverack, New York, where she remained until 1899, when her father asked her to come home to help nurse her mother, who was by then dying of cancer and TB. Her mother's death that year evidently influenced Margaret's decision to seek a career in nursing, a vocation that was aided by the mother of one of her friends at Claverack, who arranged for Margaret to enroll in a nursing program at a hospital in White Plains. Upon graduation, she began her nursing career and met and later married her first husband, architect William Sanger.

The two were wed in 1902 and although they became estranged in 1913, the divorce wasn't finalized for another eight years. The couple settled in the town of Hastings-on-Hudson, where they lived until a fire destroyed their home in 1912, prompting them to move to New York City, where Margaret went to work as a nurse in the slums on the east side of Manhattan. The move would have lasting and far-reaching consequences for both Margaret and William, bringing them into contact with the *avant-garde* culture then flourishing in Greenwich Village, whose denizens were a veritable "who's who" of radical thought and social activism, and included advocates of "free love" and libertine behavior such as John Reed, Upton Sinclair, and Emma Goldman, who would become leaders of the Communist Party USA.

Margaret's work in nursing led her to observe the woeful conditions of women's health, a situation made worse by the absence of reliable information on the subject, and she set out trying to find it in the city's public libraries in an effort to help women who were suffering and/or dying from the effects of frequent childbirth and self-induced abortions. However, due to the prevailing social and political climate of the time, this effort came to naught. First, the Comstock Law made it a federal offense to distribute information on birth control; second, the existing religious and social morals of the time were not exactly conducive to such efforts; and third, people just didn't discuss such issues.

Frustrated by this, Sanger decided to publish a number of pamphlets on her own, titled *What Every Mother Should Know* and *What Every Girl Should Know*, which first appeared in the pages of the Socialist magazine *The New York Call* in 1910 and 1911. The pieces were often frank and graphic, and they caused more than a little consternation among many of the publication's readers, some of whom cancelled their subscriptions to the *Call.* Others lauded the articles for their "candor" regarding this delicate subject.

Sanger's writings on family planning and later on in eugenics were influenced to a large degree by her own life experience. After all, she had come from a large family, she had seen her mother lose nearly as many children as she had borne, and she had watched her die of two horrible diseases, cancer and tuberculosis. She had become convinced that coming from a family of 11 children and an additional eight failed pregnancies had contributed directly to her mother's demise. As she wrote in her autobiography *My Fight for Birth Control,* "I associated poverty, toil, unemployment, drunkenness, cruelty, quarreling, fighting, debts, jails with large families." [2]

Margaret herself nearly died when her first child, Grant, was born in 1905. The events that surrounded his birth were not pleasant. First, she had to retreat to the Adirondack Mountains to strengthen herself for what was to come. For another, for all the rest and preparation, Grant's birth was no picnic; Sanger described the experience as "agonizing," an exercise in "mental torture" and "a factor to be reckoned with." However, mother and child survived the ordeal and Sanger bore another son, Stuart, and a daughter, Peggy, a few years later. Grant and Stuart both lived to adulthood, but Peggy died in 1915 at age five. It isn't hard to surmise that her experience with childbirth, her nursing work, her frustration in not obtaining the information she sought, and the fact that Sanger came from a large family were all factors that shaped her worldview going forward.

And go forward she did, in a big way. Over the next decade Sanger continued to publish and distribute both *What Every Mother Should Know* and *What Every Girl Should Know*, and in 1914 she launched *The Woman Rebel,* an eight-page newsletter aimed at promoting birth control. Using the slogan "No Gods, no masters" [3] *The Woman Rebel*'s main purpose was to promote birth control, but there was another, larger goal: to provoke a challenge to anti-obscenity statutes such as the Comstock Act, which made it a crime under federal law to disseminate information on contraception. It is not a stretch to come to the conclusion that she had reached the end of her rope and now felt that the time had come to force the issue. To her, it had become a matter of free speech, thus the pending confrontation in the courts. Sanger had also planned to write a book on birth control, and since the law prohibited her from getting information here, she began looking elsewhere for it, eventually getting most of it from England.

This information was published in her pamphlet titled *Family Limitation*, and it was a direct violation of the Comstock Act. Named for anti-obscenity crusader Anthony Comstock as a response to the widespread availability of pornography that had taken place in the Civil War, the Comstock Act was passed into law by Congress on March 3, 1873. Under this act it was unlawful for anyone to "sell or shall offer to sell, or to lend, or to give away, or in any manner to exhibit, or shall otherwise publish or offer to publish in any manner, or shall have in his possession for any such purpose or purposes, an obscene book, pamphlet, paper, writing, advertisement, circular, print, picture, drawing or other representation, figure, or image on or of paper or other material or any cast instrument, or other article of an immoral nature."

Further, the Act stipulated that it was illegal for anyone to use "any drug or medicine, or any article whatever, for the prevention of conception, or for causing unlawful abortion, or shall advertise the same for sale, or shall write or print, or cause to be written or printed, any card, circular, book, pamphlet, advertisement, or notice of any kind stating when, where, how, or whom, or by what means, any articles in this section...can be purchased or obtained, or shall manufacture, draw, or print, or in any wise make any of such articles, shall be deemed guilty of a misdemeanor, and on conviction thereof in any court of the United States...he shall be imprisoned at hard labor in the penitentiary for not less than six months nor more than five years for each offense, or fined not less than one hundred dollars nor more than two thousand dollars, with cost of court."

Given these restrictions and Sanger's outspoken advocacy for birth control, it was inevitable that matters should come to a head, and so it was in August of 1914 she was indicted on three counts of violating obscenity laws and a fourth of "inciting murder and assassination," the incitement charge being based on an article which appeared in *The Woman Rebel*. Fearful that a court trial would focus on the incitement charge and deny her a platform to espouse her views on birth control, she left the United States for England, taking up the pseudonym "Bertha Watson" in order to keep from being arrested. It would be an enlightening and profound experience, in more ways than one.

While in England, Sanger came into contact with several prominent Britons who advocated the practice of eugenics, such as author H.G. Wells (with whom she became romantically involved during her estrangement from her first husband), playwright George Bernard Shaw, and economist John Maynard Keynes. She also traveled the Continent, and while visiting a Dutch birth control clinic in 1915 she learned about diaphragms, which she became convinced were more effective than the douches and suppositories she had been handing out to women back home. These devices were illegal under the Comstock Law and were thus next to impossible to obtain. When she returned home later that year, she and others began to import them into the country in direct violation of U.S. law.

While she was in Europe, things began to change after William was arrested for giving a copy of *Family Limitation* to an undercover postal worker, an offense that carried a term of 30 days behind bars. An open letter on Margaret and William's behalf written by Upton Sinclair appeared in the Socialist newsletter *The Masses*. It garnered them enough support for her to feel comfortable returning to the U.S. in October. The noted attorney and agnostic, Clarence Darrow, offered to take her case *pro bono,* but the government, bowing to public pressure, dropped the charges altogether in early 1916.

Through it all, Sanger continued publishing her birth-control and "family planning" tracts and, by 1915, had issued her first handbook for adolescents, titled *What Every Boy and Girl Should Know.* A companion to her other pamphlets *What Every Mother Should Know* and *What Every Girl Should Know*, this publication focused on eugenics and population control, as borne out in this passage: "It is a vicious cycle; ignorance breeds poverty and poverty breeds ignorance. There is only one cure for both, and that is to stop breeding these things. Stop bringing to birth children whose inheritance cannot be one of health or intelligence. Stop bringing into the world children whose parents cannot provide for them." [4]

By 1916, Sanger had begun to crisscross the country, giving lectures on the subject of contraception and "family planning," in which she laid out a number of conditions of life that, in her view, mandated the use of birth control, including "when parents, though normal, have subnormal children," "when husband or wife are adolescent," and "when the earning capacity of the father was inadequate." [5] These statements harked back to the first birth-control pamphlets that had aroused such ire in some of the subscribers to *The New York Call.* But Sanger remained undeterred by the public criticism her speeches engendered, lamenting that "anyone, no matter how ignorant, how diseased mentally or physically, how lacking in knowledge of all children, seemed to consider he or she had the right to become a parent." [6]

To Sanger, this attitude was clearly the core issue. Too many children were being born to parents who could not support them. Too many were being sired who were sickly or mentally defective. Too many came into the world whose parents were little more than children themselves. And from her own experience, large families such as the one from which she came, were simply the cause of so much of the world's evils and misfortunes.

Sanger's continued advocacy for the cause was bound to get her into more scrapes with the authorities, and it did after she opened a family planning and birth control clinic in a Brooklyn neighborhood in October of 1916. She was arrested nine days later and was charged with breaking a New York State law that banned distribution of contraceptives.

When she went on trial the following January, she was convicted of the charge, the judge ruling that women did not "have the right to copulate with a feeling of security that there will be no resulting conception."

But the court was not altogether averse to being magnanimous. Sanger was offered a more lenient sentence on condition that she promise not to break the law in the future. But she was, for her part, defiant, telling the court, "I cannot support the law as it exists today." This statement earned her a sentence of 30 days in a workhouse, a decision she decided to appeal. The plea was initially turned down, but she earned a measure of vindication in 1918 when Judge Frederick Crane of the New York Court of Appeals issued a ruling allowing doctors to prescribe contraceptives to their patients. The publicity surrounding Sanger's arrest, trial, and appeal earned her additional sympathy and support, and encouraged birth control advocates around the country to get behind her. But more significantly, it also resulted in badly-needed financial backing from several wealthy donors, who agreed to bankroll her future activities.

One such donor was John D. Rockefeller, Jr. The son of the oil billionaire gave large sums of money to Sanger's causes beginning in the 1920s and continuing on more or less surreptitiously through the next several decades. Sanger had, by the end of World War I, abandoned the radical approach as her goals had begun to be realized through the courts, which had ruled that doctors could prescribe birth control information, as long as it was done for medical reasons. In 1921 Sanger established the American Birth Control League (ABCL) to increase her donor base and, whereas her efforts were previously aimed at women on the lower end of the income scale, they would now include those in the middle class as well. In 1917, she started *The Birth Control Review,* a periodical which examined contraceptive issues for the next 23 years until ceasing publication in 1940.

In 1923, Sanger opened the Clinical Research Bureau (CRB), the nation's first legal birth-control clinic, to take advantage of the medical exemption to the laws prohibiting the distribution of contraceptive information to women. It was also the first clinic to be staffed entirely by female doctors and social workers. That same year and again in 1924, Rockefeller contributed a sum of $5,000 to her American Birth Control League, gifts that were kept quiet so as not to arouse the opposition of the Catholic Church.

These amounts were donated anonymously because the Rockefeller family was Catholic, and any support of contraception on its part could prove problematic if not damaging or fatal to its members' political aspirations. One member of the family who could have been adversely affected by such a disclosure was future New York Governor Nelson D. Rockefeller, who had set his sights unsuccessfully on the White House in 1964, and who had served as Gerald Ford's Vice President after Richard Nixon was forced to resign the Presidency in disgrace in 1974 in the wake of the Watergate scandal.

The financial support that Sanger enjoyed from the Rockefellers and other well-heeled donors allowed her to make several trips to the Far East, visits than included stops in China, Korea, and Japan beginning in 1922.

While in China, she discovered that the primary method of "family planning" was to kill the female child (a chilling foreshadowing of the genocide to come under that country's infamous "one child" policy, in which the female child is almost always aborted as opposed to the male, who rarely, if ever, is). And, on a subsequent visit, she worked with novelist Pearl S. Buck (author of *The Good Earth*) in establishing a birth-control clinic in Shanghai. Sanger visited Japan frequently during the decade, as well, traveling there on no less than six occasions to promote the cause of birth control and "family planning."

Now, Sanger did not spend all of the 1920s as a globe-trotting advocate for birth control. During her time back in the States, she continued working with the ABCL and the CRB, publishing her birth-control pamphlets and handbooks and lecturing around the country to any group that would provide her a platform to promote her cause. These talks would sometimes place her in front of some rather interesting groups, to say the least, and ones that, to put it mildly, could arouse some curiosity if not outright suspicion as to just what exactly her motives might involve. One such occasion arose in 1926 when she agreed to address the Ladies' Auxiliary of the Ku Klux Klan, and it wasn't in some sleepy backwater town in the racist South; rather, it was virtually in her own backyard, namely, the little community of Silver Lake, New Jersey. By her own account, it was not exactly a run-of-the-mill experience.

According to the second edition of Sanger's autobiography, which was published in 1938, the address she gave was "one of the weirdest experiences I ever had in lecturing," and that she had "had to use only the most elementary terms, as though I were trying to make children understand." [7] One cannot help but marvel at her choice of audience in this case. The fact that she was speaking to the wives and daughters of the members of the most notorious white supremacist organization in the country didn't seem to cause her even the most momentary of concerns. The audience evidently liked what it heard that night; indeed, her remarks were so well-received, she later wrote, that "several more invitations to similar groups were proffered." [8]

At this point, it would be useful to ask a few basic questions, such as: 1) How could she not have been aware of the mission of the Klan prior to addressing its New Jersey Ladies' Auxiliary? 2) Did not the fact that the Klan was infamous for the atrocities it was committing against blacks, Jews, and Catholics throughout America (routinely assaulting, beating, raping, and even lynching blacks in the Deep South in particular) mean anything to her at all? 3) Given that some of her most ardent supporters included prominent blacks like W.E.B. Du Bois and James Hubert, how could she have had anything to do with such a vile and despicable group? And 4) Given that she would eventually be the driving force behind the Negro Project in the future, was she actually signaling her solidarity with the goals and agenda of those gathered in New Jersey on that occasion? These are questions, hard questions that cry out for answers that Sanger's supporters, to this day, have not yet given to anyone's satisfaction. Only time will tell whether they ever will. Surprisingly, Sanger enjoyed widespread support in the black community. In 1930, she opened a clinic in Harlem at Hubert's suggestion with backing from the Julius Rosenwald Fund.

Sanger's clinic opened four years after her remarks at the New Jersey Klan function and was staffed by black doctors, nurses, and social workers. It received the *imprimatur* of none other than Du Bois himself, and before long it seemed that everyone was getting in on the act, as even the black churches and press dutifully did their part. Nevertheless, how would they have reacted had they known that this woman had lectured to the very group that was dedicated to their destruction? Or, did they even know this at all?

In 1928, Sanger resigned from the American Birth Control League, which she had founded, and took undisputed leadership of the Clinical Research Bureau, which she had also started, changing its name to the Birth Control Clinical Research Bureau (BCCRB). She also continued to write, lecture, and lobby in favor of birth control and "family planning."

Three more books appeared in print during the decade, *Woman and the New Race, The Pivot of Civilization,* and *Motherhood in Bondage.* Brisk sales of these books helped convince her that the tide was turning, so Sanger took the next step in her crusade and formed the National Committee on Federal Legislation on Birth Control (NCFLBC) in 1929. As the name implied, the goal of the Committee was to lobby for legislation to overturn laws banning birth control (e.g., the Comstock Law), but its efforts failed to bear fruit, so in 1932 Sanger, hoping to bring about a decisive battle in the courts, ordered a diaphragm from Japan, which was then confiscated by the U.S. government. Although she had to wait until 1936 to have her day in court, this strategy ultimately proved successful when a key portion of the Comstock Law, prohibiting doctors from prescribing birth control to their patients, was overturned. This was followed by a decision in 1937 by the American Medical Association to recognize contraception as a normal medical service and to begin teaching it to medical school students on a regular basis.

Flushed with victory, Sanger decided that it was now time for a change in scenery and moved to Arizona in 1936, settling in Tucson with her second husband, James Noah H. Slee, whom she had married in 1922 after divorcing her first husband, William, in 1921. This union would last until 1943. Although she had achieved pretty much all that she had set out to do and had intended to take more of a low profile in the birth control movement, this proved to be more difficult than she thought, and her involvement would, subsequently, last another several years, well into the decade of the 1950s.

In 1937, a year after she and James had relocated to Arizona, Sanger assumed the presidency of a new group, the Birth Control Council of America, which had come into conflict with the BCCRB. She found herself called upon to intervene in the dispute and was able to get the feuding parties to resolve their differences. This led to a merger of the BCCB and the BCCRB in 1939, the new organization calling itself the Birth Control Federation of America (BCFA), with Sanger serving as President.

This new title amounted more to a figurehead position than one with any real power, and this was reflected by the group's decision in 1942 to change its name to Planned Parenthood Federation of America. Sanger had objected to the change because she felt it was, in her words, "too euphemistic." Her name, however, still carried a great deal of clout, and she would remain active in the movement for several more years. By the end of World War II, Sanger took her crusade overseas, organizing the International Committee on Planned Parenthood in 1946. In 1952 it became the International Planned Parenthood Federation, with Sanger serving as President until she departed in 1959 at the age of 80.

During her remaining years, Sanger continued her advocacy on behalf of birth control and "family planning." She continued to be the beneficiary of large contributions from donors like the Rockefeller family and philanthropists like Katherine Dexter McCormick to further the work of Planned Parenthood and other groups promoting contraception. It would be several more years before her organization would take the fateful final step and embark on an all-out campaign to legalize abortion on demand across the entire country. In the meantime, Sanger had prevailed on McCormick to provide financial support for the development of an oral chemical form of birth control that we know today as "the pill," which was created by biologist Gregory Pincus.

The Planned Parenthood founder continued to benefit in her later years from the legal decisions that were rendered striking down the existing prohibitions against birth control. In 1965, a year before she died of congestive heart failure in Tucson, the U.S. Supreme Court issued a ruling in the landmark case of *Griswold v. Connecticut.* In this case, the Court struck down one of the final remaining Comstock Laws in Connecticut and Massachusetts, but this only applied to those who were not married. It wasn't until 1972, in *Eisenstadt v. Baird,* that the Court finally struck the provision down altogether when it extended the *Griswold* decision to married couples. [9]

By the 1960s, it was becoming clear that American society had begun to change dramatically and was becoming more liberal in its attitudes and morals than at any other time in our history, including the "Roaring '20s. Entire institutions, from the American military to the university, the popular culture and probably most critically the nuclear family, were being questioned as never before. And the sexual taboos that once were in force were not immune to this seismic shift, falling one after another like dominos before a seemingly non-stop tide of self-gratification and hedonistic behavior. The changes that were part of a sweeping "progressive" social agenda would, over time, have lasting and far-reaching consequences, and most of them weren't good. And, though it wasn't at all apparent to most at the time, black Americans paid a particularly heavy price.

For example, the "welfare reform" that had been enacted as part of Lyndon Johnson's Great Society Program in 1965 had an especially deleterious effect on poor families, and the hardest hit was the black family. This is a situation that continues to this day, with seemingly no end in sight. According to two distinguished black economists, Thomas Sowell and Walter Williams, during the decades leading up to the '60s, blacks had been making tremendous strides in almost every aspect of American life with the exception of the segregated South (and even there the days of "separate but equal" and Jim Crow were clearly numbered). Sowell and Williams both point out that up to and through the '50s, blacks were faring better in many ways than whites. Black families were stronger and more intact, with more of them attending church services, than whites. Black Americans enjoyed higher high school graduation rates than whites, crime rates were lower among black Americans, and probably most important, there were fewer black children being born out of wedlock during that time. Both men point out that much, if not all, of this was due to a strong male presence in the black home. And they point to LBJ's Great Society as the main reason all this began to change, and not for the better.

Since the new guidelines in effect expelled the father from the home, entire families were now ripped asunder. The stabilizing effect of having the father at home was (and remains) critical to strong families and the inculcation of solid values in children. Simply put, by any statistical or other analysis, kids do far better in stable, intact homes where both mother and father are present. The presence of strong fathers is *particularly* essential to the success of any family, especially the black family in America.

However, that was now gone under the new system. Instead of a paycheck that the father would go out and earn once a week or twice a month, families were now receiving a monthly government stipend. The ill effects of this were many. For one thing, it began to foster an atmosphere of entitlement and dependency where once before people worked hard to earn their keep and appreciated the value of getting up every day and going to a productive job.

For another, where once before the kids learned the value of hard work and all the benefits that were involved from seeing Dad getting out and working, they now began to learn that it was easier to be handed something which they did not have to earn. This lesson was both a powerful and, as time marched on, a devastating one. Instead of helping those most in need of economic aid, government policy now perpetuated a vicious cycle where dependency was fast becoming an acceptable way of life for more and more Americans.

It is revealing to note that study after study on social policy conducted over the years has shown that the highest percentage of those who have been adversely affected have been black Americans, in particular the black family. Williams and Sowell are not alone in their assessments. Social scientists like Charles Murray and politicians like the late Daniel Patrick Moynihan (D-NY) saw the disastrous effects of the cycle of dependency that the new welfare state and the loosening of societal morals were beginning to have, in particular among black Americans, and they warned that such a cycle directly threatened to destroy the progress that blacks were making, often, as in the case of the Civil Rights movement, at the cost of their very lives.

Sowell and Williams have pointed out that, up until the mid-1960s, the black family unit was stronger and more intact in many ways than in other segments of society. Again, black Americans went to church far more faithfully than did whites; black students stayed in and graduated from high school at a higher rate than whites; fewer illegitimate births took place in the black community than among white Americans; and black Americans benefited from a much lower crime rate, including violent crime, than their counterparts in other segments of society. Nonetheless, all of that began to change with LBJ's War on Poverty, Model Cities Program, and other components of the so-called "Great Society."

And probably most important, since the father was now absent, this helped trigger an unprecedented explosion in single-parent households, ones that were headed largely by the mother with no strong, committed male presence. Indeed, during the 1960s, the very idea of fatherhood itself took a hit with the rise of feminism and its assertion that women didn't need men in their lives, and they especially didn't need a husband in the home to raise a family. Gloria Steinhem boiled this attitude down to its essence with her now-infamous contention that "a woman needs a man like a fish needs a bicycle." But the feminists weren't alone in this; the popular culture played a devastating role, as well.

For example, popular 1950s television shows such as *Leave It to Beaver, The Donna Reed Show, Father Knows Best* and *The Ozzie and Harriet Show* that emphasized strong two-parent families headed by a productive, loving father, now were being ridiculed as "out of date," "old-fashioned" or "unrealistic" depictions of an America that never really existed in the first place. In the early '60s, programs like *Make Room for Daddy* and *The Dick van Dyke Show* continued the same theme and were joined by sitcoms like *The Andy Griffith Show, Bachelor Father* and *My Three Sons,* and westerns like *Bonanza*, which centered around fathers who had been widowed, not who sired their sons outside of marriage. But as time marched on, they were eventually replaced by shows like *Married...* *.with Children,* programs that ridiculed Dad as buffoonish or even downright incompetent in dealing with his wife and children. Even worse, by the first decade of the twenty-first century, programs like *Modern Family* have openly glorified same-sex parenting, equating it with traditional child-rearing with two homosexual men raising a young girl in the *same household* as the rest of its straight characters.

The behavior of Hollywood celebrities whose "anything goes" attitude involving drug usage, promiscuity, and a host of other social ills began to emerge during the 1960s, with a crippling and corrosive effect on American culture. To be sure, such things had been going on in "Tinsel Town" for decades, but they were largely kept from public view and were certainly not championed or trumpeted. However, that too began to change with the onset of the "Woodstock generation," named for the infamous display of casual sex, drug usage and general hedonism that took place in New York State in 1969 disguised as a rock 'n roll festival.

Academia played a huge part as well in the destruction of the nuclear family in the 1960s. The decade saw the rise of "women's studies" programs on campus after campus that de-emphasized the traditional male role in the family and often taught that the man had *no* part to play whatsoever in any kind of male-female relationship, save as a sperm donor. Incredibly, some academics even cast the male as not merely the villain, but as a mindless sexual predator. Even today, 50 years later, we look aghast as feminist leaders on college campuses across the country stage so-called "take back the night" demonstrations against a perceived "epidemic" of sexual assaults on female students, even though no credible evidence of such an "epidemic" exists. Even more appallingly, we see increasing instances of male students on campuses from UC-Berkley to the University of Michigan to Columbia being hauled before kangaroo student "courts" on charges of sexual harassment to rape, all too often without any of the due process rights defendants in the criminal justice system are granted, little legal niceties such as presumption of innocence until proven guilty, facing one's accuser in open court, or examination of the evidence presented by the accuser.

All of these factors have greatly and adversely affected American society in ways that seemed almost unimaginable when they first occurred, and the toll they have taken has been nothing short of devastating to the black family in America today. Once one of the strongest threads in the American social fabric, it has now been stretched almost to the breaking point. Consider these facts for a moment. Drug abuse is rampant among black Americans; the high school dropout rate among black Americans is at its highest point in our history; the out-of-wedlock birthrate for black women now stands at a staggering 74%; the rate of violent crime is higher among blacks than any other segment of the population (including black-on-black crime), so more of them are in prison than ever; blacks suffer a higher rate of poverty than other Americans; the number of single-parent households that are headed by a black female is at its highest point in our history, and most importantly, the abortion rate is higher among black women than any other segment of society, with fully *one-third* of all such procedures being performed on black women. If this can happen to them, what guarantees do we have that we will not be next?

The answer, of course, is none, none whatsoever. The changes wrought over the past fifty years can hardly be described as beneficial in any way where blacks are concerned. In fact, under the programs that were enacted under LBJ and expanded under succeeding presidents from both political parties, it can be argued that black Americans, whose ancestors fought and died in the heroic struggle to abolish slavery and later to secure their civil rights, have, in effect, been returned to a new kind of plantation. This one, however, has social engineers such as Sanger as the new overseers with the willing participation of so-called black "leaders" like the "Reverends" Jesse Jackson, Al Sharpton, and many more who are running interference for them. In fact, Sanger had exactly such preachers in mind when she conceived the Negro Project in 1939, writing to Clarence J. Gamble that "we don't want the word to go out that we want to exterminate the Negro population. The most successful educational approach to the Negro is through a religious appeal, and the minister is the man who can straighten out that idea if it ever occurs to any of their more rebellious members." While Sanger's supporters claim that the goal of the Negro Project was humanitarian in nature and that her statement has been distorted by her detractors, the fact that she regarded those she deemed inferior as "human weeds" in need of eradication renders this claim highly suspect, to say the least.

Also, in using the word "rebellious" to describe some members of the targeted black congregations, it could be argued that Sanger was engaging in the racist view that they didn't "know their place" or were somehow being "uppity" at questioning her motives. Sanger had always considered light-skinned races superior to those with dark skins, so it is quite possible that her decision to staff her Harlem clinic entirely with minorities was made to provide cover against anyone who just might ask some rather uncomfortable and inconvenient questions. Again, what would her black supporters have said had they known that she addressed the Klan's New Jersey Ladies' Auxiliary in Silver Lake in 1926? But Sanger wasn't alone in her views regarding minorities. Not by a long shot.

Her American Birth Control League was a repository for racist views espoused by people like Dr. S. Adolphus Knopf, Lothrop Stoddard, and Dr. Harry Laughlin. These men were avowed racists of whose views Sanger could not have been unaware. Knopf, for example, addressed an international birth control conference in New York in 1925, a full year before Sanger spoke to the New Jersey Klan, issuing a warning against the "menace" posed by "the black and yellow peril." [10] Stoddard was a graduate of Harvard who wrote the book *The Rising Tide of Color against White World Supremacy.*

He was a fervid proponent of eugenics who believed that the Nazis' efforts in that field were not only "scientific, but "humanitarian" as well. [11] Laughlin, a member of the ABCL Board, believed that America's breeding stock was in dire need of "purification" and that it must be purged of what he called its "bad strains." In his view, these "bad strains" were typical not only of blacks and other minorities, but "the shiftless, ignorant, and worthless class of anti-social whites in the South" as well. [12] Now, unless Sanger was completely clueless in this matter, how could she not have been aware of the views of such people?

The obvious answer, in light of some of her own writings on the subject, is that she was not clueless; indeed, she was "all in," to use the current phraseology, on the subject of eugenics. As previously noted, during her time in exile in England, she had kept company with many prominent supporters of the practice. This could not have helped but reinforce her notions of "selective breeding." She had stated that sterilizing those she saw as being "unfit" would be the "salvation of American civilization," [13] and she doubled down on this theme by publishing a number of articles on eugenics during the decade of the 1920s, which included *Some Moral Aspects of Eugenics* (June 1920), *The Eugenic Conscience* (February 1921), *The Purpose of Eugenics* (December 1924), *Birth Control and Positive Eugenics* (July 1925), and *Birth Control: The True Eugenics* (August 1928). Eugenics was a major theme of Sanger's *Birth Control Review,* which first appeared in 1917, shortly after she had returned from England.

While race played a key role in her view of eugenics, it cannot be denied that religion was a determining factor as well, especially where the Catholic Church and its longtime opposition to birth control were concerned. Recall that Sanger's own father was a devout Catholic who later became an atheist, so it could be argued that his experience influenced her later views on religion. By the time she had come to embrace the practice of eugenics, she had become so anti-religious that she characterized those who opposed her and others like her on the basis of their faith as "irresponsible and reckless" for daring to have large families. She denigrated those "whose religious scruples prevent them from exercising control over their numbers," and further stated that "there is no doubt in the minds of most thinking people that the procreation of this group should be stopped." [14]

Once again, the race factor enters into the equation, the congregations of black churchgoers in particular. Keep in mind that for more than 300 years of our history, blacks had been held in the unspeakable bondage of the institution of slavery. They had been forcibly taken from their homes in Africa to become the property of others and were stripped of even the most basic human dignity. However, under the most savage conditions one can imagine, they were able to take solace in one thing: their religion. Their faith in God and their belief that one day they would overcome their brutal lot at once sustained them and strengthened their resolve that they would ultimately gain their freedom.

And when that happy day arrived and the bonds of their wretched condition were finally loosed, their faith in God became that much stronger and more unshakable. As we have seen thus far, black Americans are among the most ardent and passionate practitioners of their faith, with the strongest attendance at weekly church services of any demographic group.

As a result of this, black Americans were historically considered to be strong social conservatives, and many who do so today cite their religious faith as a key reason for this. And, many blacks had large families precisely because of their faith in God. This was unconscionable to Sanger and her fellow eugenicists, and it put blacks squarely in the crosshairs of the movement. Knowing all of this and owing to her own racist and anti-religious views, is it any wonder then that Sanger devised her Negro Project precisely to achieve the goals she had stated in her letter to Clarence Gamble in December of 1939?

The Negro Project afforded Sanger the opportunity to eliminate a group that, in her view, was the most problematic: members of so-called "inferior races" who possessed a strong belief in God. And as stated to Dr. Clarence Gamble of the Proctor & Gamble Co., it was the black ministers who would help keep "some of the more rebellious members" of their congregations in line. The Negro Project was an ingenious way for Sanger and the eugenicists to achieve their aim without drawing undue attention to it. After all, what better way in which to exterminate an entire race or class of people? One could go the route of the German Nazis *vis-à-vis* the Jews and shoot or gas them (although forced sterilization and euthanasia programs like *Aktion T-4* also reduced the number of Jews and other "useless eaters," as Heinrich Himmler described them); or, one could opt for a strategy aimed at getting these "undesirables" to exterminate themselves with the aid of ministers who were deliberately kept in the dark. Diabolical. Duplicitous. Dangerous. Disastrous and deadly. All of these words described Margaret Sanger's Negro Project to a "T."

Although her intended targets were the black Baptist congregations, she reserved her religious intolerance for the Catholic Church in particular, which as noted earlier, was adamantly opposed to birth control. When they traveled to Washington in the winter of 1926 to lobby Congress and the Senate to amend the Comstock Act, Sanger and her cohorts were firmly rebuffed by no less than 40 Senators and 14 Representatives. The Comstock Act was sponsored by a Protestant, passed by a Protestant Congress, and signed into law by a president who was also a Protestant. Yet, Sanger attacked the *Catholic* Church for opposing her agenda, telling her supporters that "everywhere there is a general acceptance of the idea (birth control), except in religious circles. The National Catholic Welfare Council has a special legislative committee organized to block and defeat our legislation. They frankly state that they intend to legislate for non-Catholics according to the dictates of the Church." [15]

The fact that no such committee existed did not matter. Nor did the fact that nearly two dozen *non*-catholic lay or religious groups joined with the NCWC to stand against her attempts to amend the Comstock Act. She continued to press the issue over the next several years, returning to Congress in 1934 for yet another go-around, and this time she had the support of "the Old Gray Lady" herself, The *New York Times*. Reporting on the first day of hearings, the paper took note of "the almost solidly Catholic opposition to the measure," which was itself a bald-faced lie. Running interference for the mastermind behind the Negro Project, it further stated, "This is now, according to Margaret Sanger, the only organized opposition to the proposal." [16] This wasn't the first time America's "Newspaper of Record" would seek to make the news rather than report it, nor would it be the last.

Needless to say, the legislation in question went nowhere, but Sanger would not give up. She attacked the Catholic Church yet again, accusing it of a concerted effort "not to present the facts to the committee, but to intimidate them by showing a Catholic block of voters who (though in the minority in the United States) want to dictate to the majority of non-Catholics as directed by the Vatican in social and moral legislation."

She even equated the Church's principled opposition to contraception with the actions of the nation's most notorious white supremacist group. In an article appearing in *The Birth Control Review,* Sanger wrote: "Today, by the Roman Catholic clergy and their allies, public opinion in America I fear, is too willing to condone in the officials of the Roman Catholic Church what it condemns in the Ku Klux Klan." [17] Quite a statement, especially coming from a woman who was only too happy to address that same group in New Jersey in 1926.

But, Sanger didn't do this all by herself. She had plenty of help in her attacks on the Catholic Church, personified for instance by Norman E. Himes. Himes opined in one of her journals that genetic differences existed between Catholics and members of other faiths, to wit: "Are Catholic stocks genetically inferior to such non-Catholic libertarian stocks as Unitarians and Universal Free Thinkers? Inferior in general?" Let us pause here at this point and remember that Sanger's father had renounced not only his Catholicism, but *all* religion when he became an atheist and "Free Thinker," so Himes' statement must have been music to her ears. At any rate, he continued, "My guess is that the answer will someday be made in the affirmative, and if the supposed differentials in net productivity are also genuine, he situation is anti-social, perhaps gravely so." [18]

Another who aided Sanger in her crusade against those who opposed her eugenic agenda on religious grounds was the Reverend Worth Tippy, the executive secretary of the General Council of Churches, who in April of 1931 sought to head off a firestorm of protest from Protestants following publication of Sanger's *Moral Aspects of Birth Control.* Tippy took note that the controversy had aroused "more opposition within the Protestant churches than we expected," and offered his assistance in settling things down: "Under the circumstances, and since we plan to carry on a steady work for liberalizing laws and to stimulate the establishment of clinics, it is necessary that we make good these losses and also increase our resources. Could you," he asked Sanger, "help me quietly by giving me the names of people of means who are interested in the birth-control movement and might help us if I wrote them?" [19]

Tippy's use of the word "quietly" in his letter to Sanger speaks volumes about the insidious nature of the birth-control movement at that time. A large majority of the public was resolutely opposed to it on moral and religious grounds, thus, the need for such secrecy on its part. After all, it wouldn't do to have the eugenic aspects of the movement exposed for all to see, and this was especially true later on of Sanger's Negro Project.

Sanger was ready, willing, and able to comply with Tippy's request, and he thanked her profusely for her offer. True, they expected continued opposition from "fundamentalist groups" like the Catholic and Protestant Churches, but to a much lesser extent than had been the case up to that point. It is interesting to note that one Protestant who did buy into the movement's goals was Mrs. John D. Rockefeller, Jr., the socially-prominent wife of the man whose Catholic family would lavish such generous (and often secret) financial support on Sanger's ABCL and later Planned Parenthood over the next several decades.

Conversely, one Protestant who stood with the Catholics in resisting the attempts by Sanger and her group to reform the existing laws, in this case in New York State, was the Reverend John R. Stanton. The Pastor of the Calvary Baptist Church in New York City issued a stinging rebuke of Sanger and her ABCL, blasting their support of such changes as being "subversive of the family. It is revolting, monstrous, against God's Word, and contradicts American traditions."

In response, Sanger again went after the Catholic Church, prompting the Reverend John A. Ryan to opine that Sanger and her group were more interested in preventing children from being born to poor families than in helping them improve their economic standing. "Their main objective," he wrote, "is to increase the practice of birth prevention among the poor. It is said that the present birth-prevention movement is to some extent financed by wealthy, albeit philanthropic, persons."

"As far as I am aware," he continued, "none of these is conspicuous in the movement for economic justice. None of them is crying out for a scale of wages which would enable workers to take care of a normal number of children." [20] Remember that one of the conditions requiring the use of birth control that Sanger had laid down in her standard lectures was the inability of the father to earn enough to support a larger family than she judged was acceptable. Given this, one wonders if the Reverend Ryan knew how close to the truth he really was.

When one takes a closer look at the reasons for Sanger's animus toward religion, it is helpful to bear in mind that one of the main tenets of virtually all faiths is the emphasis placed on helping the less fortunate, i.e., charity. She had taken an increasingly dimmer and dimmer view of this trait in religious believers, and she made no effort to hide her contempt for it. In *The Pivot of Civilization,* which was published in 1922, she wrote disparagingly, "organized charity itself is the symptom of a malignant disease. Those vast complex, interrelated organizations aiming to control and diminish the spread of misery and destitution and all the menacing evils that spring out of this sisterly soil, are the surest sign that our civilization has bred, is breeding and perpetuating a constantly increasing number of defectives, delinquents and dependents." [21]

Elsewhere in *Pivot,* Sanger blamed charity for saddling society with what she called "human waste." Wrote Sanger, "It encourages the healthier and more normal sections of the world to shoulder the burden of unthinking and indiscriminate fecundity of others, which brings with it, as I think the reader must agree, a dead weight of human waste. Instead of aiming to eliminate the stocks that are most detrimental to the future of the race and the world, it tends to render them to a menacing degree dominant." [22] Her solution? Not private and religious charities offering a helping hand to those less fortunate, but a *government*-administered program to encourage those she thought a burden on society to sterilize themselves so as not to bring any more of those she deemed "unfit" into the world. Sanger proposed this "solution" in a speech titled *The Function of Sterilization,* which she delivered at Vassar College's Institute for Eugenics on August 5, 1926.

Part of her remarks, which were carried in the October issue of *The Birth Control Review,* went as follows: "It now remains for the U.S. government to set a sensible example to the world by offering a bonus or yearly pension to all obviously unfit parents who allow themselves to be sterilized by harmless and scientific means." In language that today would undoubtedly be considered demeaning and insensitive, Sanger elaborated further, explaining, "In this way the moron and diseased would have no posterity to inherit their unhappy condition. The number of the feeble-minded would decrease, and a heavy burden would be lifted from the shoulders of the fit." [23]

These remarks come right out of Darwin and Malthus, and are to be soundly rejected by any sane, rational person. Moreover, it is important to bear in mind that these views were held by many eugenicists of the time and they are still in vogue today, echoed by such "intellectuals" as Paul Erlich, author of *The Population Bomb,* and the Australian Peter Singer, Chair of the Department of Bioethics at Princeton University in New Jersey.

Erlich, whom we will examine at greater length in a subsequent chapter, wrote his book in the late 1960s and predicted widespread death from famine less than a decade later. These deaths, he contended, would be caused by famines and diseases resulting directly from overpopulation, scarce natural resources, and other environmental factors. Compulsory sterilization of the "unfit" was just one of his "solutions" to what turned out to be largely a non-existent crisis. Singer, for his part, has gone on record as favoring the killing of disabled children up to and including the age of two. Charming fellows, to say the least, whose ideas are right in keeping with those of Sanger, Knopf, Stoddard, and Laughlin.

Sanger's views on race and religion were a toxic mix, and that poison was to be doled out in heaping doses over the next several decades to one special group of people above all others— black Americans. By masking her intentions behind such benevolent-sounding euphemisms as "women's health," "family planning" and, later on, "a woman's right to choose," she was able to dupe a great many unsuspecting members of this group into beginning the long, slow, inexorable descent into what today is being called by many black Americans an "extinction-level event."

Demographers have determined through long and exhaustive research that 2.1 live births per female is the *minimum* number required for a people to survive, let alone thrive. But with the inordinate abortion rate among black women, combined with premature deaths from other causes (disease, drug abuse, and violent crime being among them), the replacement level in the black community is less than *half* that number. Abortion is the leading cause of death in black America, eclipsing all others by a substantial margin. Abortion wipes out the lives of unborn black children to the tune of nearly 500,000 every year. Moreover, most of Planned Parenthood's abortion clinics are located in the black inner city, a fact that can hardly be called a coincidence. These numbers are so alarming that the Reverend Walter Hoye, whose ministry is based in Oakland, California, has stated that if this trend continues, the black race in America will, in effect, become extinct by the turn of the twenty-second century. But where black women were concerned, Sanger's aim was never to "help them control their own bodies," contrary to what she had been saying, in part to justify the birth-control movement.

In fact, many blacks took notice and were gravely concerned that Sanger and her ABCL were doing virtually nothing to address the scourge of grinding poverty and other obstacles that were preventing so many of them from accessing the mainstream of life in America. They saw through the benign-sounding rhetoric employed by Sanger promoting "better health" for blacks through the code words of "family planning" and they rightly sounded the alarm that birth control was, in point of fact, aimed at getting blacks to reduce their numbers and, in turn, any influence, either social, political, or economic, that they might have in the future. This is exactly what Sanger had feared, that some of "the more rebellious members" of the black community just might figure out the true purpose of the birth-control movement as it applied to them, thus the need for black ministers to step in and "straighten out" said members.

Clearly, something needed to be done to quell the brewing unrest, and this was where the strategy involving the black clergy was to come into play. One such minister who bought into this strategy was Dr. Adam Clayton Powell, Sr. of the Abyssinian Baptist Church, who invited Sanger to address his congregation. Sanger presented her program, packaging birth control in the positive language of "better health," helping families to "space out" the births of their children to assist in the mother's recovery, etc., but many members weren't buying it. Powell received harsh criticism from one unnamed minister who was "surprised the he'd (Powell) allow that awful woman in his church." [24]

Another member of the black clergy who was, to put it mildly, suspicious of Sanger's motives but who became an unwitting dupe, was J.T. Braun, the editor-in-chief of the National Baptist Sunday School Publishing Board in Nashville, Tennessee. In a letter he sent to Sanger on December 8 , 1941, two years after she had launched the Negro Project, he expressed his very deep concerns about birth control, telling her, "The very idea of such a thing has always held the greatest hatred and contempt in my mind." He implied, however, that his mind remained open on the subject by adding, "I am hesitant to give my *full* endorsement of this idea until you send me, perhaps, some more convincing literature on this subject. (emphasis added)." [25] In other words, "give me a reason."

Sanger seized on this opportunity in two ways. First, she sent him a pamphlet on the subject from the Federal Council of Churches' Marriage and Home Committee two weeks later on December 22. It endorsed her position and was enthusiastically supported by David Sims, Pastor of the African Methodist Episcopal Church and a member of the ABCL's National Negro Advisory Board. Sims sought to relieve Braun's angst by writing, "There are some who believe that birth control is an attempt to dictate to families how many children they should have. Nothing could be further from the truth." This assurance seems to have quelled any lingering misgivings that Braun may have had.

And, just in case that wasn't enough, Sanger sent along more material in favor of BCFA's position along with a copy of her autobiography, which he gave to his wife to read. Sanger's hidden agenda, cloaked in the stated objective of improving women's health and lowering the rate of infant mortality, had the desired effect on both the reader and her husband.

Braun relented and allowed his church to be used as forum to promote birth control. He later wrote Sanger of his experience, telling her, "At first glance I had a horrible shock to the proposition because it seemed to me to be allied to abortion, but after careful thought and prayer, I have concluded that it is sometimes necessary to save the lives of mother and children." [26]

Braun's comments clearly illustrate the extent to which Sanger's deceptive message had worked in indoctrinating this minister, and he was not alone. In addition to Braun, black leaders from all fields were taken in, such as sociologist and author W.E.B. Du Bois, who was also a founder of the National Association for the Advancement of Colored People; Charles A. Barnett, director of the Associated Negro Press in Chicago; Charles S. Johnson, President of Fisk University; Eugene Knickle Jones, Executive Director of the National Urban League; Dr. Dorothy Boulding Ferebee, President of Alpha Kappa Alpha; Dr. Mary McLeod Bethune, President of the National Council of Negro Women, and many others. They all bought into Sanger's seductive message, never once questioning either her stated views on race or her associations with the likes of Knopf, Stoddard, or Dr. Laughlin, all of whom, as noted earlier in these pages, were avowed racists and members of Sanger's American Birth Control League. We will examine them later on in this book, but for now it will suffice simply to bring them to the reader's attention.

Let us now turn briefly to Dr. Clarence J. Gamble, the heir to the Proctor & Gamble Soap Company fortune and a key partner in and financial backer of the Negro Project. In a 1939 memo he sent to Sanger, he had expressed concerns that some blacks would see the plan for what it was, an attempt to exterminate the black race eugenically, and she agreed that it would be wise to "train the Negro doctor at the clinic (presumably the one set up by the ABCL in Harlem)" in order to go out among blacks "with enthusiasm and knowledge, which will have far-reaching effects among the colored people." [27] It was in this reply to Gamble that she made her infamous proposal to use the black minister to "straighten out" those "rebellious" members of their congregations lest they discover what really lay behind her scheme. [28] The "far-reaching effects" that Sanger set in motion would forever remain her legacy, and the black community would, in the end, pay dearly for it.

Margaret Sanger died in Tucson, Arizona, on September 6, 1966, and was buried in Fishkill, New York. It is often said that a person should be judged based on the totality of their actions. Margaret Sanger is to be treated no differently in this regard. She is seen in elite circles as a pioneer in the fight for women's rights, particularly their "reproductive freedom," which is nothing more than the manufactured "right" to an abortion at any time and at any place, right up to the moment of birth, under the United States Constitution.

Never mind that this "right" can be found nowhere in this document. Sanger is memorialized by having several public buildings named after her, and every year since her passing, Planned Parenthood, ostensibly a "women's health organization" (but which in reality is the nation's largest private abortion provider with $540.6 million in tax money flowing into its coffers in 2013), issues its Margaret Sanger Award. The "Maggie," as it is sometimes called, is presented to those "individuals of distinction in recognition of excellence and leadership in furthering reproductive health and reproductive rights."

It is often pointed out by her adherents that Sanger herself was opposed to abortion because she considered it the taking of a life. This may be true as far as it goes, but if such is the case, why then is Planned Parenthood performing procedures she herself found to be so reprehensible? And, why is it that so many black ministers, politicians, business leaders, media representatives, etc., are so supportive of the goals of Planned Parenthood?

Margaret Sanger is, in many ways, the patron saint of birth control and abortion, largely due to the fact that very few of those who know better have either the inclination or the will to take a good look at this woman and what she came to represent: a culture of death that pervades seemingly every aspect of our society. This is especially true of too many of our so-called black "leaders," too many of whom are too often willfully blind to the racist eugenic agenda that drove Sanger and her disciples.

The same people who rightfully condemn the actions of the Ku Klux Klan say nothing of the fact that this woman not only had direct dealings with this group; she put, as we have seen in these pages, avowed racists on the Board of Directors of her American Birth Control League. They ignore the fact that she was an avid supporter of Malthusian eugenics and social Darwinism. And they gloss over or refuse to acknowledge that she was an anti-religious bigot who belittled people of faith for their beliefs regarding charity and the sanctity of unborn human life.

They recoil at the thought that the atrocities of the Holocaust, so many of which were committed in the name of "improving" the human race, could have taken place in such an "enlightened" nation as Germany. Yet, at the same time, they ignore or, far worse, even *endorse* the holocaust taking place right here, right now, in "the land of the free." Sanger herself supposedly condemned the actions of Hitler's regime, probably because she saw them as the "negative" variety of eugenics, while her brand was of a "positive" nature. But the fact remains that the practice of eugenics itself was evil, and it remains so, even after all these years, regardless of intent.

Margaret Sanger did not come into this world as an evil person; no one does, not even Hitler, Stalin, or Mao. Evil, like good, is a *learned* behavior. Sanger's work as a nurse was based on a genuine desire to do something about the dangerous and often fatal conditions women faced in childbirth. She also wanted to help these women avoid the same fate that befell her mother and very nearly took her own life, all of which was quite laudable and very commendable. She had "the best of intentions." But as the old adage goes, "the road to hell is paved with good intentions." And Sanger's racism, her religious bigotry, and her adherence to the ideas of the radical Left in the early 1900s which have been cited here, as well as her dealings with eugenicists both in the United States and in other countries, all served to effectively destroy whatever good works she performed earlier in her life.

By the time the ABCL had changed its name to Planned Parenthood Federation of America in 1942, the Negro Project was in full swing, supported and promoted with the unwitting participation of prominent black Americans from the clergy (whom Sanger had targeted from the outset), academia, health care professionals, financiers, media, and just about everyone in between. Sanger had snookered them so well with her stated goal of helping women to improve their health and, by limiting the number of children they would bear, do their part in contributing to the financial stability of their families. But the real hidden agenda, though not as apparent at the time, would one day wreak untold havoc on an entire group of Americans, and for one simple reason: those behind it saw many of their fellow citizens as inferior, simply because of the color of their skin.

This plot was carried off so well, so cleverly, that with the exception of a very few people, no one saw it coming until it was far too late. This is a stark, sad fact with which Margaret Sanger's apologists have yet to come to grips, most of all those who refer to themselves as our so-called black "leaders." After all, the Negro Project was directed at this segment of the population; therefore, the onus is on these "leaders" to demand a full accounting so that the facts surrounding this disgraceful and disturbing chapter in our history can be laid bare for all to see.

Only then can the healing truly begin.

NOTES

1. *Wikipedia,* the free encyclopedia.
2. www.blackgenocide.org, *The Truth about Margaret Sanger.*
3 Sanger got the slogan "No Gods, no masters" from a flyer distributed by the Marxist group International Workers of the World during the 1912 Lawrence Textile Strike. *Wikipedia*, the free encyclopedia.
4. www.backgenocide.org, *The Truth about Margaret Sanger.*
5. Sanger, Margaret, *An Autobiography,* Second Edition, c. 1938.
6. www.blackgenocide.org, *The Truth about Margaret Sanger.*
7. Sanger, Margaret, *An Autobiography,* Second Edition, c. 1938, pp. 366-67.
8. Ibid.
9. *Wikipedia*, the free encyclopedia, Note 7
10. www.blackgenocide.org, *The Truth about Margaret Sanger.*
11. www.blackgenocide.org, *The Truth about Margaret Sanger.*
12. Ibid.
13. Ibid.
14. www.blackgenocide.org, *The Truth about Margaret Sanger.*
15. www.blackgenocide.org., *The Truth about Margaret Sanger.*
16. Ibid.
17. www.blackgenocide.org, *The Truth about Margaret Sanger.*
18. www.blackgenocide.org, *The Truth About Margaret Sanger.*
19. Ibid.
20. www.blackgenocide.org
21. Sanger, Margaret, *The Pivot of Civilization,* c. 1922, p.108.
22. Ibid.
23. The *Birth Control Review,* October 1926.
24. Birth Control Clinical Research Bureau memo, February 3, 1933. From *The Negro Project: Margaret Sanger's Eugenic Plan for Black America,* c. 2001 by Tanya L. Green, Concerned Women for America.

25. Letter from Braun to Sanger, December 8, 1941. From *The Negro Project: Margaret Sanger's Eugenic Plan for Black America,* c. 2001, by Tanya L. Green, Concerned Women for America.
26. *The Negro Project: Margaret Sanger's Eugenic Plan for Black America,* May 10, 2001.
27. Sanger's letter to Gamble, December 10, 1939. From *The Negro Project: Margaret Sanger's Eugenic Plan for Black America,* May 10, 2001.
28. Ibid.

Chapter 2:

A Brief History of Eugenics

> "Eugenics: *The movement to improve the human species by controlling heredity.*"
>
> —Webster's New World Compact Desk Dictionary & Style Guide. c. 2002, p.168

In this chapter, we will examine the origins of the eugenics movement in the United States, including those who were prominent in carrying forward, the motivations behind their actions, and the connections between the eugenics movement and Margaret Sanger's Negro Project.

Varying means of "strengthening the race" have been used by many civilizations in differing forms throughout human history, one example being the practice engaged in by the ancient Greeks which involved abandoning sickly infants on mountainsides to be left to the tender mercies of Mother Nature. This typically involved exposure to the elements and attacks by wild animals, among other things. Eskimo tribes in the Far North, at one time, would practice a similar form of eugenics, leaving the sick and elderly on ice floes to meet their fates. While these are not examples of eugenics as we have come to know it, the goal was the same: to preserve the race (or tribe) by assuring that its strongest elements are preserved by sacrificing the weakest, and such forms of "mercy killing" can be said to come clearly within its scope.

But it wasn't until the advances in genetics that began in the latter half of the nineteenth century that the notion that it was possible to engineer "undesirable" traits out of an entire race of people seemed within reach. The work of early geneticists like Gregor Mendel and Luther Burbank involved developing hybrid types of plants in an effort to develop strains that were resistant to disease and pests, thereby increasing crop yields and allowing farmers to make better use of their land. Such research, in fact, continues up to the present day in the field of bioengineering, and the breakthroughs and advances that scientists in the specialty have made have opened up a world of opportunities for poor and developing nations to feed their increasingly hungry populations.

Eugenics, however, involved much more than the development of new strains of plant life, much more. It involved the bioengineering of *human beings,* ostensibly to fight the spread of disease and a whole host of other maladies common to the human condition. If, it was argued, these undesirable traits could somehow be eliminated through the use of scientific means, the human race would be healthier, happier, more productive, and would be possessed of longer life spans in the process. This was all well and good, and the study of genetics has indeed brought about many beneficial results for humanity, and very few (usually those subscribers to the discredited theories of Thomas Malthus) can argue that less disease, a longer lifespan, and more productivity are bad things.

And, if these undesirable traits were confined only to such things as disease, early deaths, and birth defects, that would have been one thing. However, many proponents of eugenics were not prepared to stop there. They expanded their definition of "undesirable" to include the weak, the mentally disabled, those who belonged to other races, etc., and argued that these individuals were imposing an undue burden on the "fitter," "healthier" elements of society.

If, they reasoned, there was some way of breeding these elements out of those in question, Mankind would be better off in the long run. The field of eugenics held out the opportunity for Man to achieve a long-dreamed of goal: the realization of a kind of utopia, a "heaven on earth," if you will. It offered him the chance to "remake" himself through scientific means by eliminating those "unwanted" traits from the human species and strengthening those that were most desirable.

Two forms of eugenics have been practiced both here and abroad down through the years, "positive" and "negative" eugenics. The proponents of the former saw it as a means to reduce human suffering by eradicating "unwanted" genetic traits before birth, and much of this kind of research that is being conducted today, both in adult stem cell studies and the more controversial embryonic variety, is aimed at bringing about the same result. While the use of adult stem cells has yielded solid, tangible results in fighting a number of diseases and physical handicaps, the jury is still out on the use of embryonic stem cells, which necessarily involves the killing of living human organisms so that such cells may be harvested. In fact, those who advocate the use of embryonic stem cells cannot, as yet, point to any successes, nor is it likely that they will ever be able to do so.

"Negative" eugenics, on the other hand, has as its focus the elimination of "inferior"elements, based on a Darwinian vision of "survival of the fittest." Some of these so-called "inferior" elements include the mentally ill and handicapped, epileptics, lepers, those of different races or ethnicities (blacks, Orientals, Asians, Jews and Slavs), or just those which a society has labeled "useless eaters" (a phrase used by Heinrich Himmler in Nazi Germany to describe anyone who could not contribute to the realization of Hitler's "Thousand-Year Reich"). The idea that society could be improved by eliminating these elements by any means necessary had a strong appeal to many Germans, and the Nazi brand of eugenics would have vast, lasting, and significant consequences for all of humanity, many that remain with us long after the demise of its most notorious supporter and practitioner, Adolf Hitler.

Indeed, because eugenics was so deeply embedded in Germany under Hitler, many people think that the practice was devised in that nation. After all, the Third Reich used it in its conduct of domestic and foreign policy and embodied it in the infamous Nuremburg Laws, Reinhard Heydrich's RHSA (Reich Office of Race and Resettlement); the *Aktion T-4* forced euthanasia program, and finally the "Final Solution to the Jewish Question." And many people believe that American eugenicists got their ideas from the Germans.

That, however, is a huge mistake. Sadly, the concept of eugenics as a legitimate scientific discipline that was taught for over a hundred years in classrooms all across America and the world actually originated in England, and was inspired by the beliefs of the British biological determinist Sir Francis Galton. [1] Galton was a first cousin of Charles Darwin, [2] who wrote the evolutionist work *The Origin of Species* in 1859. Galton had spent much of his time studying the upper classes of British society and came to conclude that their success in life was due to the notion that their genetic makeup was "superior" to that of other members of the social strata in England.

Galton coined the term "eugenics" by combining the Greek prefix *"eu"* ("good" or "well") with the suffix *"genes"* ("born") in 1883. He defined the new word as "the science which deals with all influences that improve the inborn qualities of a race; also with those that develop them to the utmost advantage." [3] Galton then compiled his observations in a book titled *Inquiries into Human Faculty and Its Development*, [4] which he published that same year.

As was mentioned earlier in these pages, his theories that the human race could "remake" itself through scientific means found an enthusiastic following among many prominent Britons such as H.G. Wells, George Bernard Shaw and John Maynard Keynes. But the list didn't stop there. Other adherents to the theory of eugenics included J.B.S. Haldane, Marie Stopes, Julian Huxley, and future British Prime Minister Winston Churchill.

Although the field of eugenics originated in England, Galton's theories found fertile ground in the United States and were embraced by some very important and wealthy Americans, among them Stanley Webb, Presidents Theodore Roosevelt and Woodrow Wilson, Clarence J. Gamble, and, of course, Margaret Sanger. Many of them bought into the idea of "positive" eugenics (i.e., encouraging reproduction in the "fitter" elements of society, while discouraging it in those perceived to be more "unfit"), although, as we have seen in Sanger's case, the aspects of "negative" eugenics *vis-à-vis* the black population became a prime mover behind the implementation of her Negro Project.

In the last decade of the nineteenth century, the United States was experiencing an influx of new immigrants from Europe, many of whom were poor, uneducated, and also had large families. This stirred much anxiety and animosity in the existing population, which feared rising rates of poverty, illiteracy, crime, and disease among these new arrivals. Although laws limiting immigration in America had been on the books for years, the new field of eugenics offered a unique angle from which to approach the problem. For instead of limiting by law the number of immigrants coming into the U.S., whom the largely Protestant population had come to resent in part because they were largely of the Catholic faith, now a new, "scientific" way to attack the problem was within reach. They may not have been able to keep these people out entirely, but they could do something to limit the number of children they bore once they were here.

Galton's ideas, as stated earlier, found ready acceptance in the United States, due in no small part to the idea that it was somehow scientifically possible to "get rid of" the bottom tenth" of American society. [5] This segment was defined by the eugenicists by its racial, economic, educational and social standing, and they hoped that the numbers of such "undesirable" or "unfit" people could be reduced or limited, if not eliminated entirely, through laws aimed at restricting immigration (for example, the Immigration Restriction Act of 1924), or by prohibiting miscegenation (interracial marriage), or other coercive measures such as forced sterilization.

For a number of reasons including race, almost every state in the Union enacted such barbaric laws to their everlasting shame and regret, including Virginia, which only ended all forms of legally-enforced sterilization in 1974. In a more ominous example, a Nazi eugenicist cited the U.S. Supreme Court's ruling upholding California's eugenics law when he faced justice in the Nuremburg War Crimes Trial following World War II. [6] We will examine some of said laws later on in this chapter.

The popularity of eugenics and the theory that it was possible to breed away our "less desirable" traits was clear all across America in the early decades of the twentieth century. For instance, county fairs began staging "better baby" contests in 1908 in which so-called "desirable" children were give awards ranging from blue ribbons to bronze medals based on a set and eventually led, beginning in 1920, to so-called "fitter family for the future" contests, in of predetermined criteria. [7] These competitions proved highly popular with the general public which entire families were encouraged to take part, with the first prize sometimes being a health checkup free of charge at a local hospital or clinic. [8]

Such programs received funding from a number of sources, including money from several wealthy families and private philanthropic foundations, among them the Harriman family, which made its fortune in the railroad business, the Carnegie and Ford Foundations, and J.H. Kellogg, who in 1906 provided seed money to establish the Race Betterment Foundation in Battle Creek, Michigan. [9] As we have seen previously, Margaret Sanger's work in birth control and eugenics was bankrolled to a large degree by a number of anonymous grants from the Rockefeller family and the foundation it created.

The Race Betterment Foundation was followed in 1911 by the establishment of the Eugenic Records Office in Cold Spring Harbor, New York. Founded by biologist Charles H. Davenport, it received its initial funding through grants issued by the Harriman family and the Carnegie Foundation. Over a span of several years, the ERO compiled a mountain of data (called "family pedigrees") that purported to show that those from socially and economically poor backgrounds fit the eugenicists' definition of someone who was "unfit" and thus a candidate for sterilization, or in the view of conservationist Madison Grant, a candidate for extermination. [10]

In his book *The Passing of the Great Race* (1916), Grant went so far as to call interracial marriage "a social and racial crime," and warned that social acceptance of such marriages would lead America to what he called "racial suicide" and eventually the disappearance of white civilization.

Such "family pedigrees," as the ERO called them, were, according to author Edwin Black in his book *War on the Weak,* often faulty and cobbled together out of equal portions of "gossip, race prejudice, sloppy methods, and leaps of logic, all caulked together by elements of actual genetic knowledge to create the glitter of a genuine science." [11]

Eugenicists were convinced that Mendel's success in cross-breeding plants could be applied to people, as well, and they pointed to the thousands of years of human experience in the breeding of different varieties of domestic animals such as dogs, cats, and livestock to bolster their case. In their view, eugenics was the wave of the future, and they believed that it was only a matter of time before similar successes could be achieved with human beings. But humans are not plants; nor are they animals. They are, as the saying goes, "a horse of a different color," and breeding a race of "perfect people" would soon prove to be an even more difficult, and as history has shown, a much more disastrous proposition than even they themselves had imagined.

Although eugenics later proved to be a pseudo-science, it was all the rage in the U.S. during the early decades 1900's, especially at the college and university level. In fact, no fewer than 376 courses were offered on the subject by 1928. [12] One prominent member of academia who endorsed the study of the field was David Starr Jordan, President of Stanford University in Palo Alto, California. Starr, along with Alexander Graham Bell, the inventor of the telephone, and geneticist Luther Burbank, was a member of the American Breeder's Association (ABA), which was founded in 1906 with Charles Davenport as its director. [13]

According to its mission statement, the ABA was established to "investigate and report on heredity in the human race, and emphasize the value of superior blood and the menace to society of inferior blood." [14] If one did not know better, one would rightly think that these chilling words came right out of Nazi Germany. Sadly, such is not the case. They were the sentiments of the members of a supposedly respectable *American* organization that included some otherwise very honorable people.

But the ABA was not alone in its mission. Soon similar groups sprang up around the country, including the American Association for the Study and Prevention of Infant Mortality, the first group to begin studying infant mortality rates utilizing the principles of eugenics. [15]

Although their efforts were concentrated in other areas of social and political activities, women's groups like the National Federation of Women's Clubs, the Women's Christian Temperance Union and the League of Women Voters soon were on the eugenics bandwagon as well. [16]

These and other groups were instrumental in getting state governments across the nation to enact forced-sterilization laws based entirely on eugenic principles, often with long-term and catastrophic consequences. Indiana was the first state to adopt such legislation, and was followed over a number of years by Connecticut, California, North Carolina and Virginia, among others. As noted earlier, California's eugenic sterilization law (under which more than 20,000 people were forcibly sterilized) served as a basis for much of Nazi Germany's infamous "racial purification" statutes and was upheld by the United States Supreme Court.

Virginia's law, euphemistically titled the "Racial Integrity Act," was passed in 1924 and was a direct result of the efforts of eugenics supporters like Dr. Harry Laughlin, Ernest Cox, John Powell, and Walter Plecker. Laughlin's role in promulgating the law was especially odious. In 1914, he issued a Model Eugenical Sterilization Law as one of his first major acts at the Eugenic Records Office.[17] Aimed at passing legislation that authorized sterilization of the "socially inadequate," the law would cover a laundry list of institutionalized individuals who were housed in facilities that were "maintained wholly or in part at public (i.e. taxpayer) expense."

Those people who came under this definition included the "feeble-minded, insane, criminalistic, epileptic, inebriate (drunk or alcoholic), diseased, blind, deaf, deformed, and dependent." Further, Laughlin proposed that "orphans, tramps, ne'er do-wells, the homeless, and paupers" all be candidates for coercive sterilization procedures. [18] How different would things be today if the parents of Helen Keller or Stephen Hawking, two shining examples of the unique human ability to overcome unspeakable handicaps, had been sterilized and rendered unable to bring them into the world? For they clearly would have found themselves in the crosshairs of the "compassionate" Dr. Harry Laughlin, who himself was epileptic and, therefore, would have been a prime candidate for sterilization under his own proposed law.

The state passed its law on the grounds that "heredity plays an important part in the transmission of insanity, idiocy, imbecility, epilepsy, and crime" and targeted those "defective persons" whose reproduction supposedly presented a "menace to society." The first victim of this law was a 17-year old girl named Carrie Buck, who had had a child out of wedlock. She was forcibly sterilized on the dubious grounds that her mother, Emma, who was confined at the Virginia Colony for the Epileptic and the Feebleminded, had passed the "undesirable" genetic traits of feeblemindedness and sexual promiscuity on to her daughter. A trial soon followed that sought to challenge the constitutionality of the state law under which Carrie was to be coercively sterilized.

The State brought forth several witnesses who testified against Carrie, including Albert Priddy, the superintendent of the asylum where Emma was confined. He testified that Emma had "a record of immorality, prostitution, untruthfulness, and syphilis" and that the Buck family were members of the "shiftless, ignorant, and worthless class of anti-social whites of the South." [19] Other witnesses at Carrie's trial included Arthur Easterbrook, a sociologist from the ERO, and a nurse who examined Vivian, the child whom Carrie had borne and found her to be "below average" and "not quite normal."

Even Laughlin himself got into the act and, although he had never even met Carrie let alone examined her, he wrote a deposition endorsing Priddy's contention regarding her alleged "feeble-mindedness" and "moral delinquency." [20] It was later discovered that Carrie had become pregnant because she had been raped by a relative of her foster parents and not because she was sexually promiscuous.

It was also shown that Vivian was not "feeble-minded" at all, but was actually a normal little girl who did so well in school that she was on the honor roll (with an "A" average, no less); and it was also later discovered that Carrie's defense lawyer was in on what could only described as a "fix" of monstrous proportions in seeing that the Virginia law was upheld. The judge ruled that Carrie was indeed mentally defective and was, therefore, to be sterilized to prevent other "defective" children from being born.

The verdict was appealed to the U.S. Supreme Court, and that body rendered its final decision in 1927 in *Buck v. Bell* with Justice Oliver Wendell Holmes presiding. Holmes was a proponent of eugenics and thus should have Stepped down from the case. However, it was his ruling that doomed young Carrie, and the words he used in justifying his decision will undoubtedly be regarded in the same vein as those of Chief Justice Roger B. Taney in justifying slavery in the *Dred Scott* case. "It is better for all the world," Holmes wrote, "if instead of waiting to execute degenerate offspring for crime or to let them starve for their imbecility, society can prevent those who are manifestly unfit from continuing their kind." He concluded, "Three generations of imbeciles are enough." [21]

Holmes' ruling was all the impetus needed to promulgate more sterilization laws across the country, particularly in the Deep South. And, in a sad footnote to the story, the Virginia law the Court upheld has never been overturned.

Another case (*Skinner v. Oklahoma)* was heard by that body in 1942 after the state tried under its 1935 law to sterilize one Jack Skinner, a thief who was convicted three times for crimes ranging from stealing chickens to armed robbery. On this occasion, Justice William O. Douglas struck down the state law, noting that while a three-time chicken thief could be sterilized, a three-time embezzler could not. He ruled that Skinner could not be sterilized for his crimes, writing, "We have not the slightest basis for inferring that the inheritability of criminal traits follows the neat legal distinctions which the law has marked between those two offenses." [22]

Despite the ruling in the *Skinner* case, forced sterilization laws continued on the books, and at one time or another 33 states had statutes permitting coercive measures of one kind or another to rein in the number of those deemed "unfit" of "defective" by the respective states. We have already seen how eugenicists like Harry Laughlin defined such people, often through the use of highly subjective, erroneous, and biased "criteria."

And, while Carrie Buck and her daughter were white, as was Jack Skinner, there were those eugenicists who, as shown, believed that sterilizing members of other races simply *because* they were members of other races was not only desirable and acceptable, it was a necessary remedy and a solemn obligation. Remember the words of Margaret Sanger in calling members of minority groups "human weeds" in justifying her Negro Project, or the sentiments of Madison Grant, who believed that minorities should be exterminated should they dare to forget their "place" and marry others outside their race. And it is absolutely stunning how many prominent black Americans were taken in by the notion of race-based eugenics, in particular where the Negro Project was concerned.

For example, Charles S. Johnson, the President of Fisk University, supported the idea of what he called "eugenic discrimination," writing in the June 1932 issue of *The Birth Control Review* that such a program was necessary because of high maternal and infant mortality rates and to lower the incidence of diseases like malaria, tuberculosis, typhoid, and venereal infection. He contended that "the status of negroes as marginal workers, their confinement to the lowest branches of industry, the necessity for the labors of mothers as well as children to balance their meager budgets, are factors that emphasize the need for lessening the burden, not only for themselves, but of society, which must provide the supplementary support in the form of relief." [23] Johnson later served on the National Negro Advisory Board of Sanger's Birth Control Federation of America.

W.E.B. Du Bois lent his support of eugenics in an article titled *Black Folk and Birth Control*, in which he belittled those who opposed contraception on religious grounds as somehow not "getting it," citing what he called "the inevitable clash of ideals between those Negroes who were striving to improve their economic position and those whose religious faith made the limitation of children a sin." He took these people to task for their stubborn intransigence, calling them "the mass of ignorant Negroes who breed carelessly and disastrously so that the increase among them is from that part of the population least intelligent and fit, and least able to rear their children properly." [24]

Du Bois suggested that blacks would be open to "intelligent propaganda of any sort" in order to foster, in his words, "a more liberal attitude" among churchgoing blacks. This was just the kind of opening eugenicists like Sanger needed to ingratiate themselves with their unsuspecting targets. The black media joined in as well, and carried Sanger's articles on birth control in the pages of such newspapers as *The Afro-American* and *The Chicago Defender.* [25]

Author Walter Terpenning was even more blunt in his criticisms than either Johnson or Du Bois. In an article that appeared in the June 1932 issue of *The Birth Control Review* that was titled *God's Chillun*, he excoriated poor blacks for siring more children, calling it a "pathetic" situation: "The birth of a colored child, even to parents who can give it adequate support, is pathetic in view of the unchristian and undemocratic treatment likely to be accorded it at the hands of a predominantly white community, and the denial of choice in propagation to this unfortunate class is nothing less than barbarous." [26]

Note if you will the corruption of the word "children" that Terpenning used in the title of his article. It is doubtful that such a deliberate attempt at mocking the speech patterns of some black Americans would be tolerated today if it were employed by a white author, but this was the work of a respected black man, so no one evidently challenged him on this point. It is also revealing to learn that the phrase "denial of choice" goes back as far as the early 1930s before being picked up by the feminist movement some 40 years later to promote its pro-abortion agenda.

From the inception of laws mandating forced sterilization beginning in 1907, tens of thousands of people were victimized by this practice. While the actual number of these operations may never be known, it has been estimated that by the time Oregon had performed the last legally-enforced sterilization in the U.S. in 1981, at least 64,000 people had their lives irreparably damaged by the effects of forced sterilization in the United States, often for the most frivolous and specious of "reasons." California led the way in this dubious category with an estimated 20,108 such procedures. Two states performed more than 5,000 (Virginia with 7,162 and North Carolina with 6,297). Michigan (3,786), Georgia (3,284) and Kansas (3,032) were the states with the next-highest number of these operations. New York (42), Idaho (38), and Arizona (30) had performed the fewest. [27] But forced sterilization wasn't the only method that the eugenicists employed to curb the number of "undesirables," however. They also promoted euthanasia, or "mercy killing" to achieve their ends.

"Euthanasia" comes from the Greek work *euthanatos,* which means "good death." It is defined as "the act of causing death painlessly, to end suffering." [28] Euthanasia has been practiced for centuries all around the world, going back as far as the time of the Roman Emperor Augustus and was first referred to as a specific medical procedure by Francis Bacon in the 1600s [29] Although the debate on the ethics of ending life prematurely in this manner has been going on for most of recorded history, the discussion in the U.S. began in earnest in the latter stages of the nineteenth century.

Robert Ingersoll and Felix Adler were two of the more prominent early advocates for euthanasia in this country, Ingersoll arguing in 1894 that in the case of devastating diseases such as terminal cancer patients should have the right to commit suicide to end their suffering, and Adler for the same three years later. Adler also added that doctors should be able to assist their patients who were suffering from overwhelming pain in taking their own lives. [30] The dawn of the twentieth century saw the first attempts to legalize euthanasia on the state level when Henry Hunt introduced a bill to that end in the Ohio Legislature in 1906, and a similar one was introduced in the Iowa Assembly that same year by Ross Gregory.

Both bills sought to alleviate human suffering by allowing patients to end their lives through the use of lethal doses of anesthesia, and each contained numerous caveats and provisions (e.g., the patient's age, proof of terminal illness, the level of pain suffered by the patient, and the number of doctors required to give their consent and be present at the act of ending that patient's life, the number of witnesses needed to attest to the patient's state of mind, etc.) before such a drastic remedy could be used. Although similar in intent, Gregory's bill differed from Hunt's in two ways.

and Holland. We now know, for example, that both types of euthanasia were widely practiced during Hitler's Third Reich and were a major factor in implementing his "Final Solution to the Jewish Question." We also know that the death toll from this scheme, which was conducted in almost complete secrecy, was absolutely staggering with more than *200,000* either physically or mentally disabled people done in by lethal injection, starvation, and gassing between 1933 and the end of World War II. [35] This, in addition to the six million Jews who were exterminated during his reign of terror in Germany and the occupied lands to the East. We also know that this figure was not confined just to the Jews alone. Non-Jews were murdered by the bushel by the Nazis, as were Catholics, gypsies, homosexuals, Hitler's political enemies, and just about anyone else whom the Reich determined was "unfit."

Holland's program has been in place for the last couple of decades with a death toll of more than 130,000 as of 2010 resulting from voluntary, involuntary, and non-voluntary forms of euthanasia (non-voluntary euthanasia being administered in situations where the patient's consent is unavailable). [36] This is an alarming development, to say the least. The Dutch law was originally intended to help the incurably ill end their suffering by terminating their lives with specific restrictions.

But evidence is now emerging that shows that the program is being extended to those who do not just have terminal illnesses, but those who suffer from depression or who are just plain "tired of living" at all. The gift of life is the most precious of all and is one on which the very existence of civilization itself is based. Such a cavalier attitude is a very dangerous one to have, one which bodes ill indeed if such reasoning is ever accepted on a worldwide basis.

The euthanasia movement purportedly has always revolved around the idea that if one possesses a right to life, one must also have a concurrent "right to die," as long as they have the ability to give their consent. But what happens if that ability is not present through no fault of one's own (such as a debilitating injury or illness that renders one incapable of doing so), or through their failure to provide notice to a loved one or other party of their intentions in this regard? Who will make this critically important decision? The family? The spouse? Doctors or the courts? Maybe even the government? Probably the most high-profile example of this dilemma in recent years is the case of Terri Shiavo, a Florida woman whose life was ended through involuntary euthanasia following a lengthy battle involving her husband, her immediate family, her doctors, the courts, and even the United States government itself.

Terri was born Theresa Marie Schindler on December 21, 1963, in the Philadelphia suburb of Lower Moreland Township, Pennsylvania. She had weight issues throughout her early life, but was able to control them through adolescence and into her college years, which were spent at Bucks County Community College. It was there that she met Michael Schiavo, whom whom she began dating in 1982 and would later marry on November 10, 1984. Two years later, Terri and Michael would move to Florida, settling in St. Petersburg.

Terri was originally diagnosed as having suffered massive brain injuries that were caused by a fall in her apartment on February 25, 1990. She was taken to the Humana Northside Hospital, where she was intubated and placed on a ventilator after attempts were made to resuscitate her. It was determined that her injuries led to a lack of oxygen to her brain that caused her to lapse into a comatose state. During admission, she was found to be suffering from a condition known as hypokalemia, brought on by low potassium levels in the bloodstream, even though her sodium and calcium levels were normal. Electrolyte imbalances such as hypokalemia can be caused by vomiting, either self-induced or otherwise, as well as by drinking excessive amounts of fluids, and can result in heart rhythm abnormalities like sudden arrythmia death syndrome. [37] Self-induced vomiting, it should be noted, is common among many of those who suffer from bulimia, a debilitating eating disorder from which Terri had been suffering.

At the hospital, her medical chart read that Terri "apparently has been trying to keep her weight down with dieting by herself, drinking liquids most of the time during the day and drinking about 10-15 glasses of iced tea." [38] During her stay at Humana Northside, she was attended by Doctors Garcia DeSousa, a board-certified neurologist who had treated her before, and Victor Gambone, an internist who was also the Schiavo family physician. Together, they determined Terri had lapsed into a permanent vegetative state.

This diagnosis, which DeSousa and Gambone had reached about a year before, after she had suffered her sudden cardiac arrest, was soon followed by a long, protracted battle between the Schindler family and Michael Schiavo that ultimately involved no less than 14 separate appeals in the Florida courts, not to mention several motions, hearings, and petitions on the state level; five suits in federal district court; state laws which were struck down by the Florida Supreme Court, and four denials by the United States Supreme Court.

Terri's feeding tube was removed and reinserted on several occasions over the next few years until it was ordered removed for the last time. The case even reached the U.S. House and Senate, which passed special legislation ordering that the feeding tube be reinserted to provide nourishment to the stricken woman after Judge George Greer ordered it removed yet again. President George W. Bush made a special trip back to Washington from his vacation in Crawford, Texas to sign the legislation ordering the feeding tube to be reinserted.

At issue was whether or not Terri would have wanted her feeding tube removed so that she could die in peace. But due to her condition, she could not make her wishes known about what to do. Her husband, Michael, maintained that Terri would not have wanted to remain on the tube and that she had made this clear to him, but her parents disputed this contention, saying that their daughter was a devout Catholic who would never have made such a request due to her religious upbringing. The Schindlers were so confident that she could still function that they offered to care for Terri on their own, but they were denied the opportunity to do so. They also maintained that her cognitive abilities were still intact to the point that she was able to respond to certain external stimuli, which they attempted to prove using videotaped evidence. Again, they were rebuffed. The matter was further complicated by the fact that she had not prepared a "living will" laying out her wishes in the case of such a catastrophic event as that which actually befell her. In fact, no one, neither her husband nor her parents, knew exactly what she wanted.

The whole thing was a mess, to put it mildly, and Michael certainly did himself no favors when it was revealed that he had begun an affair with another woman and had fathered a child with her while he was still married to Terri and was still her legal guardian. He also had reportedly asked on one occasion, "When is the bitch going to die?" Schiavo's relations with the Schindlers, which were once so amicable that he was allowed to live rent-free in their condominium for a number of months from 1990-93, were now beyond repair. [39]

An autopsy that was conducted on Terri following the removal of her feeding tube on March 21, 2005, was inconclusive as to the cause and manner of her death. It was conducted by Jon R. Thogmartin, M.D., the Chief Medical Examiner for Pinellas and Pasco Counties, who worked in consultation with neuropathologist Stephen J. Nelson. [40]

While they found extensive damage to Terri's brain and nervous system, there was no sign of any trauma to the neck area, which seems to rule out the possibility that Terri was strangled before her fall.

The autopsy also revealed that her heart and blood vessels were healthy, which ruled out that her initial collapse was the result of myocardial infarction. Interestingly, Dr. Thogmartin found no evidence of bulimia, contrary to the initial diagnosis made at Humana Northside Hospital on February 25, 1990. The autopsy results were released to the public on June 15, 2005, and they seem to have raised more questions than they answered. In it, Thogmartin wrote, "Mrs. Schiavo suffered severe anoxic brain injury, the cause of which cannot be determined with reasonable medical certainty. The manner of death will, therefore, be listed as undetermined." [41] While the results of Terri's autopsy may have laid the matter to rest for many, including Michael, the Schindlers were far from satisfied. Terri's brother, Bobby Schindler, issued a statement on the family's behalf, which read as follows: "The fact that the medical examiner ruled out bulimia and ruled out a heart attack without a doubt asks more questions." [42]

Since Dr. Thogmartin issued his findings in the Schiavo case, relations between the Schindlers and Michael have remained, to put it charitably, icy at best. Each side has kept the "right to die" issue alive in its own way. Michael established the Terri PAC (political action committee) in 2005 with the goal of electing legislators who favor enacting such laws and penned a book titled *Terri: The Truth* (2006). Schiavo shut down his PAC in 2007 following a Federal Election Commission judgment against it for failure to file complete and timely records.

The Schindlers were busy as well, and formed the Terri Schindler-Schiavo Foundation in 2000 to garner support for their side of the issue. Three years later, they changed the name to the Terri Schiavo Life and Hope Network. They also published a book of their own, *A Life That Matters: The Life of Terri Schiavo-A Lesson For Us All* (2006), the same year that Michael's book was released. [43]

Charges of financial improprieties have also flown back and forth between the two sides. For example, Michael has alleged that Terri's family has benefited from improperly using her name in the foundation's fund-raising activities, a name he contends they have no right to use since he owns it, while the Schindlers argue that they have the right to use her name since the attention resulting from the case had made her a public figure. Such developments as this have made it fairly safe to say that the effects of the Terri Schiavo case will be with us for quite some time to come. They have also made it clear that the euthanasia discussion, regardless of what name is attached to it ("right to die," physician-assisted suicide, etc.) isn't going away

solution, as shown by her Negro Project, was to make sure that "human weeds" like minorities or those who were mentally and/or physically handicapped never had the opportunity to reproduce at all!

And, as horrific as the idea of butchering a defenseless life in the womb is, there are those who believe that it is perfectly permissible to snuff out a life *after* it has come into this world if the parents are being "burdened" by that life in some fashion. Chief among them is Peter Singer, the Chair of Bioethics at Princeton whom we met earlier in this book. Singer has publicly stated that parents should have the right to kill a child whom they determine has an "inferior" quality of life, a rather subjective term, to say the least. It should also be noted that Singer is the author of *Animal Liberation,* a book that has been called the "bible" of the animal "rights" movement.

It's bad enough that Singer holds such anti-human views, but what's far worse is that he is allowed to teach such toxic ideas to hundreds of students each year. What is the university's position on all this? And where is the public outcry, especially among the parents, many of whom are paying tens of thousands of their hard-earned dollars in tuition every year so their precious offspring can attend such a prestigious Ivy League school?

And, we cannot, before we are finished, let this aspect of eugenics pass without mentioning that the man who currently holds the highest office in the land, the Presidency of the United States, Barack Obama, voted on numerous occasions against the Illinois version of the federal Born Alive Infant Protection Act while he was a state Senator in Springfield. In fact, he was the *only* state senator to vote against this measure, which would provide basic medical services to the survivors of abortions in the Land of Lincoln. His reasoning? That voting for the bill would have "gone against" the intention of the mother and her doctor to end that baby's life. It is a sad commentary on the American voter that a man who holds such a view was not only elected President after this was discovered, he was rewarded with *four more years* in the Oval Office! Worse still is the revelation that abortions are now being used to select the sex of the baby. And here we thought this only happened in China. Eugenics may have lost most of its appeal, but from what we have seen, it is still very much alive, and we ignore this lesson at our grave and everlasting peril.

NOTES

1. *Eugenics in the United States. Wikipedia*, the free encyclopedia.
2. Kieves, Daniel, *A Brief History of the Eugenics Movement.* Investigator No. 72, May 2000.

3. Galton, Sir Francis, *Eugenics: Its Definitions and Aims.* From *The American Journal of Sociology,* July 1904.
4. Galton, Sir Francis, *Inquiries into Human Faculty and Its Development,* c. 1883.
5. Torgesen, Lara, *The Powerful People Behind the Eugenics Movement.* From *Indy Week,* March 24, 2010.
6. Ibid.
7. *Eugenics in the United States. Wikipedia,* the free encyclopedia.
8. Ibid.
9. Ibid.
10. *Eugenics in the United States. Wikipedia,* the free encyclopedia.
11. Torgeson, Lara, *The Powerful People behind the Eugenics Movement. Indy Week,* March 24, 2010.
12. *Eugenics in the United States. Wikipedia,* the free encyclopedia.
13. Ibid.
14. Ibid.
15. Ibid.
16. *Eugenics in the United States. Wikipedia,* the free encyclopedia.
17. Lombardo, Paul, University of Virginia, *Eugenic Sterilization Laws.* From *Social Origins of Eugenics.*
18. Lombardo, Paul, University of Virginia, *Eugenic Sterilization Laws.* From *Social Origins of Eugenics.*
19. Lombardo, Paul, University of Virginia, *Eugenic Sterilization Laws.* From *Social Origins of Eugenics.*
20. Ibid.
21. Lombardo, Paul, University of Virginia, *Eugenical Sterilization Laws.* From *The Social Origins of Eugenics.*
22. Ibid.
23. Johnson, Charles S., *A Question of Negro Health.* From *The Birth Control Review,* June 1932, pp. 167-169.
24. Green, Tanya L., *The Negro Project: Margaret Sanger's Eugenic Plan for Black Americans.*
25. Ibid.
26. Terpenning, Walter, *God's Chillun.* From *The Birth Control Review,* June 1932, p. 172.
27. Wellerstein, Alex, *States of Eugenics: Institutions and Practices of Compulsory Sterilization in California* in Sheila Jasonoff's *Reframing Rights: Bioconstitutionalism in the Genetic Age,* MIT Press, c. 2011, p. 30.
28. *Webster's New World Compact Desk Dictionary and Style Guide,* Second Edition, c. 2002, Wiley Publishing Co., p.168.
29. "Euthanasia." *Wikipedia,* the free encyclopedia.
30. "Euthanasia." *Wikipedia,* the free encyclopedia.
31. Ibid.
32. "Euthanasia." *Wikipedia,* the free encyclopedia.
33. "Eugenics in the United States." *Wikipedia,* the free encyclopedia.
34. Ibid.
35 Action T-4. *Wikipedia,* the free encyclopedia.
36. Patients' Rights Council, *CBS Statline.*
37. The Terri Schiavo Case, *Ask.com Encyclopedia*
38. The Terri Schiavo Case. *Ask.com Encyclopedia.*
39. The Terri Schiavo Case, *Ask.com Encyclopedia.*

40. Ibid.
41. The Terri Schiavo Case. *Ask.com Encyclopedia.*
42. Ibid.
43. The Terri Schiavo Case. *Ask.com Encyclopedia.*

Chapter 3:

Margaret Sanger's Nazi Connection

"We prefer the policy of immediate sterilization, of making sure that parenthood is immediately prohibited to the feeble-minded."

— Margaret Sanger, *The Pivot of Civilization*

"The demand that defective people be prevented from propagating equally defective offspring is the most humane act of mankind."

— Adolf Hitler, *Mein Kampf,*

By the time Adolf Hitler and his National Socialist German Workers Party (NSDAP) took power in 1933, Margaret Sanger was already an internationally-known advocate for birth control and eugenics. She had traveled the world over to preach her message of contraception and "family planning," and this message found fertile ground in places like China, Japan, Korea, England, and Holland. However, it was in Hitler's Germany that the ideas put forth by Sanger and her cohorts received their most enthusiastic reception.

As stated earlier in these pages, we are justly repulsed by the thought that any nation or people could actually embark on a policy of breeding "perfect" human beings. We are even more outraged, as we look back over the gulf of more than 80 years, that such a supposedly civilized country as Germany was doing exactly that, using eugenics to bring into existence a so-called "Master Race" that would someday come to rule not only over the German people, but the rest of the world, as well.

Further, we recoil at the thought that such schemes as *Lebensborn* (the breeding of children for the Fatherland), the Nazi policy of forced sterilization of "useless eaters," or the infamous *Aktion T-4* forced euthanasia program could ever have been devised in the minds of Germans, much less carried out on such a massive scale. We are sickened that such policies reached their logical conclusion in "The Final Solution to the Jewish Question," otherwise known as the Holocaust, an event which led to the deaths of six million Jews in Germany and the vast majority of the European continent, which fell under the Nazi reign of terror during World War II. To this day. the effects of such a horrible blight on humanity remain so powerful that we have vowed that something so unspeakable will never happen to anyone, anywhere, ever again.

Margaret Sanger's supporters are quite vocal in their assertions that she decried the actions of the German government in carrying out its eugenic policy under Adolf Hitler, Hermann Goring, Heinrich Himmler, Adolph Eichmann, and Reinhard Heydrich. And they point to the public denunciations of such policies as forced sterilizations, gassings, and "mercy killings" as proof or her abhorrence of Hitler's regime and its actions. True, she had written to Edith How-Martyn that "all the news in Germany is sad and horrible and to me more dangerous than any other war going on because it has so many good people who applaud the atrocities and claim it is right." [1]

"The sudden antagonism in Germany against the Jews and the vitriolic hatred of them," Sanger continued, "is spreading underground here and is far more dangerous than the aggressive policy of the Japanese in Manchuria." They also point out that her books were among those tossed into the fire at the book-burnings all over Germany in a disgusting orgy of hatred that also consumed the works of Sigmund Freud, Thomas Mann, and Albert Einstein in the wake of Hitler's accession to the Chancellorship on January 30, 1933. Remember that this was the same woman who lectured the Ku Klux Klan's Ladies' Auxiliary in Silver Lake seven years earlier. And, bear in mind as well, that Jews held a very high position on the Klan's hit list.

So, was Margaret Sanger a Nazi? Did she subscribe to the Party's philosophy and its attendant ideology? Did her actions and associations in this country comport with her denunciations of Hitler's regime and the unspeakable atrocities it committed against so many of its own citizens while at the same time acting in the name of the German people?

These are questions that have rarely, if ever, been asked, questions that cry out for answers from Sanger's supporters and apologists. As the saying goes, one can judge a person by the company they keep, so let us now do exactly that. Let us examine the company that Margaret Sanger kept, the associations and alliances she maintained, and judge for ourselves the validity of her supporters' claims and assertions.

While it is true that Sanger was never a member of the Nazi Party or of its American offshoot, it cannot be denied or wished away that she was in sympathy with many of its goals regarding eugenics. It has already been established quite clearly that the American eugenics movement and its German counterpart each had the same objective: each sought to "improve" or "purify" its respective gene pool through the use of scientific means. In the U.S., this was carried out in various ways such as sterilization (either voluntarily of coercively), anti-miscegenation statutes, immigration laws limiting the number of people coming into this country from a particular part of the world, and so on, and so forth.

Germany's approach to "racial hygiene," as it was called, took on a far darker tone, especially after Hitler's accession to the Chancellorship. His rise to power took the German eugenics movement, which had originated in the late 1800s, in a wholly new and different direction. His role as the leader of the failed Beer Hall *Putsch* (or coup) on November 9, 1923, put him in Landsberg Prison from 1924-25, a time during which he had ample opportunity to entertain visitors, steep his fellow inmates in Nazi doctrine, and just as importantly, to read, and read he did, voraciously.

During his time behind bars, Hitler read everything he could get his hands on, and he pored over the texts of American eugenicists like Harry Laughlin, Lothrop Stoddard, and Margaret Sanger. During his confinement at Landsberg, he also dictated his autobiography *Mein Kampf* ("My Struggle") to his faithful Secretary Rudolph Hess, who was also jailed for his part in the botched military takeover of the government in Munich. Hess would later be named Deputy *Fuhrer* by Hitler until his fateful and inexplicable flight from Germany to England in 1941 at the height of World War II. The American eugenicists spoke to Hitler through the pages of their books, and their ideas on the subject reinforced his own. Hitler was especially struck by the Darwinian theme of "survival of the fittest" that they conveyed, and their notions seemed to confirm his own racist views.

This was especially true concerning Europe's Jews, whom he had come to despise as *untermensch,* or "subhuman," (an attitude that began to form following his encounters with them during his time as a wandering vagabond in Vienna in the early 1900s), and on whom he would later unleash the full fury of his hatred upon becoming Germany's head of state. Hitler wrote at length in *Mein Kampf* of his revulsion at seeing hundreds of orthodox Jews strolling along the wide thoroughfares of the city dressed in long black robes and wearing the traditional head covering, the *yarmulke*, and he spared no effort to hide his contempt for them.

In his 2000 book on Nazi Germany, *The Third Reich: A New History*, author Michael Burleigh provides us with an insight into the future German leader's attitudes toward the Jews in this passage from Hitler's tome: "In a short time," Hitler wrote, "I was made more thoughtful than ever by my slowly rising insight into this type of activity carried on by the Jews in certain fields. Was there any form of filth or profligacy, particularly in cultural life, without at least one Jew involved in it? If you cut even cautiously into such an abscess you found, like a maggot in a rotting body, often dazzled by the sudden light—-a little Jew." [2]

The pages of *Mein Kampf* are filled to the brim with such a visceral, vitriolic brand of hatred for Hitler's "chosen people," chosen for extermination, that is. Hitler blamed the Jews for all kinds of social and economic ills that befell his later-to-be adopted country of Germany (he was actually born in the town of Braunau-am-Inn in Austria) and what he would call the "Aryan" race. To him, the Jews controlled everything: the banks, the press, the military, and, seemingly, everything in between.

They were, after all, the ones who started World War I (or The Great War of 1914-1918, as it was called at the time), and they were among the "November Criminals" who sold out the German Army, in which he had served as a courier, and the German people by "stabbing them in the back" on November 11, 1918. What was worse, in his view, it was the Jews who were despoiling the "pure" racial stock of the superior Nordic peoples. Hitler vowed to revenge himself on them, thus saving the Aryan race from being annihilated and avenging Germany's defeat at the hands of its external enemies and those within who had so cravenly betrayed the Fatherland in the Great War. Hitler claimed that by eradicating the Jews he would be doing "God's work." But this would have to wait until he was released from prison and embarked on a political career. In the meantime, he continued to study eugenics, a field which would play a prominent role in the future of the German state and the world at large.

During Hitler's readings on the subject, he became so enamored of Harry Laughlin, Lothrop Stoddard, Margaret Sanger, and Madison Grant that he even sent a letter to Grant praising Grant's book *The Passing of the Great*

Race, calling it his "bible." [3] He became so convinced that it was possible to breed a "Master Race" that when he became Chancellor on January 30, 1933, he immediately tasked the German medical community with making his vision a reality.

One of Hitler's first official acts as Chancellor was passage of the *Gesetz zur Verhutung Ebkranken Enchases Nachwacheses* (the Law for the Prevention of Hereditary Diseased Offspring), which he signed into law on July 14, 1933. [4] Under its auspices, more than 200 eugenic courts were created, and all German doctors were required to report patients who were mentally retarded, mentally ill or blind, or who were deaf or physically deformed. Even alcoholics were included in this rather lengthy laundry list of those deemed "unfit" by the regime. The law also stipulated that any doctor who did not properly report such individuals was subject to stiff fines in order to force compliance with its provisions.

Those patients in question had their cases reviewed by eugenic courts consisting of Party officials and public health officers who would take a look at their medical records and interview their friends and colleagues before issuing their decisions as to whether to order them sterilized. The patients themselves never had any choice in the matter; in fact, if they did not submit to the courts' demand that they appear willingly, they would be forced to do so. By the time the Third Reich collapsed around Hitler in a nightmarish *gotterdamerung* in April 1945, the Law for the Prevention of Hereditary Diseased Offspring had exacted a frightful toll on Germany's populace, claiming over 400,000 victims of the Nazis' rabid obsession with creating a "Master Race."

The aforementioned law and others like it were the product of Hitler's and the Nazis' tortured belief in the doctrine of "blood and soil," which among other things preached the superiority of the "Aryan" (or northern Indian) race over all others, especially those of Jewish descent. In addition to being the source of all the world's ills, Jews simply did not fit into Hitler's notion of the ideal man and, therefore, must be eliminated along with a whole slew of people who did not measure up, people like Slavs, gypsies, Poles, and, yes, those physically and mentally deficient people who were subjected to the tender mercies of Hitler's eugenic courts.

Hitler's ideal of the perfect man was a tall, blond, fair-skinned Adonis, who would be possessed of almost super-human strength and who would use those attributes to fight Hitler's wars and usher into existence a "Thousand-year Reich." And *Der Fuhrer* (The Leader) would have plenty of help in realizing this dream from the likes of Heinrich Himmler, *Reichsfuhrer-SS,* and a former chicken farmer, fanatical Propaganda Minister Joseph Goebbels, Gestapo Chief Reinhard Heydrich, Adolph Eichmann, the architect of the "Final Solution to the Jewish Question," and thousands more.

As cruel and inhuman as this first law was, however, it paled in comparison to the enactment of the so-called "Nuremburg Laws," passed by the German *Reichstag* on September 15 , 1935. Now effectively stripped of the same basic protections that all other Germans enjoyed, Jews in Germany were no longer citizens in their own land. The preamble of the Law for the Protection of German Blood and Honor states: "Imbued with the insight that the purity of German blood is prerequisite for the continued existence of the German people and inspired by the inflexible will to ensure the existence of the German nation, the Reichstag has unanimously adopted the following law, which is hereby promulgated." [5]

The restrictions placed on German Jews were immediate and far-reaching, and included prohibitions on marriages between Jews and "subjects of German and kindred blood," extramarital intercourse between the same, and hiring of Jews by "female subjects of German and kindred blood" who were under the age of forty-five. [6] Notice, if you will, the use of the word "subject" instead of "citizen" in the new law. The difference between the two could not be clearer. Citizens possess certain rights and their corresponding responsibilities, which include having a voice in how the affairs of state are conducted. Subjects have no such rights. They are not participants in the democratic process, but are rather little more than onlookers who are waiting for the next *diktat* from on high. It is both telling and tragic that the Nazis viewed not only the Jews, but the rest of their own *populace* in such a condescending fashion. What is even more astonishing is that, with very few exceptions, the German people just sat there and took it. This is the nature of a dictatorship, not a nation of free men. Indeed, as Frederick Osborn stated, "Germany's rapidity of change with respect to eugenics was possible only under a dictator." [7]

However, the Nuremburg Laws, as the new legislation came to be known, extended to far more than just sexual intercourse between Jew and Gentile. All aspects of Jewish life in Germany were affected, from the refusal of shops and restaurants to serve Jewish patrons to the denial of a chance to receive a college education, to prohibitions on employment in the trades and professions, and practically everything else. Drawing on how blacks in the United States had been and were being treated, Hitler succeeded in making the lot of the German Jews so unbearable that many of them (those who could afford to do so after the Reich confiscated most, if not all, of their property first) would leave the country.

And they did, many of them, ranging from the noted physicists Albert Einstein, father of the Theory of Relativity, and Edward Teller, father of the atomic bomb, to renowned actress Marlene Dietrich, who took their brains and talents with them to their new homes. Because of the "brain drain" that resulted from the mindless and breathtakingly racist laws now in place in the Third Reich, Germany became educationally and culturally impoverished and would pay dearly a few short years hence for its leaders' warped ideas of what constituted a "Master Race." For those Jews who remained, racist sterilization laws and denial of their rights as German citizens turned out to be the least of their worries compared with what awaited them at places like Dachau, Treblinka, Bergen-Belsen, Sobibor, and worst of all, at Auschwitz. For "The Final Solution to the Jewish Question" was also part and parcel of the Nazi eugenic program.

At this point, let us refer back to Margaret Sanger's May 21, 1933 letter to Edith How-Martyn in which she expressed such shock and outrage at and sympathy for the plight of the Jews living in Hitler's Germany. One would have thought that someone with her stature and high public profile would be doing everything possible to assist these horribly oppressed souls, like lobbying the U.S. government to amend the Immigration Restriction Act of 1924 to allow more, not fewer, Jews to escape Hitler's tyranny.

Sadly, no record exists of her ever having made such an effort. Indeed, she and her colleagues in the eugenics movement did the exact *opposite*, and resolutely opposed any such increase in the number of people, including the Jews, who were seeking to come to this country. Of this we do have a record, which is contained in the April 1932 issue of *The Birth Control Review.* In this piece, Sanger left no doubt as to her position on this question. Sanger was quite blunt, writing that America should "keep the doors of immigration closed to the entrance of certain aliens whose condition is known to be detrimental to the stamina of the race, such as feebleminded, idiots, morons, insane, syphilitic, epileptic, criminal, professional prostitutes, and others in this class barred by immigration laws of 1924." [8]

Because of her views and those of other eugenicists, the U.S. made no provisions to allow an increase in the number of Jews who were attempting to flee Hitler's reign of terror to come to America. In fact, as David Wyman writes in *The Abandonment of the Jews: America and the Holocaust 1941-45*, only 21,000 Jews were admitted during the entirety of our involvement in World War II. [9] We like to pride ourselves on the idea that the words inscribed on the Statue of Liberty, words that read, "*Give me your poor, your tired, your wretched refuse, your huddled masses yearning* to *breathe free*," actually mean something, but, in this case, they did not. It will be to our everlasting shame as a nation that we knew what was happening to the Jews in Germany, yet, deliberately chose to do next to nothing because of Margaret Sanger and her ilk. But knowing what we know about her racist views and associations, could one have expected anything less from one of the country's leading eugenicists?

There exists a common misperception that the German eugenics program originated with the onset of Hitler's regime, but, in reality, the sterilization of so-called "unfit" persons was promoted at least as far back as the First World War. A number of writers have commented on this subject, including author Gisela Bock, who writes that by the end of that conflict, "sterilization was widely and passionately viewed as a solution to urgent social problems."

Paul Wiendling reveals that the emphasis on coercive sterilization "predated the Third Reich and had been developed and lobbied for during the Weimar years," [9] and some eugenic researchers were not happy about the new regime's actions. He cites one German geneticist, Richard Goldschmidt, as complaining that the Nazis "took over our entire plan of eugenic measures." [10] Wiendling elaborates further: "The authoritarian politics provided favorable circumstances for eugenicists to exert influence on social policy in the planning of sterilization legislation" [11] Moreover, the Nazi policy of coercive sterilization, contrary to popular belief, was not a homegrown one; far from it. In fact, it had lots of help.

As stated earlier, Hitler read voraciously during his imprisonment and had taken a keen interest in the progress of the eugenic movement in the United States. So, by the time he was released in 1925, he was well-versed in the subject. He spoke with particular pride to one fellow Nazi that "I have followed with great interest the laws of several American states concerning prevention of reproduction by people whose progeny would, in all probability, be of no value or be injurious to the racial stock." [12] One state whose eugenic policy Hitler followed quite closely was California, which led the U.S. in the number of forced sterilizations.

The California law, signed in 1909 by Governor James Gillette, sought to reduce the number of social "misfits" by sterilizing their parents and read as follows: "Whenever in the opinion of the medical superintendent of any state hospital, or superintendent of the California Home for the Care and

Training of Feebleminded Children, or of the resident physician in any state prison, it would be beneficial and conducive to the benefit of the physical, mental, or moral condition of any inmate of any said state hospital, home or state prison, to be asexualized, then such superintendent or resident physician shall call in consultation the general superintendent of state hospitals and the secretary of the state Board of Health, and they shall jointly examine into all the particulars of the case with the said superintendent or resident physician, and if in their opinion or in the opinion of any of the two of them, asexualization will be beneficial to such inmate, patient or convict, they may perform the same." [13]

As Alex Wellerstein writes in his book *States of Eugenics*, " 'Whenever in the opinion' is the crucial phase that defined the character of eugenics in California; operations were performed at the discretion of the superintendents." [14] Also worth noting is that nowhere in the California law is the word "sterilization" mentioned; rather, the procedure is called "asexualization." The use of such a euphemism, it could be argued, would be rather like an abortion supporter using the phrase "pro-choice" to mask their real sentiments.

It was this law and others like it around the country which would inspire Margaret Sanger's cohort Harry Laughlin in crafting his proposed Model Eugenical Sterilization Law in 1922. Interestingly, Laughlin also helped get Congress to pass the Immigration Restriction Act two years later. This was the same law, the reader will recall, which Sanger was so vocal in citing when she opposed any increase in the number of Jews who were seeking to flee Hitler's Germany. Wellerstein goes on to inform us that because California's original law was seen as being too vague, it was repealed in 1913 and replaced with a new, stronger sterilization mandate that allowed the State Department of Mental Hygiene (whose precursors were the State Commission on Lunacy and the State Department of Institutions) to sterilize a patient.

"The first section of the 1913 statute," Wellerstein writes, "specified that the patient must be afflicted with hereditary insanity or incurable chronic mania or dementia." What follows in Section Two, Wellerstein notes, "is simply an exact duplicate of the 1909 statute, which enabled sterilization at the discretion of physicians, with no further specifications of the kinds of reasons that had to be given." [15]

The 1913 law that so inspired the Nazis and some of their allies in the U.S. was amended in 1917 and again in 1923, on the first occasion to add "those suffering from perversion or marked departures from normal mentality" or from "disease of a syphilitic nature," and on the second to expand the list to include prisoners who were convicted of molesting young girls under the age of ten. Wellerstein writes that "no further changes to this legislation took place until 1951, when the law was substantially rewritten as part of a general overhaul of health legislation." [16]

Laughlin had issues with the California law, but they were more in the way in which it was worded than in how effective it was. For instance, he believed it lacked specificity and relied too much on the use of the word "may," which appeared no less than seven times in its original form when it came to who had the authority to order a sterilization procedure. To him, the use of such a word defeated the very idea of compliance. "For a law to be compulsory (for the physicians)," he wrote, "then of course there must be no gaps in its chain of mandates, which begins with the order for appointment of executive officers and ends with the actual surgical procedure of sterilization. A single 'may,' inserted in the chain of execution, makes the whole procedure an optional one, or at least a non-compulsory one." To Laughlin, the absence of any language mandating action on the part of doctors was not only pointless, but totally unsatisfactory and unacceptable.

Nonetheless, despite his misgivings, Laughlin could not argue with the results. In fact, he couldn't help but express his admiration for the way the Golden State was carrying out its eugenic program. "To California," he wrote effusively, "must be given the credit for making the most of her sterilization laws. The history of the application of these statutes shows an honest and competent effort to improve the racial qualities of future generations." [17]

Note here the use of the words "racial qualities" that Laughlin employed in his paean to the California eugenicists. Nowhere in the text of the original 1909 law were these words used; nor were they in the 1913 statute that replaced it, nor were they when the law was amended in 1917 and in 1923. One is tempted to ponder what went through the minds of these folks upon reading these sentiments. But, since they have all long since departed this world, we will never know. One thing we do know for certain is that the German eugenicists and the *Fuhrer,* who commanded them to do his bidding, looked time and again to their counterparts across the Atlantic Ocean for guidance in creating the "perfect" race of men, a race of men that was unlike any the world had ever seen before.

A race of men free from all human frailty. A race of men who would be unburdened by disease, by physical deformity or mental illness. And, a race of men that, in their view, would come to dominate the world through the new "science" of selective breeding. One example of such guidance was Harry

Laughlin's aforementioned Model Eugenical Sterilization Law, which the head of the Eugenic Records Office hoped would serve as a template for a program of selective breeding in every state. It was this law which served as a model for future German race and population-control policy. Not surprisingly, it was enthusiastically supported by German eugenicists like Dr. Ernst Rudin, the director of the Kaiser Wilhelm Institute for genealogy in Munich. Rudin and other German eugenicists were so taken with Laughlin's work and the proposed law that resulted that they bestowed a special award on him in 1936 from Heidelberg University for his work in "the science of racial cleansing." Laughlin was delighted with the award and wanted to accept it personally, but was unable to do so because he could not make the trip to Germany himself, so he picked it up from the Rockefeller Foundation instead.

Rudin was one of the foremost German researchers in the field of selective breeding, and along with Dr. Alfred Ploetz, was part of the Expert Committee on Questions of Population and Race Theory. The group was assembled by German Interior Minister Wilhelm Frick on June 2, 1933 "to plan the course of Nazi racial policy." [18] Under this mandate, the group quickly went to work and by July 14 had devised a number of recommendations that would soon become known as the Law for the Prevention of Genetically Diseased Offspring, the first of the Nazi sterilization statutes and which would take effect on January 1, 1934.

Rudin and others repeatedly credited American eugenicists like Harry Laughlin, Lothrop Stoddard, and Dr. Paul Popenoe as their inspiration in crafting their race hygiene Legislation, and they specifically cited California's coercive sterilization law as the basis for the new German legislation. In her article "Legal and Medical Aspects of Eugenic Sterilization in Germany," author Marie Kopp wrote, "The leaders in the German sterilization movement state repeatedly that their legislation was formulated after careful study of the California experiment as reported by Mr. Gosney and Dr. Paul Popenoe. It would have been impossible, they say, to undertake such a venture involving some one million people without drawing heavily on previous experience elsewhere." [19] We will examine the case of Dr. Popenoe and his connections to Margaret Sanger later on, but for the moment let us continue to focus on Rudin and his work.

As previously mentioned, German eugenicists had been hard at work at least since the years following the First World War and their recommendations had been in place since the years of the Weimar Republic, but they were never really acted upon by any of the succession of German governments.

This understandably frustrated many of them, but all of that changed when Adolf Hitler took over on January 30, 1933. Now, for the first time, their work would not only be taken seriously, it would be made a top priority under the new regime.

Rudin, for one, could hardly contain himself at the change in course. In his address to the German Society for *Rassenhygiene* ("race hygiene"), he expressed his delight and gratitude: "The significance of *Rassenhygiene* did not become evident to all aware Germans until the political activity of Adolf Hitler," Rudin gushed, "and only through his work has our 30-year long dream of translating *Rassenhygiene* into action finally become a reality." [20] Calling the new policy "a duty of honor," he continued, "We can hardly express our efforts more plainly or appropriately than in the words the *Fuhrer*: 'Whoever is not physically or mentally fit must not pass on his defects to his children. The state must take care that only the fit produce children. Conversely, it must be regarded as reprehensible to withhold healthy children from the state.'" [21] Margaret Sanger's disciples are quick to dismiss any links to the German eugenicists, yet, the evidence to the contrary is quite clear. For example, her *Birth Control Review* carried an article penned by Rudin titled "Eugenic Sterilization: An Urgent Need," which appeared in print three months before the landmark "sterilization" legislation was passed in Germany. [22]

Although her supporters go to great lengths to try to assure us that Sanger was no Nazi sympathizer, they cannot deny the fact that she also corresponded with Rudin and never once repudiated or condemned his views. In fact, despite her professed outrage at what happened to six million Jews in the Holocaust, Sanger and her cohorts in the American eugenics movement at some point must be held accountable for supporting the eugenic policies of the German government, which made the whole thing possible in the first place, and which destroyed so many innocent lives in pursuit of the mad dream of establishing a "Master race."

Rudin's sentiments weren't reserved just for the German people; he wrote an essay tailored *specifically* to his counterparts in the U.S. that in his words were "concerned only with sterilization as a voluntary practice, that is, undertaken with the consent of the patient himself or his statutory guardians." [23] How different this was from the policy of coerced sterilization that he and other leaders in the field were preparing for enactment into law in his own homeland!

But Rudin, like so many American eugenicists, knew that the people in this country would never support a national policy of coerced sterilization, despite the efforts of those like Harry Laughlin to bring it about. Therefore, in Rudin's estimation, a program of "systematic and careful propaganda should be undertaken where sterilization is advisable. Such propaganda should, of course, be gradual and should be directed in the first instance at the medical directors in institutions and schools, medical officers of health, and finally at private practitioners." [24] If one did not know better, this would sound eerily similar to the "religious appeal" Sanger advocated be made to the "rebellious" black congregations who opposed her Negro Project as an act of genocide against them.

American eugenicists, including Lothrop Stoddard, whom Sanger appointed to the Board of Directors of her American Birth Control League, often traveled to Germany to compare notes with their brethren in the Fatherland. In Stoddard's case, he journeyed to Germany in 1934 and was granted an exclusive audience with Hitler himself. Needless to say, Stoddard, who applauded the German dictator's rise to power in 1933, was greatly impressed by his tete-a-tete with *der Fuhrer.* In his book *The Nazi Connection: Eugenics, American Racism and German National Socialism,* author Stefan Kuhl writes about how Stoddard lauded his German hosts for "increasing both the size and the quality of the population" [25] and how he praised them for encouraging "sound" citizens to reproduce with "a drastic curb of the defective elements." [26]

Stoddard did not stop there, however. According to Kuhl, he spoke in glowing terms of how the Nazis were "weeding out the worst strains in the Germanic stock in a truly scientific and humanitarian way." [27] And, when it came to the Jews, whom the Nazis targeted not only for persecution but for forced sterilization and abortion (to say nothing of their ultimate annihilation in the Holocaust), Stoddard would write in *Into the Darkness: Nazi Germany Today,* (1940), "The 'Jew problem' is already settled in principle and is soon to be settled by the physical elimination of the Jews themselves from the Third Reich." [28]

Was Stoddard writing about only the coerced sterilizations and forced abortions of German Jews? Was he referring to the Nazi policy of driving Germany's Jews from the country to seek refuge in other lands such as England and the United States? Did he also mean the deportations of the Jews to places like Poland, where they would be forcibly resettled? Or, did Hitler, in the course of their time together in 1934, give him some peek into what was to eventually become first of Germany's and then all of Europe's Jews?

By its title, *Into the Darkness* may have been an attempt by Stoddard to engage in second-guessing the motives of Hitler's regime *vis-à-vis* the Jews. So be it. Nonetheless, the fact remains that Stoddard, like his fellow ABCL Board member Harry Laughlin, and their boss Margaret Sanger, were all avowed racists who looked at eugenics as a primary weapon in the extermination of "inferior" human beings.

Stoddard, however, was by no means the only American eugenicist with whom the Nazis attempted to curry favor. Another was Leon Whitney, the executive director of the American Eugenics Society. Whitney was an enthusiastic supporter of Germany's forced sterilization program and looked upon it with a rather *macabre* combination of both wistfulness and envy, saying of Germany's headlong leap into the eugenic abyss, "While we were pussy-footing around, the Germans were calling a spade a spade." [29] Whitney's sentiments were echoed by some very high profile and otherwise respectable Americans.

One of these people was Joseph DeJarnette, the superintendent of Virginia's Western State Hospital, who in an interview with the *Richmond Times-Dispatch* groused, "The Germans are beating us at our own game." [30] Whitney's work was so highly regarded in German eugenic circles that Hitler himself requested a copy of his book *The Case for Forced Sterilization*. Whitney complied immediately and received a letter from Hitler thanking him for his indulgence. According to Whitney's unpublished autobiography, he later met with Madison Grant and showed him the German dictator's correspondence, whereupon Grant showed him a letter from the *Fuhrer*, which thanked him for writing *The Passing of the Great Race*. Hitler described the book as his "bible," and Whitney concluded that, given his actions, "one could believe it." [31]

Let us now turn to another American eugenicist whom the Germans credited with serving as their inspiration, Dr. Paul H. Popenoe. Popenoe, William Tucker tells us, was the author of the most widely used American eugenics text and the editor of the *Journal of Heredity*. Popenoe had served in the U.S. Army in World War I and specialized in the study of sexually-transmitted diseases before turning to the field of eugenics, and had advocated the practice of eugenic sterilization, which, he wrote in an article that appeared in the April 1933 issue of Margaret Sanger's *Birth Control Review*, "is one of the many indispensable measures in any modern program of social welfare." He called it "an integral part of a general system of protection, parole, and supervision, for those who by reason of mental disease or deficiency are unable to meet the responsibilities of citizenship."

"Sterilization," Popenoe continued, "promotes eugenics by cutting off some of the lines of descent that are spreading mental disease and mental defects throughout the population." He went on to observe that at that time there were approximately 5 million people in the United States who would at some time be committed to state hospitals as being insane and another 5 million or more who "were so deficient intellectually (with less than 70% of average intelligence), as to be, in many cases, liabilities rather than assets to the race." [32] He warned his readers, "the situation will grow worse instead of better if steps are not taken to control the reproduction of the mentally handicapped" and that "eugenic sterilization represents one such step that is practicable, humanitarian, and certain in its results." [33]

To Popenoe the German eugenic program was a virtual godsend. The Nazis had done their homework and were showing the world how to do things the right way. He saw how Hitler had read the definitive German work on heredity by researchers Baur, Fischer, and Lenz, and concluded that the Nazis were basing the results of their findings "solidly on the application of biological principles to human society." [34] It is little wonder, then, that Popenoe was so bullish on Germany's eugenic program.

After all, he had been both directly and intimately involved in the passage of California's notorious coercive sterilization law in 1909, a law under which the reader will recall more than 20,000 people had their lives permanently and unalterably damaged.

Like a proud father whose child had not only learned from him, but had gone him one better, now Popenoe, in his own words, had given his enthusiastic blessing to the ruination of millions of *German* lives. By praising the efforts of the Nazi regime, he had linked himself forever to one of the most despicable, cruel, and inhuman governments in all of human history.

Just how lethal Popenoe's eugenic views were can be found in his endorsement of executing the "unfit." In his textbook *Applied Eugenics* he stated, "From an historical point of view, the first method which presents itself is execution...Its value in keeping up the standard of the race should not be underestimated." [35] Elsewhere in *Applied Eugenics,* Popenoe advanced other methods of what he called "lethal selection," even devoting an entire chapter to the idea. In it, Popenoe wrote that lethal selection involved the destruction of the individual "by some adverse feature of the environment, such as by cold, or bacteria, or by bodily deficiency." [36]

We have all read of the atrocities committed by the Nazis in World War II, horrible, unspeakable abuses involving the gas chambers and ovens at

Auschwitz, the hideous experiments performed on prisoners by "Doctor" Josef Mengele, and the duplicitous part that was played in all of this by German companies like I.G. Farben, which supplied the poison gas *Zyklon-B* to the death camps. And we wonder where the Nazis got such barbaric ideas. Since Hitler had such high praise for American eugenicists like Paul Popenoe, is it not at least plausible to posit that they may have gotten them from him?

American philanthropic organizations were also deeply involved in the German eugenic movement, such as the Carnegie Institution, the Rockefeller Foundation, and the Harriman railroad fortune. Carnegie, the reader will recall, set up the first eugenic laboratory complex at Cold Spring Harbor, New York, in 1904. It will also be recalled that it was there that Harry Laughlin established his Eugenic Records Office. The Rockefeller Foundation, in addition to funding Margaret Sanger's birth control programs in the U.S., also helped found the German eugenic program that employed Mengele before he went to Auschwitz, where he soon acquired the infamous title of "the Angel of Death." [37]

The Harriman fortune, for its part, concentrated its efforts on bankrolling local charities in New York, for example, the city's Bureau of Industries and Immigration, with the express objective of identifying Jewish, Italian, and other immigrants in New York and other crowded cities and targeting them for deportation, imprisonment, or even worse, forced sterilization. [38] These organizations worked closely with their cohorts in California in aiding and abetting their German colleagues by publishing racist eugenic literature and fake scientific journals and exporting them for circulation in Germany. [39]

Hitler and his followers eagerly read this trash and used it to justify their despicable and murderous program of forced sterilization, euthanasia, human experimentation, and genocide. Despite the fevered denials and professed outrage that American eugenicists like Sanger, Laughlin, Stoddard, and Popenoe voiced over what was taking place across the Atlantic Ocean, the record is clear and damning. They could not escape the fact at that time that the horrors the Nazis unleashed first in Germany and later on in the rest of Europe were heavily influenced by their brethren in the United States, any more than their apologists can escape it today.

Two other areas of the German eugenic agenda that bear examination were the Third Reich's *Lebensborn* (German for "spring of life") [40] and *Aktion* (German for "Action") *T-4* programs. *Lebensborn* was a secret project that came into existence on December 12, 1935, and involved the breeding of racially "pure" children for the regime by the members of the Nazi SS *(Schutzstaffel,* or Security Service), and the *Wehrmacht* (the German Army). It was overseen by Hitler's faithful henchman, *Reichsfuhrer-SS* Heinrich Himmler, and would be in keeping with his leader's admonition that it was "morally reprehensible to withhold children from the state."

Himmler founded the *Lebensborn* program (which was officially titled *Lebensborn E.V. (Eingetragener Verein,* or "registered association" in German) to reverse Germany's declining population that had occurred over the preceding decades due the country's high abortion rate. As many as 800,000 of these procedures a year had been performed in the years between World Wars I and II. [41] *Lebensborn* was intended to reverse that trend by encouraging the breeding of as many children as possible who would, in the Nazis' view, be of "superior" racial stock and would embody the genetic characteristics that were deemed preferable by them at a time when those whose genetic makeup was deemed to be "undesirable" were either being sterilized or aborted out of existence. Some of these "desirable" characteristics included, but were not limited to fair skin, blue eyes, and blond hair, in short, as many of the Nordic or "Aryan" qualities that the Nazis favored as was possible. In this way, Himmler hoped that Germany's population would rise to 120 million within a few decades. The organization was partly an office within the Nazi *SS* with the responsibility for certain family welfare programs, and partly a society for Party bigwigs.

In a letter to members of the *SS* that surfaced after World War II, Himmler laid out *Lebensborn's* aims and objectives. On September 13, 1936, he wrote: "The organization '*Lebensborn E.V.* ' serves the SS leaders in the selection and adoption of qualified children. The organization *Lebensborn E.V.*' is under my personal direction, is part of the race and settlement central bureau of the SS, and has the following obligations:

1. Support racially, biologically, and hereditarily, valuable families with many children;
2. Place and care for racially and biologically and hereditarily valuable pregnant women who, through their and their progenitor's families and the race and settlement central bureau of the SS, can be expected to produce equally valuable children;
3. Care for the children;
4. Care for the children's mothers.

It is the honorable duty of all leaders of the central bureau to become members of the organization '*Lebensborn E. V.*' The application for admission must be filed prior to 23 September, 1936." [42]

The requirements of the *Lebensborn* program were stringent and included not only the physical characteristics of the parents, but their family backgrounds as well. For example, each parent had their genealogy traced back at least three generations in order to assure that any "suspect" bloodlines (usually Jewish) were not present. There could be no doubts whatsoever about the fitness of prospective parents under *Lebensborn*. Just how rigorous the requirements for inclusion in the program were reflected in the fact that only 40 percent of women who applied passed the racial test and were accepted, and that the majority of the mothers who took part were unmarried (57.6 percent until 1939, and 70 percent a year later). [43] The German people, despite their fanatical support of Hitler, still thought that bearing children out of wedlock was immoral, hence, the utter secrecy surrounding the *Lebensborn* program.

Children born under the program were taken to *SS* nurseries and later to *Lebensborn* homes, the first of which was opened in 1936 in Steinhoering, a small village a short distance from Munich. During World War II, *Lebensborn* homes also were set up in Norway (9), Austria (2), and Belgium, Holland, France, Luxembourg and Denmark (1 each). Here the mothers were provided with the means of bearing their children in an environment of safety, comfort, and secrecy, free of the social stigma attached to being an unwed mother. The surroundings were often lavish and were furnished with items and accessories that the Nazis looted from the homes of Jews who were sent to Dachau, the first of the concentration camps set up by the Hitler regime. In many cases, the homes had also, at one time, been Jewish residences or nursing facilities. Himmler himself took a personal interest in these homes to the extent where he visited them often, chose the mothers, and favored children who were born on his birthday, October 7.

Himmler had high hopes for his project, but within four years of its inception it had not produced the results that he wanted. By that time Germany was deeply involved in World War II, and the casualties were already beginning to mount despite the impressive number of victories the Nazis were rolling up on the battlefield. Therefore he issued a direct order to all *SS* members and the police to father as many children as possible to make up for the deaths suffered on the battlefield. However, he was forced to rescind it when the public outcry became too great. The German people still regarded the idea of unwed mothers as immoral, this despite the fact that their own country was conducting the most immoral and destructive war in human history with their fanatic approval. But Himmler was not alone in his goal. Hitler too had his own ideas on the subject.

In 1942, the *Fuhrer* instituted a policy that expanded Himmler's program to include non-German mothers. As the *Werhrmacht* continued to overrun Europe, the policy of non-fraternization with women in the Occupied Territories was changed to allow German soldiers not only to mingle with them, but also to have children with them. The racially "fit" girlfriends or one-night stands of *SS* officers would then be invited to a *Lebensborn* home to have their children in safety and privacy.

But, as bad as all this was, it paled in comparison to another aspect of the *Lebensborn* program, the kidnapping and indoctrination of "Aryan-looking" children in the countries to the east that the Nazis invaded and subjugated in World War II. Desperate to increase the German population by any means necessary, the regime instituted a policy whereby any children who appeared German were forcibly taken and spirited off to Germany, where they would be brought up as if they had been born there. Many of these children had been orphaned in the War, but they weren't the only victims of this scheme; it is well-documented that *thousands* of children were seized from their families and brought to the Reich to be "Germanized" at the *Lebensborn* homes. [45] Although the exact number of children who were kidnapped by the *SS* for this purpose may never be fully known, it is estimated that as many as 250,000 of them were taken, with approximately 100,000 of them from Poland alone. [46]

Once they had arrived at their destinations, these children were subjected to all forms of psychological, and in many cases, physical abuse at the hands of their captors. For example, the *SS* nurses at the homes would attempt to brainwash their young charges into believing that their parents had abandoned them. [47] In some cases, these attempts to get the children to forget their parents were successful. But most of these victims weren't stupid; they knew what had happened to them, and they knew who had done it, although they weren't sure exactly why. Those who refused to be brainwashed paid a heavy price, indeed, for their insolence. Many of them were beaten or abused in other ways, but were eventually ticketed for extermination, invariably at the Kalish death camp in Poland. [48]

A particularly horrifying footnote to the infamous *Lebensborn* experiment came in 1942, when Czech partisans bombed the car carrying *SS* Governor Reinhard Heydrich. The faithful lackey of Heinrich Himmler, and who also served as the chief of the Reich Security Office (RhSA), Heydrich was severely wounded and later died of blood poisoning. In reprisal, the *SS* set fire to and destroyed the small village of Lidice, murdering the entire male population in the process.

Ninety-three children were sent to Germany to be assimilated, while the rest were taken to special children's camps at Dzierzazna and Litzmannstadt before they were eventually exterminated. [49] Lidice itself was wiped off the face of the earth and never again appeared on any German map of Czechoslovakia. However, time was running out on the Third Reich and the mad scheme of its leaders to strengthen and purify its "racial stock."

As the War neared its end in the spring of 1945, the Allies liberated thousands of cities and towns along their path to Berlin. One of those towns was Steinhoering, the site of the first *Lebensborn* home. As American troops marched into the town on May 1, they found upwards of 300 children aged six months to six years at the *Lebensborn* home. [50] At other homes near Bremen and Leipzig, British and Soviet soldiers reported having similar encounters.

Though the *Lebensborn* program ended mercifully with the fall of Hitler's Germany, nearly a quarter of a million young people had been horribly damaged by this attempt to accelerate the creation of the "Master race." After the War, every effort was expended to make them whole again by either putting them up for adoption to loving families or reuniting them with their own families. However, many of those who were kidnapped and forcibly assimilated had become so thoroughly brainwashed that they were judged "too Germanic" to fit back into normal society. [51]

Then there was the matter of *Aktion* (German for "action") *T-4,* the Nazi forced euthanasia program. Operating from the beginning of World War II in September 1939 and lasting, at least officially, until August 1941 (it would continue unofficially until the end of the conflict), *Aktion T-4* was named for TiergartenstraBe-4, the address of a villa in the Berlin borough of Tiergarten. The villa served as the headquarters of the *Gemeinnutzige Stiftung fur Heil-und-Anstaltplege* (Charitable Foundation for Curative and Institutional Care) and was overseen by *Reichsleiter* Phillip Bouhler, the head of Hitler's private chancellery, and Dr. Karl Brandt, Hitler's personal physician. [52]

Euthanasia had been promoted since the early part of the twentieth century by German eugenicists such as Alfred Hoche and Karl Binding as a way to end "life unworthy of life," a phrase they coined in 1920, several years before Hitler came to power. This was especially true in the case of racial "hygiene." Hitler himself weighed in on the subject, writing the following in *Mein Kampf*: "He who is bodily and mentally not sound and deserving may not perpetuate this misfortune in the bodies of his children. The *volkische* ("people's") state has to perform this gigantic child-rearing task here. One day, however, it will appear as a deed greater the most victorious wars of our past bourgeois era." [53]

When Hitler came to power in 1933, he immediately set about implementing laws aimed at eliminating perceived racial and social "defects" among certain segments of the German people, among them the so-called Law for the Prevention of Hereditary Diseased Offspring, which we examined earlier, as well as the Nuremburg Laws, which followed in 1935. But while these dealt with sterilization and segregation against the Jews, mercy killing was another matter entirely. Hitler strongly advocated ending "life unworthy of life," and he was quite blunt about who should be put to death and why. In a conference in 1939 that was attended by Health Minister Leonardo Conti and Hans Lammers, head of the Reich Chancellery, Hitler cited severely mentally ill people who could only lie down on sawdust as those he would euthanize because "they perpetually dirtied themselves" or "who put their own excrement in their mouths, and so on."

As Lammers and Conti testified after the War, Hitler told them that he favored killing the incurably ill as early as 1933, but that he hesitated to do so because the public would never accept such a drastic step. [54] No, he reasoned, the time was not right, but that did not prevent him from acting in one specific instance. That instance came in 1938 when a German family petitioned him for permission to kill their severely handicapped infant son. The boy was blind and physically and mentally disabled, and the family turned to Hitler for help. He instructed Karl Brandt to evaluate the petition and the family's request was granted in July of 1939. Hitler further directed his chief doctor to act similarly in a number of other cases. In 1939, the parents of Gerhard Kretschmar, who was born with severe physical deformities, asked Hitler for permission to put their son to death. Hitler agreed and greenlighted the formation of the Reich Committee for the Scientific Registering of Serious Hereditary and Congenital Diseases. [55]

This body, which came under the supervision of Karl Brandt and was administered by Herbert Linden and *SS Oberfuhrer* Viktor Brack, was authorized to approve applications to kill children in circumstances such as the aforementioned cases. The details were left to be hashed out by such Nazi underlings as Brack and *SA* (*Sturmabteilung*, or "storm detachment") *Oberfuhrer* Werner Blankenburg.

This soon opened the door to the wholesale slaughter of untold numbers of children who had committed no crime other than to be born in such dire physical straits. Under the new mandate, the Interior Ministry required doctors and midwives to report all cases of newborns with severe physical or mental handicaps. The reports were assessed by a panel of doctors, who would then make their recommendation. The consent of at least three doctors had to be obtained before a subject could be put to death. Those children aged three and under who exhibited such "serious hereditary disabilities as "suspected idiocy," "Down syndrome (especially the blind and deaf)," "microcephaly, hydrocephaly, malformed limbs, heads, and spinal columns, paralysis, and spastic conditions" were all put to death by lethal injection. [56]

The new policy was sure to raise the opposition of many parents, particularly those of the Catholic faith, so the regime used various forms of deception in order to gain their consent. One such form was to tell the parents that their children were being sent to so-called "Special Sections" where they would receive treatment to improve their sorry condition. To further the lie, the parents were then told that their children would be kept at these places for a few weeks while their cases were "being assessed." After a time, the children would be administered the aforementioned injections, usually of phenol, and the cause of their deaths would be listed as "pneumonia." The *piece de resistance* to the Nazis' cynical campaign of lies and deceit came when the children's autopsies were conducted. Samples of their brains were taken to be used for what was euphemistically called "medical research," and the parents were never any the wiser. This story worked so well that they came to believe that their children had not died in vain after all. [57]

Hitler had always believed that the wholesale killing of "life unworthy of life" was not possible in peacetime because of the firestorm of protest that was sure to result. As he told Dr. Gerhard Wagner, "Such a program could be more smoothly and easily carried out in war." [58]

Hitler's intent, he wrote, was, "in the event of war, radically to solve the problems of the mental asylums." [59] Needless to say, when the *Wehrmacht* invaded Poland on September 1, 1939, Hitler's golden opportunity finally presented itself in spades. One month later he backdated an order to September 1 which authorized Bouhler and Brandt to set the *Fuhrer's* wishes in motion, to wit: "Reich Leader Boulher and Dr. med. Brandt are charged with the responsibility of enlarging the competence of certain physicians, designated by name, so that patients who, on the basis of human judgment [*menschlichem ermessen*], are considered incurable, can be granted mercy death [*Gnatentod*] after a discerning diagnosis." [60]

As the war went on, the casualties inevitably began to mount and the wounded would need medical care upon returning to Germany. This presented a problem, as hospital beds were being taken up and resources were being expended caring not only for the soldiers, but for those with severe disabilities. Many in the regime became openly resentful that these people were being accorded treatment in asylums and hospitals when they believed that caring for Germany's fighting men and those made homeless by the war should take precedence. Why, it was argued, should they have to take a back seat? Or, as one prominent Nazi doctor, Hermann Pfannmuller, put it, "The idea is unbearable to me that the best, the flower of our youth must lose its life at the front in order that feebleminded and irresponsible asocial elements can have a secure existence in the asylum." [61] Hitler's backdated euthanasia order of October 1 helped quell the kind of resentment that was expressed by people like Dr. Pfannnmuller, and there were many of them, to be sure.

The regime went all-out to gain as much public support for euthanasia as possible. But despite such books promoting it as *The Permission to Destroy Life Unworthy of Life* (1920) [62] and a whole host of propaganda leaflets, posters, and short films that the National Socialist Racial and Political Office produced (*The Inheritance,* 1935, *The Victims of the Past,* 1937, and *I Accuse,* 1941), the German public eventually turned against it and Hitler was forced to discontinue the program in August 1941, at least officially. As mentioned earlier, it continued in secret, even after the German surrender on May 7, 1945. For example, the last child killed under *T-4* was Richard Denne, who died on May 29 in the children's ward of the Kaufbeuren-Irsee State Hospital in Bavaria. [63] During the official phase of *T-4,* 70,273 people were killed before Hitler had to give in to mounting public opposition. Much of that opposition came from the Catholic Church, which paid a heavy price, indeed, for its courage.

Catholic institutions that cared for the disabled were closed as a result, their patients transferred to squalid and overcrowded state facilities where they were denied decent medical care, and were cynically used by the regime to promote its "mercy death" program, and it was there that they eventually met their fates. Many parents of disabled children also protested vehemently and were threatened with having them forcibly taken if they did not comply, especially those parents who did not believe the official line about what was really happening. If that failed, they were threatened with being called up for what was termed "labor duty." [64]

Children were not the only targets of the Nazi program to "purify" the Aryan race. Adults were also dispatched with frightening regularity for a host of genetic "defects" that included virtually everything from physical and psychological infirmities such as epilepsy and insanity to chronic alcoholism or simply being racially "inferior." The Nazis went after those who fit this latter category with a vengeance, first executing their murderous agenda not on their fellow Germans, but on the Poles. A secret meeting was held in July of 1939, which was attended by Dr. Leonardo Conti and Professor Walter Hyde, the head of the *SS* medical department, and from which a national register of all institutionalized patients with mental illnesses or physical handicaps was created. [65]

The policy was carried out at first by members of the *SS Einsatzkommando* 16, whocleared out the hospitals and asylums in the Polish region of the Wartheland following the German invasion of the country on September 1. From Danzig to Posen, quite literally thousands of Poles were either shot or gassed by roving German "action squads," or *einsatzgruppen*. Over time gassing proved to be a more efficient and inexpensive means of dispatching the hapless victims than lethal injection, and when Himmler witnessed one such operation in 1939, he enthusiastically endorsed the practice with monstrous and unimaginable consequences, as history has shown us all too well.

Hitler himself endorsed the use of carbon monoxide gas to do away with thousands of people at a time, personally recommending it to Brandt, who later called it "a major advance in medical history." [66] The gassings carried out under *T-4* began in earnest in January of 1940 and lasted (at least officially) for the next two and-a-half years until July of 1942, starting at the Brandenburg Euthanasia Center where 9,772 people were killed dead), Linz, Austria (more than 8,000), Saxony (a body count of 15,000), and Hesse (with 14,494 dead). [67] The helpless victims were taken from their institutions to the killing centers where they invariably met a quick end, often within 24 hours of their arrival. As with the children, the Nazis employed a sophisticated web of lies and deceit to keep the families of handicapped adults from discovering what was really happening to them.

Such tactics included dressing *SS* men in white coats to give them an air of medical authority when they came to take someone away, using buses from the euphemistically-titled "Community Patients Transport Service" to shuttle the condemned to their demise, and sending letters to the families telling them that, because of wartime conditions, it would not be possible to visit their stricken relatives. Those designated for "mercy death" had their cases assessed by a panel of medical experts, who were required to make their judgments based solely on the reports of the staffs of the institutions where the patients were confined. These experts did not refer to the detailed medical histories of the inmates, nor did they examine any of the patients themselves. Reports were marked with a "+" for death, a "-" for life, or a "?" when the panel was unable to decide. Three "death" verdicts sufficed to dispatch the patient in question. The death panel often dealt with hundreds of these reports at once, a testament to the frightening level of efficiency with which the program was being carried out. As time went on, the guidelines for determining who was to live and who would die became more relaxed, the medical criteria broader, and Nazi underlings carried out the euthanasia program themselves in ever-increasing numbers. [68]

Like the *Lebensborn* program, the regime went to great pains to keep *T-4* hidden from the German public. Hitler, mindful of the strong negative reaction that would result if the people ever discovered what was happening, had said as much to Bouhler at its inception, telling him, "the Fuhrer's Chancellery must under no circumstances be seen to be active in this matter." [69] But the air of secrecy could only last so long, given the fact that thousands of doctors, administrators, and other medical personnel were involved and some of them would inevitably talk about what was happening, despite being under strict orders to keep quiet. And, the German people themselves began to ask questions when many families received suspicious death notices, for example, in cases involving deaths resulting from "appendicitis" when the patients had had them removed several years before, or when several families in the same community would receive death notices of loved ones on the same day.

It wasn't long before people began catching on to what was happening in the towns where the killing centers were located and began putting two and two together. Residents could see the buses arriving and the patients entering the facilities, but they also saw that no one ever came out. Further, they could see and smell the smoke belching out of the chimneys of the crematoria, and they couldn't ignore the ashes that fell to the ground like snow flakes. In one particularly gruesome episode, people in the town of Hadamar witnessed not only human ashes wafting down, but human *hair*, as well! [70] In her book *Into That Darkness: An Examination of Conscience,* Gitta Sereny relates how even the children of Hadamar came to a horrifying conclusion about *Aktion T-4*. In May 1941, Sereny writes, Justice Minister Franz Gurtner received a letter from Frankfurt County Court describing how the children of the town were shouting in the streets that people were being taken away to be gassed. [71]

Incidents like the one at Halamar gave rise to an increasing number of protests from the German public, including many Party members themselves, and the outcry became so widespread and intense that it led to the cancellation of the official phase of *Aktion T-4* on August 21, 1941. However, this did not mean that the Nazis stopped killing the disabled. Under the unofficial phase of the program, German and Austrian doctors continued the policy even after the end of the War. Only now, it was carried out less systematically and at the initiative of local doctors and Party leaders. [72] The use of poison gas was then discontinued and people were once more either given lethal injections or they simply were starved to death. Once the Nazis had invaded and occupied the territories to the east, they unleashed the full fury of *Aktion T-4*, especially in the Soviet Union after the Germans invaded on June 22, 1941. Personnel who had served in the program back in Germany found new opportunities to kill on a far grander scale, one which would come to be known as "The Final Solution to the Jewish Question," or simply, the Holocaust. And they did not focus just on those who were physically or mentally handicapped; *Aktion T-4* became an integral part of Hitler's and the Nazis' campaign of annihilation against so-called "inferior" races, especially the Jews.

We cannot end our discussion of the Nazi reign of terror without recognizing that there was another group of Germans, who although their numbers were miniscule when compared to the rest of the country's population, nevertheless were squarely in the Nazis' crosshairs and targeted for extermination: the approximately 24,000 Germans of African descent. While not subjected to the terrors of Hitler's "Final Solution," such as the gas chambers at Auschwitz and other killing factories, black Germans suffered many of the same fates as their countrymen who were white, Jewish, or who came under the regime's ever-expanding definition of what was considered to be "inferior."

The systematic campaign to eliminate Germany's black population, first by depriving it of the same rights other citizens of the country enjoyed and then, to exterminate it entirely through coercive sterilizations, shootings, gassings. and forced abortions, began almost as soon as the Nazis had gained power. Germany's black citizens were not native to the Fatherland, but rather came into the country through immigration or as a result of the country's colonial empire, which included a number of countries in Africa. In time, black Africans in time became used to German institutions, customs, and traditions, so it was only natural for them to consider themselves to, in fact, be German. But all that changed on November 11, 1918, following Germany's defeat in World War I. Under the terms of the Versailles Treaty, which Germany signed in 1919, the country was deprived of its colonial empire and many Africans chose to follow their occupiers home, which did not sit well with the native population. They did this, despite the indignities and even outright atrocities that were committed against them by their occupiers. Such atrocities included forced sterilizations of the native people and even gruesome medical "experiments" that were conducted under Germany's nascent eugenics program. These experiments were conducted in German Southwest Africa (known today as Namibia) as early as 1890 and were overseen by Germany's most senior eugenicist, Dr. Eugen Fischer. [73]

Fischer conducted his "research" to bolster his claims about the "dangerous" genetic differences that he believed existed between black Africans and white Germans, and that race-mixing between them would be nothing short of a disaster. German colonial officials refused to recognize marriages between black Africans and white Germans beginning in 1890, even though such unions were legal in Germany at the time. [74]. Once again, the German policy was based largely on eugenic arguments, and, by 1912, it had become standard operating procedure in many German colonies in Africa. The issue had become so serious that it sparked intense debate back home in the German *Reichstag*. [75] Many German lawmakers expressed concerns that black colonials who came into the country would have the full rights and benefits of German citizenship, e.g., to vote, to serve in the military, and to be employed in the civil service, among others.

Under the terms of the Versailles Treaty, Germany was not only forced to relinquish its African colonies, it also had to submit to French occupation of the Rhineland, which it had won following its victory in the Franco-Prussian War in 1871. France, too, had African colonies like Morocco and Algeria, and many of the troops who moved into the newly-demilitarized region to serve as peacekeepers came from these colonies. This meant an additional influx of blacks into what was, in effect, Germany's "backyard." It also meant contact between white German women and the black African soldiers. These encounters included a number of sexual liaisons, which resulted in the births of between 400 and 600 children of mixed-race relationships.

Many Germans resented the terms of the Versailles Treaty and believed that their country had been "stabbed in the back" by traitors in the government, as well as the victorious Allies. They saw the occupation of the Rhineland by the French and the use of its black soldiers as peacekeepers as another sign of that betrayal. The German press capitalized on this to portray black Africans as "subhuman" and ran sensational stories of incidents in which French colonial soldiers raped innocent German women who then bore them what came to be known as "the Rhineland Bastards." [76] It was the resentment of Versailles, the reader will recall, which Hitler exploited so masterfully in his quest for ultimate power, a quest which proved so monstrously successful and led to the deaths of tens of millions of soldiers and civilians in World War II.

When Hitler became Germany's Chancellor in 1933 and its absolute dictator a year later, he began to put his master plan of extermination into effect. We have seen how he went after the Jews, who had always been his number one target, but other groups came to feel his wrath as well, including Germany's black citizens. In *Mein Kampf,* Hitler took dead aim at black Germans, referring to them as "half-apes" and charging that "the Jews had brought the Negroes into the Rhineland with the clear aim of ruining the hated white race by the necessarily-resulting bastardization" of the country's "pure" Aryan blood. [77] As a result, when the Nazis took over, Germany's black population was subjected to the same oppression and persecution as its Jewish citizens were forced to endure.

Black Germans and their mixed-race children were just one of a number of groups to suffer under the newly-passed Nuremburg Laws, which went into effect in 1935. These people, like the Jews at whom the legislation was aimed, were now stripped of all of their rights as German citizens and were placed at the bottom of the country's racial hierarchy. They could not vote, they could not hold public office, they could not hold most jobs, and were prevented from serving in any of the branches of the German military and the civil service. But, as the Jews who did not get out of Germany in time were to discover, they, too, would consider this the least of their worries. They would soon be in line for much harsher treatment at the hands of the Nazis and their murderous agenda.

By 1937, the regime began to go after black Germans with a vengeance, beginning with the mulatto children of mixed-race relationships between white and black Germans. The fate of the "Rhineland bastards" was sealed when the Gestapo seized and forcibly sterilized nearly all 600 of these children, with the rest being used for "medical research," or just simply vanishing into thin air. [78] Adult black Germans would soon follow their children into oblivion, additional victims of the Nazis' insane and murderous obsession with "race hygiene." Many were forcibly sterilized, shot, gassed, and incinerated in the death camps, that is, when they weren't being worked into an early grave at these places. Not only were black Germans ticketed for extermination, many black Allied prisoners of war shared similar fates in Nazi POW camps at Dachau, Mauthausen, Buchenwald, and Sachsenhausen. There they were either deprived by their captors of protection under the terms of the Geneva Prisoner of War Convention, worked to death in construction details, or, simply, shot to death. [79]

No one can tell with any degree of certainty exactly how many black Germans met their fates under the Nazis, or how many were either sterilized or killed under the various programs they instituted in their quest to "purify" Germany's racial stock. After the War, attempts were made to raise awareness that there actually *was* a black German population that was decimated by the Nazis. There were also efforts to locate survivors of this little-known aspect of the Holocaust and provide them with financial compensation. In his 1979 book titled *Sterilisierung der Rheinlandbastarde: Das Schicksal einer farbigen deutschen Minderheit 1918-1937* (*Sterilization of the Rhineland Bastards: the fate of a colored German Minority*), German historian Professor Reiner Pommerin publicized the sterilization of these tragic souls and sought to discover what had happened to them. This was evidently the first time that most Germans had ever heard of such a thing or that there was even such a thing as a black German population. Pommerin pointed out that this was most likely because of "the lack of public interest in minorities" in Germany. [80] At least one German not only was keenly interested in the fate of black Germans and their mixed-race children, he was prepared to offer those who survived at least a small measure of financial recompense for all their suffering. This German, a Social Democrat member of the *Bundestag,* wanted to give each a sum of 3,000 marks if he could have their names, and he approached Pommerin with his proposal. Pommerin however, declined.

Pommerin turned it down, he said, because "I knew where they were living, but I didn't want to bother these people because I could tell that this was more of a political interest. And, I could see the TV cameras standing in front of the house in the village as the money is being handed over. All of a sudden the sensation is great in the village: here is someone who has been sterilized." [81] Pommerin, to his great credit, was able to leave sleeping dogs lie. He realized that these survivors of the darkest period in his nation's history and one of the greatest and most preventable tragedies in the history of the world had been through more than their share of hell on earth and that it was far better to leave them alone to live out the rest of their lives in what peace they were able to find. Besides, if any of them had wanted their story told, they would, in all likelihood, have done so by now. It was not his place to tell it for them, regardless of any amount of money that any politician was willing to give to them, regardless of motive.

Thus ended one of the least-known aspects of Hitler's eugenic war on those of his fellow countrymen whom he considered to be living "life unworthy of life." Long before he began setting his ideas to paper in *Mein Kampf,* he had developed a poisonous view of the world based on the warped ideas of humanity popularized by Darwin, Galton, Sanger, Stoddard, Fischer, Laughlin and the rest. Hitler took Germany into a nightmarish abyss from which it would not re-emerge until after a dozen years of terror, fear, carnage, and war had taken their toll. And, he not only nearly destroyed his own nation in the process, he almost single-handedly decimated the idea of eugenics as legitimate science. While we can be thankful for that, we must also measure through the prism of history what we have gained by what we have lost. We have lost a lot, too much, in fact. The example of the "Rhineland bastards" illustrates only too well that, literally, no one was safe under Hitler, not even a small enclave of black Germans who numbered less than 25,000.

Estimates of the death toll exacted by the Nazis under their "race hygiene" schemes have tended to vary over the years. For example, in addition to the 70,273 people we know were murdered by the Nazis during the official phase of *Aktion T-4,* evidence uncovered at the Nuremburg War Crimes Trial places the number killed at around 275,000 after the program officially ended. [82] Other evidence from files recovered after 1990 places the number at roughly 200,000 killed between 1939 and 1945 from starvation, lethal injection, or gassing. In all likelihood, we will never know exactly how many died through no fault of their own, or how many families, German and non-German alike, were ripped asunder by this insane policy of "racial purification." We do know the horrific price that Germany and her allies paid in World War II, a price that is still being exacted today in national guilt and international scorn, as a result. It is a lesson we can ill-afford to ignore.

While it may be true that American eugenicists like Margaret Sanger, Harry Laughlin, Lothrop Stoddard, Madison Grant, and Paul Popenoe had no knowledge of programs like *Lebensborn* or even the murderous depths to which their German counterparts descended in carrying out programs like *Aktion T-4,* many of them did indeed express public outrage over what happened during that time. But, it was more over the way in which the Germans went about implementing their eugenic program than in the morality of eugenics itself.

Nevertheless, despite their outrage, they must bear the full judgment of history, a judgment that decrees that they have the blood of millions of innocents on their hands. They served as the Nazis' inspiration; they wrote the books that Hitler read in jail; they worked to pass laws in American states which served as models for the Nazis' own policies; and they both admired and even envied them (recall Joseph DeJarnett's lament that "the Germans are beating us at our own game") and received accolades from them (Harry Laughlin's award from Heidelberg University). While Sanger and the rest may not have been Nazis, they have much for which to answer at the bar of history. It is up to us to hold them to account. Justice demands we do no less. If not us, whom? If not now, when?

NOTES

1. Sanger to Edith How-Martyn, May 21, 1933. From *The Sanger-Hiller Equation, The Margaret Sanger Papers Collection*, Winter 2002-03.
2. Burleigh, Michael, *The Third Reich: A New History*, c. 2000, p. 91
3. *Eugenics and the Nazis - The California Connection.* From *The San Francisco Chronicle*, November 9, 2003.
4. Compulsory Sterilization, *Wikipedia*, the free encyclopedia.
5. *Nuremberg Laws: Nazi Germany*, Spartacus Educational, www.spartacus.schoolnet.co.uk.
6. Ibid.
7. Mehler, Barry, *Eliminating the Inferior: American and Nazi Sterilization Programs. Science for the People*, Nov./Dec. 1987. The Institute for the Study of Academic Freedom,
8. Richmond, Mike, *Margaret Sanger's Eugenics. Life Advocate*, January/February 1998, Volume 12, No. 10.
9. Mehler, Barry, *Eliminating the Inferior: American and Nazi Sterilization Programs.* From-*Science for the People*, Nov/Dec. 1987, pp.14-18. Institute for the Study of Academic Freedom, Ferris State University.
10. Mehler, Barry, *Eliminating the Inferior: American and Nazi Sterilization Programs.* From *Science for the People*, Nov./Dec. 1987, pp.14-18. Institute for the Study of Academic Freedom, Ferris State University.
11. Ibid.
12. Black, Edwin, *Eugenics and the Nazis- The California Connection. The San Francisco Chronicle*, November 9 , 2003.
13. Wellerstein, Alex, *States of Eugenics: Institutions and Practices of Compulsory Sterilization in California.* From *Reframing Rights: Bioconstitutionalism in the Genetic Age*, by Sheila Jasonoff, MIT Press, 2011, pp. 29-58.
14. Ibid.
15. Wellerstein, Alex, *States of Eugenics: Institutions and Practices of Compulsory Sterilization in California.* From *Reframing Rights: Bioconstitiutionalism in the Genetic Age* by Sheila Jasonoff, MIT Press, 2011, pp. 29-58.

16. Ibid.
17. Laughlin, Harry. Cited in Wellerstein's *States of Eugenics.*
18. Richmond, Mike, *Margaret Sanger's Eugenics.* From *Life Advocate,* Jan/Feb. 1998, Vol. 12, No. 10.
19. Ibid.
20. Richmond, Mike, *Margaret Sanger, Sterilization and the Swastika*, From *The Ethical Spectacle.*
21. Ibid.
22. Ibid.
23. Richmond, Mike, *Margaret Sanger, Sterilization and the Swastika,* From *The Ethical Spectacle.*
24. Ibid.
25. Kuhl, Stefan, *The Nazi Connection: Eugenics, American Racism and German National Socialism*, Oxford University Press, 1994, p. 62.
26. Ibid, p. 85.
27. Ibid, pp. 61-62.
28. Stoddard, Lothrop, *Into the Darkness: Nazi Germany Today*. c. 1940, pp. 190-191.
29. Black, Edwin, *Eugenics and the Nazis - The California Connection.* From the San Francisco Chronicle, November 9, 2003.
30. Ibid.
31. Richmond, Mike, *Margaret Sanger's Eugenics.* From *Life Advocate Magazine*, January/ February 1998, Vol. 12, No. 10.
32. Richmond, Mike, *Margaret Sanger's Eugenics.* From *Life Advocate Magazine,* January-February 1998, Vol. 12, No. 10.
33. Ibid.
34. Ibid.
35. Black, Edwin, *Eugenics and the Nazis - The California Connection. The San Francisco Chronicle*, November 9, 2003.
36. Ibid.
37. Black, Edwin, *Eugenics and the Nazis - The California Connection. The San Francisco Chronicle,* November 9, 2003.
38. Ibid.
39. Ibid.
40. "Lebensborn." *Wikipedia,* the free encyclopedia.
41. Ibid.
42. Barrett, Roger, and Jackson, William E., Office of the Chief Counsel for Prosecution of Axis Criminality, 1946. *Nazi Conspiracy and Aggression (Founding of the Organization "Lebensborn E.V."),* 13 September, 1936. From *"Lebensborn,"* in *Wikipedia*, the free Encyclopedia.
43. The *Lebensborn* Project. *Wikipedia*, the free encyclopedia.
44. "The *Lebensborn* Project. "*Wikipedia*, the free encyclopedia.
45. *The "Lebensborn" Program.* Jewish Virtual Library, American-Israeli Cooperation Enterprise, 2013.
46. Ibid.
47. Ibid.
48. *The "Lebensborn" Program.* Jewish Virtual Library, American-Israeli Cooperation Enterprise, 2013.
49. Ibid.
50. Ibid.

51. *The "Lebensborn" Program.* Jewish Virtual Library, American-Israeli Cooperation Enterprise, 2013.
52. Action T-4, From *Wikepedia,* the free encyclopedia.
53 Hitler, Adolf, *Mein Kampf,* Vol.1, p. 447.
54 "Action T-4," *Wikipedia,* the free encyclopedia.
55. Proctor, Robert, *Racial Hygiene: Medicine Under the Nazis.*
56. Ibid.
57. Proctor, Robert, *Racial Hygiene: Medicine Under the Nazis.*
58. Ibid.
59. "Action T-4." *Wikipedia,* the free encyclopedia.
60. Lifton, Robert J., *The Nazi Doctors: Medical Killing and the Psychology of Genocide,* 1986, p. 64.
61. Ibid.
62. *The Holocaust.* Humanitas International.
63. Von Buttlar, Horst, *Forscher Offnen Inventor des Schreckens,* at *Spiegel Online,* October 1, 2003.
64. Lifton, Robert J., *The Nazi Doctors: Medical Killing and the Psychology of Holocaust,* 1986, p. 55.
65. *Euthanasia.* From *Wikipedia,* the free encyclopedia.
66. Lifton, Robert J, *The Nazi Doctors: Medical Killing and the Psychology of Holocaust,* 1986, p. 55.
67. *Euthanasia. Wikipedia,* the free encyclopedia.
68. Lifton, Robert J., *The Nazi Doctors: Medical Killing and the Psychology of Holocaust,* 1986, p. 72.
69. "*Euthanasia.*" *Wikipedia,* the free encyclopedia.
70. Lifton, Robert J., *The Nazi Doctors: Medical Killing and the Psychology of Holocaust,* 1986, p.66.
71. Sereny, Gitta, *Into That Darkness: An examination of Conscience,* 1983, p. 58.
72. Ryan, Donna, and Schulman, John S., *Racial Hygiene: Deaf People in Hitler's Europe,* p. 62.
73. Wikianswers, *Why did Hitler Hate Black People?*
74. *Black People in Nazi Germany. Wikipedia,* the free encyclopedia
75. Ibid.
76. "Black People in Nazi Germany." *Wikipedia,* the free encyclopedia.
77. Hitler, Adolf, *Mein Kampf,* 1925. U.S. Holocaust Memorial Museum, June 10, 2013.
78. Ibid.
79. United States Holocaust Memorial Museum, *Blacks During the Holocaust,* June 10, 2013.
80. Chimelu, Chiponda, *The Fate of Blacks in Nazi Germany,* Deutsche Welle, October 1, 2010
81. Chimelu, Chiponda, *The Fate of Blacks in Nazi Germany,* Deutsche Welle, October 1, 2010.
82. Von Buttar, Horst, *Forcsher Offnen Inventor des Schreckens,* at Spiegel Online, October 1, 2003.

Chapter 4:

The Useful Idiots of Margaret Sanger's Negro Project

> *At first glance I had a horrible shock to the proposition* (birth control) *because it seemed to me to be allied with abortion, but after careful thought and prayer, I have concluded that especially among many women, it is necessary to save both the lives of mothers and children.*
>
> -Letter from J.T. Braun, Editor-in-Chief, National Baptist Convention Sunday School Publishing Board, to Margaret Sanger, May 18, 1943 [1]

When the Communists took power in Russia in 1917, Vladimir Lenin created a unique phrase to describe those who would unwittingly support his sinister and deadly agenda for his nation and the world at large—the "useful idiot." Throughout the twentieth century, this phrase would come to be associated with a whole slew of leftist political movements from Communism, Nazism, and Socialism in the early 1900s to feminism, animal "rights," "gay" rights, and environmentalism today. Each has had its share of useful idiots, people like Walter Duranty and John Reed, who thought the future of Man lay in the new Soviet Union and Charles Lindbergh and Joseph P. Kennedy, who sang the praises of Adolph Hitler's Germany. Hollywood celebrities like Brigitte Bardot, Kim Bassinger, and Alec Baldwin mindlessly bought into the animal "rights" agenda. And, more recently, Sean Penn, Danny Glover, and Oliver Stone were incredibly duped by Venezuela's dictator Hugo Chavez. The "global warming" (now "climate change") movement has its useful idiots as well, people such as former Vice President Al

Gore and NASA Administrator James Hansen. And the feminist movement has its stable of such people, like Jane Fonda, Gloria Steinhem, and HBO actress Lena Dunham, just to name a few.

And the case is no different where the issues of birth control, sterilization, and abortion are concerned, specifically Margaret Sanger's Negro Project. When she wrote her infamous letter to Clarence J. Gamble on December 10, 1939, she all but admitted the need for the birth-control movement to enlist a number of prominent black Americans who would be unaware of the eugenicists' true agenda: to eliminate as many of these people and other minorities as possible. Sanger and her cohorts, people like Lothrop Stoddard, Harry Laughlin, and Madison Grant were all avowed racists, as we discovered in the first chapter of this work. Their aim was clear: since minority groups (especially blacks) were somehow genetically inferior to the white race, it was, therefore, necessary to eliminate as many of them as possible through various means, including sterilization and, later on, through abortion.

They also knew that it would be impossible to obtain their cooperation with this hideous agenda without the aid of a number of prominent black leaders. They also knew that black Americans were among the most ardently religious of any group in this country and thus among the most faithful attendees at Sunday church services. It would be critical to gain the cooperation of black ministers, "preferably with engaging personalities and social service backgrounds," as Sanger infamously wrote, to pull off this scheme.

This effort to deceive the ministers' unsuspecting flocks into accepting Sanger's agenda would start with the churches, but it would soon encompass nearly every segment of black life and would come to include leaders in business, entertainment, academe, and the media. In the tradition of all leftist ideology, the eugenicist agenda would be framed in such benign and noble-sounding euphemisms as "family planning," "birth control," and "disease prevention," and would rely heavily on a number of useful idiots in the black community to carry it forward. The purpose of this chapter, then, is to examine more closely the role these people played in implementing Margaret Sanger's Negro Project, not only from its inception in December of 1939, but up to and including the present day.

One prominent figure in the black community was W.E.B. Du Bois. Born in Great Barrington, Massachusetts, in 1868, Du Bois became an accomplished writer, sociologist, and a key founder of the National Association for the Advancement of Colored People (NAACP). During his long career, Du Bois became recognized at the time as "the most outspoken civil rights activist in America" and was the recipient of a number of awards, among them the Springarn Medal from the NAACP in 1932, doctorates of Letters from Atlanta University and Fisk University in 1938, and honorary doctorates from Morgan State, Berlin, and Charles Universities. [2] He was also a committed leftist and later on a member of the Communist Party. In fact, Du Bois was awarded the Lenin International Peace Prize in 1958.

His political views meshed well with the Progressive movement that was coming to the fore in the early decades of the twentieth century, including the eugenic views of Margaret Sanger, Lothrop Stoddard, Harry Laughlin, and others. Du Bois came to believe that what he called "the worst" of his fellow blacks were over breeding and, thus, adding to the social ills that were plaguing this group while "the best," as he called them, were not holding up their end of the bargain. He believed that the problem could only be resolved through the selective breeding of black children with "desirable" traits, meaning through eugenics.

These views led him to promote the idea that a so-called "Talented Tenth" of the black population would, in time, raise the whole black race up to the level of their white peers. Author Jonah Goldberg gives an insight into Du Bois' take on the subject in his book *Liberal Fascism: The Secret History of the American Left from Mussolini to the Politics of Meaning,* in which he writes the following: "W.E.B. Du Bois shared many of the eugenic views held by white progressives. He defined members of the Talented Tenth as 'exceptional men' and 'the best of the race.' He complained that 'the negro has not been breeding for an object,' and that he must begin to 'train and breed for brains, for efficiency, for beauty.' Over his long career, he time and again returned to his concerns that the worst blacks were over breeding while the best were under breeding. Indeed, he supported Margaret Sanger's Negro Project, which sought to sharply curtail reproduction among 'inferior stocks' of the black population." [3] Du Bois' disdain for his fellow blacks for bringing what he considered "useless" offspring into the world was clear for all to see.

The June 1932 issue of Sanger's *Birth Control Review,* for example, was titled "The Negro Number," and was dedicated to the question of birth control and sterilization among blacks. It featured articles by Du Bois, Charles S. Johnson, and others that attempted to make the case for wider access to birth control. In his essay titled "Black Folks and Birth Control," Du Bois gave a brief recap of the lot of so many blacks in the aftermath of emancipation and Reconstruction. He cited the "inevitable clash of ideals between those Negroes who were striving to improve their economic position and those whose religious faith made the limitation of children a sin" as a cause of their misfortune. He savaged the "mass of ignorant Negroes who still breed carelessly and disastrously, so that the increase among Negros, even more than the increase among whites, is from that part of the population that is least intelligent and fit, and least able to rear them properly." [4]

Du Bois had a solution to the problem of siring those children he believed did not make his "Talented Tenth" list: a religious approach among churchgoing blacks. And the people who could help bring this about? The eugenicists themselves. "The churches are open to intelligent propaganda of any sort," he wrote, "and the American Birth Control League and other agencies ought to get their speakers before the church congregations and their arguments in the Negro newspapers." [5] He justified his eugenic position as he concluded his piece thusly: many blacks, he wrote, "are quite led away by the fallacy of numbers. They want the black race to survive. They are cheered by a census return of increasing numbers and a high rate of increase. They must learn that among human races and groups, as among vegetables, quality and not mere quantity really counts." [6] *"As among vegetables."* Is this what "the most outspoken civil rights activist in America" really thought of his fellow black citizens? That they were no better than vegetables?

Sanger and her associates could not have been more pleased with this take from one of the most high-profile and deeply-respected black Americans of his era. And, since he had already been named to the advisory board of her Harlem birth-control clinic in 1930, this only made things better, in their view. The irony could not have been more apropos; Sanger, the religious bigot, enlisting Du Bois' help in infiltrating the black churches in order to promote the eugenic agenda and, thus, aid and abet their own destruction. But, despite their attempts, the birth-control advocates still had tough sledding ahead.

For all their efforts over the next few years, they were frustrated by the opposition of many black ministers and their congregations to their plans. Sanger and her allies clearly still had much work to do. Yet, the tide began to turn in their favor as their campaign of "intelligent propaganda" slowly began to bear fruit. As they gained more access to black churches, they were able to deliver the message that birth control was actually *good* for blacks. After all, who could be against "better health" for black women? Who could possibly be against blacks improving their economic lot by having smaller families? The arguments proved powerful indeed: birth control would be infinitely beneficial to the black community, both by improving not only its health, but its standard of living. In this way, Sanger laid the groundwork for her Negro Project in 1939.

While Du Bois was busily advocating for his fellow blacks to sterilize themselves into oblivion from his position on the Board of her Harlem clinic, other leaders in the black clergy, media, business community, and education establishment were being seduced by Sanger's message, as well. These useful idiots included some of the brightest lights in the black community. Charles S. Johnson, President of Fisk University in Nashville, wrote an article titled, "A Question of Negro Health," which also appeared in the June 1932 issue of *The Birth Control Review.* Like Du Bois, Johnson too made no bones about his support for selective breeding among black Americans.

"Now that Negro mortality has been reduced to the point at which whites stood a generation ago," he wrote, "the same *eugenic discrimination* which applies to the whites is necessary with reference to selective fertility within the Negro group (emphasis added)." [7] Johnson attempted to make the case for birth control by citing such health statistics among blacks as infant mortality, venereal disease rates, and the like. This was a favorite tactic of the eugenicists, and was intended to mask what many black Americans suspected was a deliberate attempt to severely limit their numbers, at the very least, and at the very worst, to eventually exterminate them.

Little wonder then, that when the Birth Control Federation of America tried to operate a display at the American Negro Exposition in Chicago in 1940, it was unceremoniously cancelled due to "last minute changes in floor space." [8] Sanger did not accept this and she quickly blamed the Catholic Church, charging that it had intimidated the Board into cancelling the BCFA exhibit by threatening to withhold state and federal funds from the event. She then urged that a flood of protest letters demanding an investigation be sent to Wendall L. Green, Vice Chair of the Afra-Merican Emancipation Exposition Commission, which sponsored the event.

Denying there was any pressure placed on the Commission, either religious or monetary (in either case, neither the Catholic Church nor any other religious body, for that matter, could withhold *taxpayer* money from an event), Green explained that funding had come from a number of people of all religious persuasions. Therefore, he added, "any exhibit in conflict with the known convictions of any religious group contravenes the spirit of the resolution." [9] The Commission upheld the ban despite BCFA's allegations that it confirmed their original suspicions.

Clearly then, much work still lay ahead of Sanger and her allies in carrying forth their eugenic agenda. They continued to rely on such useful idiots as Du Bois and Johnson, and they would enlist several more over time in pursuit of their goal. Another such person to whom they would turn was Dr. Dorothy Boulding Ferebee, President of Alpha Kappa Alpha, the nation's largest black sorority. Ferebee, a *cum laude* graduate of Tufts University in Boston, was another member of academia whose influence in the black community would prove critical in implementing the Negro Project in the coming years.

Ferebee first attended Simmons College, where she earned her Bachelor of Science degree, then went on to Tufts, where she earned another degree in medicine and served on the staff of the University's medical school as an instructor in obstetrics and as a medical doctor. From 1939 until 1941, she served as President of KAK, and, in the process, became its tenth International President. This list of credentials was sure to impress the BCFA high command. Here was an accomplished woman of color, a graduate of one of the most prestigious institutions of higher learning in the country, a holder of two degrees, and even better, a medical doctor to boot. This was precisely the kind of person Sanger had in mind when assembling her Birth Control Federation of the American Negro Advisory Council.

Ferebee bought into BCFA's sophisticated propaganda machine designed to promote birth control as a health issue, an approach that took the tagline titled "Better Health for 13,000,000," a slogan devised by Charles S. Johnson in an April 16, 1943 report on Negro Project demonstration programs, but most of her fellow blacks were not buying into it. This was evidenced when BCFA opened two birth control clinics in Tennessee and South Carolina in 1940. The first was located in Nashville and opened on February 13. The fact that only 25% of the city's population was black was telling, to say the least. Why BCFA did not choose to open similar clinics in other parts of town to service the other 75% of the population, which was overwhelmingly white, is a question worth pondering. The Nashville clinic reported some success (55% of women receiving birth control used it regularly), [10] but much resistance on religious grounds yet remained.

The second clinic, under the direction of Dr. Robert Siebels, opened in rural Berkeley County, South Carolina on May 1. The site was chosen because "the leaders in the state were particularly receptive to the experiment. South Carolina had been the second state to make child spacing a part of its state public health program after a survey of the state's maternal deaths showed that 25% occurred among mothers known to be physically unfit for pregnancy." [11] "Child spacing," the reader will recall, was merely one component of BCFA's strategy to couch its agenda in non-threatening and utterly misleading terms. It fit neatly into the "better health" theme that the BCFA was attempting to establish. And, as at other BCFA facilities, the emphasis was on birth control, not on better prenatal care.

On January 29, 1942, representatives of the 34 state BCFA chapters met in special session to form the Planned Parenthood Federation of America, or Planned Parenthood as we know it today. The words "birth control" disappeared from the bylaws of each state league affiliate to be replaced with the words "planned parenthood." And no wonder. As Robert G. Marshall and Charles A. Donovan wrote in *Blessed Are the Barren: The Social Policy of Planned Parenthood,* "Particularly, the New York State Federation of Planned Parenthood's old bylaws stipulated that the object was to 'organize on sound eugenic, social and medical principles, interest in and knowledge of birth control throughout the State of New York as permitted by law.' The new bylaws replaced 'birth control' with 'planned parenthood.' 'Eugenics,' " Marshall and Donavan wrote, "was dropped in 1943 because of its unpopular association with the German government's race-improving eugenics theories." [12]

At this meeting, a progress report to which Ferebee contributed heavily was presented comparing the success rates at the two clinics. It revealed that the programs did not significantly improve the lives of black families in either state and allowed that religious factors, as well as the comparison of birth control to abortion, along with conditions of grinding poverty, especially in rural South Carolina, played a major role. Despite this, Ferebee remained optimistic and wrote, "When thrown against the total pictures of the awareness on the part of Negro leaders of the improved conditions and their opportunities to even better conditions under Planned Parenthood, the obstacles to the program are greatly outweighed." [13]

Ferebee then called for disseminating more propaganda to the black community in a fashion that can only be described as chilling and highly disturbing: "The future program for Planned Parenthood," she advised, "should center around more education in the field through the work of a professional Negro worker, because those of us who believe that the benefits of Planned Parenthood as a vital key to the elimination of *human waste* must reach the entire population (author's emphasis added)." [14] Imagine, if you will, the level of public outrage that this comment would have generated had the speaker been a Klansman who was referring to black Americans or if the same thing had been said by a member of the American Nazi Party in referring to Jewish Americans. Planned Parenthood would have been discredited immediately, its members rightly ostracized by every right-thinking American. But Ferebee was neither a Klan member nor a Nazi Brown shirt. Rather, she was a highly-educated black woman who was actually *applauded* for her views, and she would continue to play a leading role in Planned Parenthood for many years to come.

But it only got worse as she continued to address the PPFA meeting. She went on, emphasizing the importance of having "Negro professionals, fully integrated into the staff, who could interpret the program and objectives to other blacks in the normal course of day-to-day contacts; could break down fallacious attitudes and beliefs and elements of distrust; could inspire the confidence of the group and *would not be suspect of the intent to eliminate the race* (again, author's emphasis added)." [15] Now, Planned Parenthood's supporters are quick to contend that Sanger's infamous statement of December 10, 1939 has been deliberately distorted by the organization's critics; yet, here we see unmistakably that her sentiments were not only shared by one of the most influential black American women of her time, they were openly and unapologetically expressed by her *in public* at the group's first annual meeting in January of 1942.

Another of Sanger's useful idiots was Walter A. Terpenning. A celebrated writer, economist, and sociologist from Kalamazoo, Michigan, Terpenning was another of the prominent blacks who contributed to the June 1932 issue of her *Birth Control Review.* Terpenning's piece was titled *God's Chillun,* and it echoed the eugenicist line that was toed throughout the issue by Du Bois, Johnson, and other black contributors. In his article, he rightly decried the level of poverty among the 1,800 black citizens of his hometown.

He also condemned the subtle discrimination against them by many in the city's white population, but it wasn't long before he turned from their champion into their attacker. Even as he praised "many of the colored citizens" as "fine specimens of humanity," he excoriated others as "a large percentage of Kalamazoo's human scrap-pile." [16] Terpenning cited a number of large black families with offspring who were in prison, on public assistance, or who had been institutionalized, and whose plight was made worse by the ugly prejudice to which they were routinely exposed. However, his solution to these ills lay not in bettering race relations, improving blacks' economic standing, or in strengthening the family unit, but in *reducing* the number of black children who were being born in the first place!

Terpenning's attack on poor, disadvantaged blacks continued: "The birth of a colored child," he charged, "even to those who can give it adequate support, is pathetic in view of the unchristian and undemocratic treatment it is likely to be accorded at the hands of a predominantly white community, and the denial of choice in propagation to this unfortunate class is nothing less than barbarous." [17] Terpenning called for an end to the "crude checks" on the black population embodied by malnutrition, disease, and death, to be replaced with "the more humane provision of birth control." [18] Calling "the denial of knowledge of such provision "one of the most hypocritical and savage illustrations of man's inhumanity to man," he argued that blacks would be more open to having their numbers controlled eugenically through "sterilization and institutionalization." [19] He continued promoting the eugenic line all the way through to the end of his piece by concluding, "The dissemination of the information on birth control should have begun with this class" of poor blacks rather "than with the upper social and economic classes of white Americans." [20] Articles like Terpenning's played directly into the hands of Sanger and her cohorts.

With "friends" like Du Bois, Johnson, Ferebee, and Terpenning, the black community, it would be safe to say, certainly did not need any enemies. But that was the whole point of the Negro Project: if enough blacks could be bamboozled and duped into exterminating themselves, so much the better. It was bad enough that racist whites were trying to kill them off, it was something else entirely to have prominent blacks telling them that they had to do it to themselves. At a time when the Great Depression was in full swing, not to mention the grinding racism that accompanied it, the useful idiots of the Negro Project were sending out precisely the wrong message to black Americans: that it was better that they had never been born at all than to try to make the world a better place. How ironic indeed then, that the man who called for the elimination of "human scrap-piles" would one day be honored by Albion College with its Walter A. Terpenning Award that "recognizes scholarship and service by a graduating senior in Economics and Management." [21] There were others, many others, who shared Du Bois', Johnson's, Ferebee's, and Terpenning's views.

As Sanger's Negro Project began to gain momentum, it ensnared more and more of the mainstream black leadership in its web of deceit. By 1942, three years into the Negro Project, Planned Parenthood's National Negro Advisory Council numbered no fewer than *three dozen* black leaders from all across the country, representing nearly every segment of society from the clergy to the professions, from academia to the black media. [22] Mary McLeod Bethune was one such member, and just as with Dorothy Ferebee, she brought an impressive list of credentials with her to her seat on Sanger's Council. For one, she was the President of the National Council of Negro Women's Groups in Washington, D.C.

From here, she was able to bend the ear of President Franklin D. Roosevelt as his special advisor on minority groups. She was a close friend of FDR's wife, Eleanor, and would remain so until her death in 1955.

Bethune was the only black woman present at the founding of the United Nations in San Francisco in 1945. She was a member of the so-called "Black Cabinet," a group of influential black leaders who had regular access to FDR during his presidency. And, she is probably best remembered for establishing the institution of higher learning that bears her name, Bethune-Cookman College in Daytona Beach, Florida.. When Bethune died, Ida Tarbell named her one of the most influential black women of the twentieth century. Her list of accomplishments is both long and very impressive, and her life story has inspired many people of all races. The fact that a woman whose parents were slaves in South Carolina was able to access the freedoms that were finally won by her fellow blacks and soared to such great heights as a result of her own drive and initiative, should make all Americans exceedingly proud.

But like so many others on PPFA's National Negro Advisory Council, Bethune sadly bought into Sanger's seductive message. She seems to never have questioned Sanger's associations with known racists like Lothrop Stoddard, Harry Laughlin, Madison Grant, or S. Adolphus Knopf. She apparently never read nor questioned any of Sanger's own racist writings such as *The Pivot of Civilization,* in which the reader will recall she wrote, "Our failure to segregate morons who are increasing and multiplying demonstrates our foolhardy and extravagant sentimentalism. Philanthropists encourage the healthier and more normal sections of the world to shoulder the burden of unthinking and indiscriminate fecundity of others; which brings with it, I think the reader must agree, a dead weight of human waste. Instead of decreasing and aiming to eliminate the stocks that are most detrimental to the future of the race and the world, it tends to render them to a menacing degree dominant...We are paying for and even submitting to, the dictates of an ever-increasing, unceasingly spawning class of human beings who should never have been born in the first place." [23] Bethune could not have been unaware of Sanger's views on severely limiting the number of immigrants coming into the U.S., which was made quite clear by her and other eugenicists' support for the Immigration Restriction Act of 1924. Neither could she not have known about Sanger's "Plan for Peace," which she advanced in a speech to the New History Society of New York on January 17, 1932.

In her speech, which was also published in that April's issue of *The Birth Control Review,* Sanger advocated a number of things, but her chief demand was for a "stern and rigid policy of sterilization and segregation to that grade of population whose progeny is tainted, or whose inheritance is such that objectionable traits may be transmitted to offspring." [24] This should have set off the alarm bells for Bethune, but she agreed nonetheless to serve on PPFA's Negro Advisory Board without a second thought. If she had done her due diligence and looked into Sanger's background, her associations and her alliances, how different might things be today?

But, sadly, Bethune and her fellow black leaders did not, and millions of Americans of all races, including the unborn, paid a terrible price for the willful blindness of so many in the black community who were entrusted to lead their people responsibly. That price is still being paid, even today, in the continuing decimation of the black population in America. Since the inception of the Negro Project, the numbers of black Americans have declined precipitously due in no small part to the thousands of men and women who either were sterilized or had birth control devices issued to them, and later through the most hideous form of contraception imaginable, abortion.

It has been stated previously in these pages that the black demographic is in dire peril as fewer and fewer children are being born to take the place of their parents. No society can survive, let alone thrive or prosper, with a replacement rate of less than 2.1 live births per female. This is especially true in the case of black Americans, whose replacement rate now stands at a staggering *0.7* live births per female! We will examine more closely the many contributing factors that so negatively affect this group in Chapter 6. For now, though, let us heed the warning of those who are closest to the situation, such as the Reverends Jesse Lee Peterson and Walter Hoye, Dr. Alveda King, and conservative advocate Star Parker, that if this trend continues, the black race in America will, for all intents and purposes, become extinct by the turn of the twenty-second century.

Could Bethune, Terpenning, Ferebee, Du Bois, Johnson, and others have foreseen such a situation coming? To be sure, no one can predict the future, but by agreeing to serve on PPFA's National Negro Advisory Board in the first place, they gave, through their good names and reputations, enormous credibility to a scheme designed to accomplish exactly what Sanger and her fellow eugenicists set out to do: reduce the number of those whom they considered "unfit" because of their own subjective, arbitrary set of criteria. And, to make matters worse, it would be done with the *unsuspecting* cooperation of people like W.E.B. Du Bois, Walter Terpenning, Charles S. Johnson, Dorothy Boulding Ferebe, and Mary McLeod Bethune. There were others who should have known better; yet, they instead swallowed whole the eugenicist line of Margaret Sanger, Lothrop Stoddard, Harry Laughlin, S. Adolphus Knopf, and Paul Popenoe. These individuals, through the power of the pulpit, academia, their influence in the business community, and in the media, would in their own way contribute to the success of the Negro Project and, in so doing, would sow the seeds for the coming decimation of the black race in America. Let us now look at some of the ministers whom Sanger targeted to promote her racist eugenic agenda in the black churches, such as the Reverend Adam Clayton Powell, Sr.

As the head of the Abyssinian Baptist Church, the largest such church in the Harlem section of New York, Powell was enormously powerful and influential in the city's teeming, vibrant black community. Due to that power and influence, he enjoyed a position of great credibility. People held him in high esteem; they listened to what he had to say and considered his opinions on many spiritual matters to hold great weight and importance. It was only natural, then, for Sanger to zero in on him to help her out. He was just the kind of person she had in mind when she wrote her infamous letter to Clarence Gamble on December 10, 1939—a minister with a background in social services who could "straighten out" those "rebellious members" of his congregation if they ever got the wrong (or, in this case, the right) idea about what she had in store for them. As a man of faith and compassion who was deeply concerned about the plight of his people, Powell was in a position to be used in the most cynical way possible by Sanger and her cohorts. It was the height of arrogance and hypocrisy that Sanger, who was not just irreligious, but openly *hostile* to organized religion (in this case, the Catholic Church) and its tenets of compassion and charity for all, was able to enlist the aid of a man who led the largest black congregation in New York City.

Sanger did this through her stated concerns for "women's health," "child spacing," and "family planning." Powell seemingly never questioned her ties to the KKK, which saw the births of more black and other minority children as the *last* thing the world needed. Neither did he grill her on her associations with racial eugenicists like Madison Grant, who penned *The Passing of the Great Race*, S. Adolphus Knopf, who delivered a racially inflammatory speech in New York in March of 1925 in which he warned against the menace posed by the "black and yellow peril," or Lothrop Stoddard, the author of *The Rising Tide of Color against White World Supremacy.*

The reader will recall that it was none other than Adolf Hitler himself who not only praised Grant's book, but referred to it as his "bible." If Powell had done his homework and vetted her properly, Sanger might not only have not been invited to deliver a lecture on birth control at his church, he himself might have become one of her fiercest opponents. It is quite possible that his opposition would have inspired other black clergymen and leaders to reject Sanger's seductive and deadly message.

This is only speculation, however, because none of that happened. In fact, Powell *did* invite her to address his congregation, which she did on December 7, 1932. [25] By failing to properly vet this woman before allowing her into his church, he unwittingly aided and abetted the coming destruction of millions of black and other children, first through sterilization and contraception, and over the next several decades, abortion. But Sanger's appearance that night was not without controversy or opposition, as we saw earlier. Powell, the reader will recall, received blistering and "adverse criticism" from a minister from a congregation other than Baptist who was "surprised that he'd allow that awful woman into his church." [26] As we also saw, the damage in the end was done. Sanger successfully hoodwinked Powell and his flock. She had gotten just what she wanted and would now move on to other targets.

One of those targets was the Grace Congregational Church, which hosted a debate on birth control. Sanger's disciples argued that it was actually good for blacks to *limit* their numbers rather than increase them. They trotted out the same arguments that birth control would help black families from a health and economic perspective. "Family planning," it was posited, was beneficial because it helped women recover physically from childbirth and that by regulating the number of children a family would have, it would also help the father, who was almost exclusively the primary bread-winner in the family, recover financially. Further, the proponents of birth control argued, it would result in the birth of healthier children, not only physically but mentally, as well, and that the incidences of communicable diseases would decrease.

Note that nowhere in these arguments is any mention made of the need to combat the horrible effects of racism on the black community, which manifested itself in so many ways. Birth control would not end discrimination against black Americans; "family planning" and "child spacing" would do nothing to end the Jim Crow laws in the Deep South; contraception would not provide black Americans with better opportunities to improve their economic station. But, this was not meant to do *any* of that. Leaders like Powell, Du Bois, Ferebee, Terpenning, Bethune, and others failed to grasp that the only way that blacks would finally win the economic and political empowerment they craved lay in increasing their numbers and influence, not in limiting or reducing them. As the old adage goes (and it's an old adage because it's true), there is strength in numbers, and they certainly did not need a woman like Margaret Sanger, whose racist and anti-religious views were certainly well-known, lecturing them on these points. Yet, that is exactly what happened. Sanger and her supporters were permitted to use the church that night to espouse these views, despite the warning signs about her racist past that should have been heeded, but, sadly, were not.

In the end, the proponents of birth control won the debate, due in no small part to their skill in framing the issue as one of "women's health." It was a difficult argument to refute unless one knew how. Again, how could anyone be against any of that? The much larger issue, i.e., the moral issue of the racism of Margaret Sanger and her birth control agenda *vis-à-vis* the black community, was thrust into the background. The leaders of Grace Congregational Church could easily have vetted Sanger and her allies and would rightly have been shocked and repelled by what they discovered, and they would almost certainly have passed the word to their fellow clergymen to be on their guard, but they evidently chose not to, to the everlasting detriment of their flock and black Americans for generations to come.

Complicit, as well, in all this were the editors of the *Amsterdam News,* a leading black newspaper of the day. [27] They, too, bought into the notion that reducing the number of children being born to black families was essential to combating the evils of racism, and they also fell for Sanger's seductive narrative regarding the "benefits" of controlling the black birthrate. In its position of prominence, the publication carried great weight with its subscribers, and Sanger quickly took advantage of this to strike directly at her targets.

A golden opportunity presented itself when the paper, in partnership with leading black civic organizations, endorsed the establishment of her birth-control clinic in the Harlem section of New York City. Sanger's use of the well-worn, but effective, message of "better health" through contraception was evident in a letter she wrote to Du Bois on November 11, 1930. In it, she invited him and a number of prominent black leaders to become involved in forming an advisory council to direct the clinic's operations "for the benefit of colored people." [28] In order to remain in business, the facility relied heavily on the generosity of private foundations such as the Julius Rosenwald Fund which, for example, donated $2,500 in 1931 as "representing the balance of our appropriation to the Harlem Birth Control clinic in 1930." [29] Sanger also appealed to doctors like Peter Marshall Murray, whom she persuaded to support the clinic, "so that our work in birth control will be a constructive force in the community." [30]

Although Sanger went to great pains to point out that the clinic, which opened on November 21, 1930 after more than a year's preparatory groundwork, was open to all residents of Harlem including poor white women, who also needed its services, the fact remains that the vast majority of women who went there were black. This is not at all surprising since the neighborhood's population was predominantly black, a situation that was borne out by these stark and sobering facts from Sanger's own clinic:

1. Blacks in Harlem were segregated in an over-populated area (224,760 of 330,000 of Greater New York's blacks lived there during the late 1920s and '30s);
2. Blacks comprised 12% of the population of New York, but accounted for more than 18% of the city's unemployment rate;
3. Blacks had an infant mortality rate of 101 deaths per 1,000 residents compared with 56 deaths per 1,000 for the city's white population; and
4. Out of all of New York, the black death rate from tuberculosis was 237 per 100,000 residents. [31]

It is little wonder, then, that Sanger's message was so eagerly received by people like Du Bois, Powell, Terpenning, Johnson, Ferebee, Bethune *et al.* They all ignored her racist dealings with the Ku Klux Klan, Harry Laughlin, Lothrop Stoddard, S. Adolphus Knopf, and Madison Grant, and they overlooked her fierce opposition to organized religion, as well as her disdain for its charitable activities, which is ironic to say the least, given her almost shameless reliance on *secular* charities to support the operations of her Harlem birth-control clinic. And, it is no less ironic that, even today, 78% of Planned Parenthood's abortion mills are located in the black inner city, a fact that is neither ever discussed nor even questioned by today's so-called black "leaders."

Apparently, black clergymen like the Reverends Jesse Jackson and Al Sharpton, and liberal/Progressive lawmakers like Representatives Maxine Waters (D-California), John Lewis (D-Georgia), and Elijah Cummings (D-Maryland) all have weightier issues with which to deal than asking some rather pointed questions of the nation's largest abortion provider. Waters, for example, has accused the CIA of introducing crack cocaine into America's black neighborhoods with no proof whatsoever. But, when it comes to the complicity of Planned Parenthood in what can only be described as the *self-imposed* extermination of more than 500,000 of her fellow blacks every year, most of whose lives are extinguished by the organization Sanger founded, the good Congresswoman's silence is deafening. It is even more damning that the NAACP, the organization Du Bois helped establish in 1909, has repeatedly stated that it has *no official policy* regarding abortion! If those who claim to represent black Americans in Congress would have done their due diligence over the years and dug as deeply into the views of Margaret Sanger and Planned Parenthood as Waters supposedly has done with her vendetta against the CIA and other purported examples of racism against blacks, who knows how many lives could have been saved or changed for the better? But, sadly, we will probably never know because these elected officials seem to be singularly disinterested in the whole business.

Rather, they have accepted a sanitized portrait of Margaret Sanger that has, over the years, seen her canonized as a saint of the political Left whose primary motivation was to help women in need to gain the right of "reproductive freedom while ignoring her racist views, not to mention her deep involvement in the now-discredited theory of eugenics. They view anyone who dares to question this prevailing meme as being "racist," "misogynist," "anti-choice," "Neanderthal," or worse. It is to their everlasting shame that so many who should have known better ignored the warning signs that arose over three-quarters of a century ago. Had they shown a bit more courage and backbone, the story quite likely would have been very different indeed. But, regrettably, that never happened. In fact, more of the black leadership of the early twentieth century fell for the eugenicists' agenda hook, line, and sinker, and Sanger, Stoddard, Laughlin, and the rest continued to rely on the useful idiots in the black clergy, academy, professions, and media to aid them in their quest.

As pastor of the African Methodist Episcopal Church in Philadelphia, Bishop David H. Sims was in a position of power and influence that made him a logical choice for a seat on the BCFA (later PPFA)

National Negro Advisory Council. As with his fellow black clergymen who accepted Sanger's eugenic line, he, too, was taken in by the flowery language and benign-sounding goals of "family planning," "child spacing," and "better health" proffered by the founder of the modern birth-control movement and her disciples.

He, too, apparently never questioned either Sanger's known racist connections or her anti-religious sentiments. Her views on both were certainly well-documented, as the reader will recall. She had, after all, addressed the New Jersey Klan's Ladies' Auxiliary at Silver Lake in 1926, a lecture she herself described as having been "well-received," and she excoriated organized religion, particularly the Catholic Church, not only for its opposition to birth control, but its charitable activities, as well. Recall further that she accused it in her book *The Pivot of Civilization* of enabling "the unthinking and indiscriminate fecundity of others."

From his acceptance of Sanger's offer to sit on her Council, it is safe to presume that Sims, in fact, never read her book, because if he had, it would have been impossible for him to have missed this passage: "The most serious charge that can be brought against modern 'benevolence' is that it encourages the perpetuation of defectives, delinquents and dependents. These are the most dangerous elements in the world community, the most devastating curse on human progress and expression." [32] How a person of deep religious conviction could or would have anything to do with anyone so provably hostile to religion, charity, or the members of his race is breathtaking to contemplate. Yet, this is exactly the course upon which Sims embarked, and he wasn't alone. The reader will remember that it was Sims who endorsed the Federal Council of Churches' Marriage and Home Committee birth control pamphlet which Sanger sent to J.T. Braun, who in turn gave it to his wife to read. The reader will further recall that it was this tract which deeply affected Mrs. Braun and which eventually helped sway her husband's opinion in favor of birth control. After reading more literature on the subject, Braun opened his church to a group of women for a discussion of contraception. Due to Sims's advocacy, Braun had now been so thoroughly co-opted by Sanger and the eugenicists that he went so far as to correspond with the founder of Planned Parenthood after the event. "I was moved by the number of prominent black Christians backing the proposition," he told her in a letter he wrote her on May 18, 1943. "At first glance I had a horrible shock to proposition because it seemed to me to be allied to abortion, but after careful thought and prayer,

I have concluded that, among many women, it is sometimes necessary to save both the lives of mothers and children." [33]

Granted, there is no telling for certain what would have happened if Bishop Sims investigated Sanger's racist and anti-religious background before he sent Braun the FCC pamphlet. If he had, it is quite likely that the meeting would never have taken place, and that Sims would have been lauded for warning his fellow clergymen about what she had in mind. What is clear is that by doing the *opposite* he ensnared an otherwise good and honorable man and his wife in the web of treachery and deceit that was being spun by Sanger and her disciples. Sims' failure to act on behalf of his flock and other black Americans illustrates clearly the wisdom of Edmund Burke's axiom that "all that is necessary for evil to triumph is for good men to do nothing."

Bishop Sims and Reverend Braun, good and compassionate men by all accounts, did nothing to stop what was happening and, thus, allowed an unspeakable evil to flourish. They did enormous damage to their flocks by failing to ask even the most basic questions about an avowed racist and anti-religious bigot, and their legacies have been severely tarnished as a result, to say nothing of the disastrous consequences for black Americans that have ensued due to their failure and that of so many other "good men" to oppose such a monstrous evil. By co-opting such men of the cloth as Powell, Braun, Sims, and the leaders of the Grace Congregational Church, Sanger had achieved much of what she set out to do, but her work was far from finished. In fact, she was just getting started.

Now that Sanger had her "three or four colored ministers, preferably with social service backgrounds and engaging personalities" in her hip pocket, she zeroed in on other prominent Americans in the media, the education establishment, the medical professions, and various social service organizations to implement and carry her Negro Project forward. Indeed, even a cursory glance at the members of her Negro National Advisory Council is quite revealing. By 1942, Sanger had assembled an impressive list of some of the leading lights in the black community, people who were highly respected by their fellow black Americans As the years went on, their power and influence would prove quite invaluable, indeed, to Sanger and her fellow eugenicists.

In addition to the editors of such black news organs as the *Amsterdam News* and the *Chicago Defender,* Sanger reeled in such respected journalists as Charles A. Barnett, the Director of the Associated Negro Press in Chicago and Dr. Peter Marshall Murray, who headed the Publications Committee of the National Medical Association in New York City. As Murray was both an MD and a journalist, this allowed Sanger to, in effect, "kill two birds with one stone." The importance of having such respected journalists as these on Sanger's Council cannot be overstated as this provided a critical forum from which the eugenic message could be easily and widely disseminated among black Americans. [34]

In addition to journalists like Barnett and Murray, the roster of the PPFA Council included a large number of medical professionals besides Dorothy Boulding Ferebee. Walter G. Alexander, MD was a Past President of the National Medical Association. Michael J. Bent, MD served on the staff of the Meharry Medical School in Nashville, Tennessee. M.O. Housefield, MD was the Director for Negro Health of the Julius Rosenwald Fund in Chicago. The Rosenwald Fund, as the reader will recall, was an important financial backer of Sanger's Negro Project. And, E.R. Carney was President of National Hospital Association in Detroit, Michigan. [35]

The top-heavy presence of medical professionals on the PPFA Council continued with Paul B. Cornely, MD, who was an Associate Professor of Preventive Medicine at Howard University in Washington, D.C. John W. Lawlah, MD was the Dean of Medicine at Howard. Walter Maddux, MD, came to Sanger's Council from the Slossfield Health Center in Birmingham, Alabama. John West was the Medical Director for Provident Hospital in Chicago. Nurses also had a place at the table in the person of Mrs. Mabel Staupers, Executive Secretary of the National Association of Colored Nurses in New York City. From their seats on the PPFA National Negro Advisory Council, these health care professionals were in a powerful position to espouse the eugenic line that by limiting their numbers, black Americans would enjoy the benefits of "better health" through the policy of "family planning" and "child spacing." And, as important as the presence of doctors and nurses on the PPFA Council was, the inclusion of a number of prominent black academics on Sanger's board was equally indispensable.

In addition to some of those whom we examined earlier, the National Negro Advisory Council held several well-respected educators such as John W. Davis, President of West Virginia State College. Davis was joined on Sanger's Council by Albert W. Dent, the President of Dillard University in New Orleans, Louisiana, Charles Hubert, DD of Morehouse College in Atlanta, Georgia, and Frederick D. Patterson, President of Tuskegee Institute in Alabama. Ira D. Reid of the Sociology Department at Atlanta University, Forrester B. Washington, Director of the Atlanta University School of Social

Work, and Emmett Scott, Secretary of the Southern Education Foundation in Washington, also lent their presence to the PPFA Council, as well. [36]

Not to be outdone by their fellows in the media, academic, and medical professions, the leaders of a number of business, labor, social, civic and civil rights organizations also got into the act. In addition to Mary McLeod Bethune at the National Council of Negro Women and W.E.B. Du Bois from the NAACP, other notable black Americans who served on Sanger's Council included Channing H. Tobias of the National Council of the YWCA, J. Finley Wilson, the Grand Ruler of the IBPOE (the Elks), and Max Yergan, President of the National Negro Congress in New York.

A.L. Holsey, Secretary of the National Negro Business League in Tuskegee, was also a member of the PPFA Council, as were Jesse O. Thomas and Eugene Knickle Jones of the National Urban League in New York, Mary Church Terrell, the Honorary President of the National Association of Colored Women in Washington, and Frank R. Crosswaith, the Chairman of the National Negro Labor Committee in New York. Du Bois was joined on the Council by NAACP Secretary Walter White, thereby lending additional credibility to Sanger's board by giving it two members of the nation's largest civil rights organization.

An impressive list to say the least, and a telling one, at that. Even a slight glance at this roster of outstanding names is striking, the more so when one considers that of the 36 members of Sanger's Council, fully one-third of them came from the Deep South. And, when one adds those who hailed from the nation's capital, the list grows to 18, or exactly one-half of those on PPFA's Council who were from below the Mason-Dixon Line. Now, given what we have learned thus far, it is clear that this was not by coincidence or mere happenstance. Since Sanger considered minorities (and especially blacks) to be inferior, it was only logical, then, that she target as many of them for elimination as possible, and if she could con a sufficient number of black leaders into going along with her plans and taking their followers with them, so much the better, as far as she was concerned.

We have seen from the writings and public statements of W.E.B. Du Bois that his position on eugenics was quite clear, but there was another black leader who, although he never served on Sanger's Council, was nonetheless firmly in the eugenic camp. His name was Marcus Garvey, the Haitian-born father of the "back to Africa" movement. Garvey was a firm believer in the eugenic doctrine and he was also the founder of the Universal Negro Improvement Association. [37] Unlike Du Bois, Garvey was highly critical of the attempts by civil-rights organizations like the NAACP to normalize race relations. In fact, he had nothing but contempt for these efforts.

Garvey stated that the integrationist policy of the NAACP and other bi-racial groups represented "a dangerous race-destroying doctrine," [38] a serious charge to be sure. It is interesting to note that Garvey's view of selective breeding came about along political lines, rather than the prevailing scientific (or pseudo-scientific, as it turned out) attitude surrounding the eugenic movement. Garvey firmly opposed interracial marriage and believed that the races should be kept apart wherever and whenever possible. In fact, he was quite clear on this point. The UNIA, he wrote, "... believes in and teaches the pride and purity of race. We believe that the white should uphold its racial pride and the black race should do likewise." [39] Garvey viewed the union of whites and blacks as reflective of a watering-down of racial integrity, if not a sign of downright racial suicide. In a speech he delivered on September 7, 1921, Garvey opined that interracial marriage should be rejected in order to strengthen the gene pool and "establish a uniform type among ourselves." [41]

While Garvey never used the word "eugenics" in any of his writings, this did not prevent him from forming what can only be described as an unholy alliance with the racial supremacists in his home state of Virginia. He openly associated with members of the KKK and the state's Anglo-Saxon Clubs of America, and with notorious racists like Ernest Sevier Cox, John Powell, and Walter Plecker, who were outspoken supporters of Virginia's Racial Integrity Act of 1924, which explicitly forbade marriage between the races. While this is correctly seen as abhorrent today, Garvey wholeheartedly supported this law. In fact, he fiercely defended his position on the matter, writing, "I unhesitatingly endorse the race purity idea of Mr. Powell and his organization (the Anglo-Saxon Clubs of America)." [41]

Garvey did not stop there. In subsequent writings and public statements, he continued to clarify and refine his "eugenics as a path to black empowerment" theme. For example, in *The Negro's Greatest Enemy* (1923), Garvey posited that "any attempt to bring about the amalgamation of any two opposite races is a crime against nature." [42] How stunning to realize that he shared the same views on this subject that Madison Grant voiced in *The Passing of the Great Race*! He theorized that race-mixing would lead to political confusion because children of mixed-marriage couples would not know which group or ideology to support. Garvey concluded that "we feel that there is absolutely no reason why there should be any differences between the black and white races if each stops to adjust (purify) itself. We believe in the purity of both races." [43]

Garvey's followers latched onto his premise of black political empowerment through selective breeding with all the energy and enthusiasm they could muster, and they spared no effort to present this message to an ever-widening audience of their fellow blacks. For instance, in *Fighting Fire with Fire: African-Americans and Hereditarian Thinking, 1900-1942*, University of Alabama Assistant Professor Michael Dorr, PhD, writes that John J. Fenner, President of the UNIA's Richmond Division, was most helpful in this regard. [44] "Fenner," Dorr relates, "worked to place eugenicist tracts 'in the hands of members of my race intelligent enough to understand them.' He also secured black audiences throughout Virginia, who listened attentively to the pronouncements of white eugenicists." [45] This approach seems to have worked quite well as Fenner elaborated, "I find an increased sentiment agreeing that THE INTEGRITY OF THE RACES IS A FINE IDEA AND THE APPROVAL OF THE SAME IS GROWING." [46] Little wonder then that Garvey's views were so well-received by the Klan, Anglo-Saxon Clubs, and all the other racists in Virginia; despite his difference in skin color, he was just as much one of their own as if he had been white, and, therefore, a most useful idiot in Sanger's scheme.

But, for all his political posturing and attempts to co-opt his counterparts at the other end of the racial divide, Garvey may well have been too clever by half. He should have known better what the true goals and aims of the eugenic movement were, even though he had his own political agenda. He did not seem to understand that there can be no increase in economic, political, or social empowerment without an increase in the number of those seeking such empowerment. This is precisely what Sanger, her fellow eugenicists, and the racists in the Ku Klux Klan and the Anglo-Saxon Clubs of America all had in mind—-as few members of "undesirable," "unfit," or "inferior" races as possible. What would Marcus Garvey, or for that matter, W.E.B. Du Bois or the members of PPFA's National Negro Advisory Council, say today if they could return and see the murderous effects of the eugenic agenda on members of their own black race?

Would they be shocked to learn that so many of their fellows have either been sterilized or aborted out of existence? What would they say if they knew of the coming extinction of black Americans if the policies of Planned Parenthood and other abortion providers are taken to their logical conclusion? And, how would they react knowing that the leading civil rights group in the country, which Du Bois helped establish in 1909, has "no official policy" regarding abortion, which takes the lives of over 500,000 unborn black babies each year? The useful idiots of Margaret Sanger's Negro Project are all gone now, but their shameful legacy survives in the persons of Jesse Jackson, Al Sharpton, former Planned Parenthood President Faye Wattleton, Congresswoman Maxine Waters and Barack Obama, who on April 25, 2013 became the first sitting President to address a Planned Parenthood conference. Obama ended by saying, "God Bless you." Philosopher George Santayana warned years ago that "those who forget their history are condemned to repeat it." When will these people ever learn? Or rather, *will* they ever learn?

NOTES

1. Green, Tanya L. *The Negro Project: Magaret Sanger's Eugenic Plan for Black Americans,* May 10, 2001.
2. Reuben, Paul P., W.E.B. Du Bois, *Perspectives in American Literature, A Reference and Research Guide - An Ongoing Project,* November 2011.
3. Goldberg, Jonah, *Liberal Fascism: The Secret History of the American Left from Mussolini To the Politics of Meaning,* c. 2008, p. 258.
4. Du Bois, W. E. B.. *Black Folks and Birth Control. From The Birth Control Review,* June 1932, p. 166.
5. Ibid, p. 167.
6. Du Bois, W. E.B., *Black Folks and Birth Control. From The Birth Control Review,* June 1932, p.166.
7. Johnson, Charles S., *A Question of Negro Health. From The Birth Control Review,* June, 1932, p.167.
8. BCFA Stationery, Margaret Sanger Papers Collection, Library of Congress, July 1940. From *The Negro Project: Margaret Sanger's Eugenic Plan for Black Americans* by Tanya L. Green, May 10, 2001.
9. Green, Tanya L., *The Negro Project: Margaret Sanger's Eugenic Plan for Black Americans,* May 10, 2001.
10. Johnson, Charles S., *Better Health for 13,000,000,* April 16, 1943, p.10.
11. Johnson, Charles S., *Better Health for 13,000,000,* April 16, 1943, p.10.
12. Marshall, Robert G., and Donavan, Charles A., *Blessed Are the Barren,* 1991, pp. 24-25.
13. Ferebee, Dorothy Boulding, *Planned Parenthood as a Public Health for the Negro Race,* January 29, 1942.
14. Ibid, p. 5.
15. Ferebee, Dorothy Boulding., *Planned Parenthood as a Public Health for the Negro Race,* January 29, 1942, pp. 4-5.
16. Terpenning, Walter A., *God's Chillun.* From *The Birth Control Review,* June 1932, p. 171.
17. Ibid, p. 172.
18. Ibid.
19. Terpenning, Walter A., *God's Chillun,* from *The Birth Control Review,* June 1932.
20. Ibid.
21. Albion College homepage listing scholarships and awards, 2013.
22. Green, Tanya L., *The Negro Project: Margaret Sanger's Eugenic Plan for Black Americans,* May 10, 2001.

23. Sanger, Margaret, *The Pivot of Civilization*, c. 1922, pp. 116, 122, 189
24. Sanger, Margaret, *A Plan for Peace*. From *The Birth Control Review*, April 1932, pp. 107-108.
25. Flyer announcing Sanger's lecture at the Abyssinia Baptist Church, December 7, 1932. *Margaret Sanger Collection*, Library of Congress.
26. BCCRB memo, February 3, 1933. *Margaret Sanger Collection*, Library of Congress
27. Green, Tanya L., *The Negro Project: Margaret Sanger's Eugenic Plan for Black Americans*, May 10, 2001.
28. Letter Sanger to Du Bois, November 11, 1930. *Margaret Sanger Collection*, Library of Congress.
29. Levin, Nathan, Comptroller, Julius Rosenwald Fund, to Sanger, January 5, 1931. *Margaret Sanger Collection*, Library of Congress.
30. Sanger's letter to Murray seeking his endorsement of the Harlem clinic, December 2, 1930. *Margaret Sanger Collection*, Library of Congress.
31. BCFA Harlem Clinic file, 1929. *Margaret Sanger Collection*, Library of Congress.
32. BCFA Harlem Clinic file, 1929. *Margaret Sanger Collection*, Library of Congress.
33. Sanger, Margaret., *The Pivot of Civilization*, c. 1922, p. 123.
34. Holley, Anna, *Margaret Sanger and the African-American Community*, July 2010, pp. 4-6.
35. Holley, Anna, *Margaret Sanger and the African-American Community*, July 2010, pp. 4-6.
36. Holley, Anna, *Margaret Sanger and the African-American Community*, July 2010, pp. 4-6. www.trustblackwomen.org.
37. Dorr, Gregory Michael, Ph.D., *Fighting Fire with Fire: Black Americans and Hereditarian Thinking*, 1900-1942, p.14.
38. Dorr, Gregory Michael, MD, *Fighting Fire with Fire: African-Americans and Hereditarian Thinking*, 1900-1942, p.13.
39. Quote from Garvey in *Racial Purity in Black and White: The Case of Marcus Garvey and Ernest Cox, Journal of Ethic Studies*, 1987, Vol. 1, p.12.
41. Garvey, Marcus, *The Marcus Garvey and UNIA Papers*, University of California Press, 1983, Vol. 4, p. 41, Robert Hill, Editor.
41. Garvey, Marcus, "Letter of Introduction for John Powell by Marcus Garvey," *Negro World*, November 7, 1925. The Marcus Garvey and UNIA Papers, Vol. 6, University of California Press, 1983, Robert Hill, editor.
42. Garvey, Marcus, *The Negro's Greatest Enemy*. From *Current History*, September 1923, Vol. 1, p.10.
43. Garvey, Marcus, *The Negro's Greatest Enemy*. From *Current History*, September 1923, Vol. 1, p. 10.
44. Dorr, Gregory Michael, Ph.D., *Fighting Fire with Fire: African-Americans and Hereditarian Thinking*, 1900-1942, p. 15.
45. John J. Fenner to Ernest Sevier Cox, June 17, 1925. *Ernest Sevier Cox Papers*, Box No. 2, p. 15.
46. Ibid.

Chapter 5:

The Horrifying Agenda of Planned Parenthood and the "Pro-Choice" Movement

> *"Human weeds, reckless breeders, spawning human beings who should never have been born."*
>
> -Margaret Sanger, Founder, Planned Parenthood.
> From *The Pivot of Civilization, 1922*

In the previous chapter of this book we learned that Planned Parenthood came into existence on January 29, 1942 when representatives of the 34 state chapters of the Birth Control Federation of America met to change the organization's name and by-laws. We also learned that there was good reason for doing this, as the public's acceptance of eugenics began to wane due to its association with Nazi Germany's race-improvement program and the atrocities Hitler's regime was committing in the name of *rassenhygiene*, or "race purity." We have seen that each state chapter included the words "birth control" in its mission statement, and that one affiliate, New York State, actually included the word "eugenic" in its by-laws. The language stated that the goal of that state's chapter was "to organize, on sound eugenic, social, and medical principles, interest in and knowledge of birth control throughout the State of New York as permitted by law."

We have also seen in these pages how these affiliates replaced the words "birth control" with the more palatable euphemism "planned parenthood" to disguise the true nature of the eugenic movement—-to wipe out those whom the eugenicists considered to be "unfit" through various means, such as segregation, anti-miscegenation laws, new restrictions on immigration, sterilization (either voluntary or coercive), euthanasia and, ultimately, through abortion.

We have detailed how Margaret Sanger, the "mother" of the birth-control movement, had a particular animus toward minorities, and at the top of her list were America's black citizens. Her supporters claim that her Negro Project had only the noblest of intentions and that she was merely trying to "empower" women, especially poor black women, by giving them access to reliable information on birth control, but a closer examination of the facts reveals that such was hardly the case.

In the first place, Sanger considered all minorities inferior and unworthy of life, and blacks held a particularly low rung on the ladder for no other reason than the color of their skin. What else can explain her alliance with the New Jersey Ku Klux Klan, whose Ladies' Auxiliary she addressed in 1926? Why would she have had anything to do with avowed racists like Lothrop Stoddard, S. Adolphus Knopf, Harry Laughlin, and Madison Grant? And why, to her dying day, did she not sever her ties with such individuals?

Secondly, given her hatred for organized religion, especially the Catholic Church, the fact that black Americans, just as they are today, were the most deeply religious people in the country must have rankled her on a most visceral level. When she wrote her infamous letter to Clarence J. Gamble on December 10, 1939, she was well aware that despite the inroads made by the birth-control movement in the black churches, opposition to her message remained quite strong among black pastors and their congregations.

To Sanger, this simply would not do. Thus, the need, as she saw it, to "hire three or four colored ministers, preferably with social service backgrounds and engaging personalities" to finally seal the deal and infiltrate these black churches with the eugenic agenda. Because of this agenda, black America has paid a frightful price at the hands of a woman who, along with her willing accomplices in the eugenic movement, established an organization that has been responsible, first, for an untold number of sterilizations of unsuspecting blacks and later on for the millions of abortions that have been performed on women of color. While we don't know for certain how many abortions were done on black women alone first by the American Birth Control League, its successor the Birth Control Federation of America, and finally by its successor Planned Parenthood prior to 1973, we do know that since then more than 3,000 such procedures have been carried out *per day* since abortion was declared a fundamental Constitutional "right" by the United

States Supreme Court, and that upwards of 35% of all abortions are performed on black women. The black community has been especially hardest hit by abortion and has paid dearly to the tune of more than 17 million of these procedures. And, this is all thanks to Margaret Sanger, her followers at the time, and those who continue to carry out her bloody legacy and her horrifying "pro-choice" agenda.

Thus, the aim of this chapter is to examine that agenda and gain a clearer insight into what Planned Parenthood and its sister organizations like the National Abortion Rights Action League (NARAL) have in store for America's citizens of black descent. When, for example, did Planned Parenthood begin performing abortions? Why are so many of its "clinics" located in America's black inner cities? Why have atrocities such as those that were committed in the Philadelphia "clinic" that was run by the late-term abortionist Kermit Gosnell not received the badly-needed coverage in the mainstream media that they so richly deserve? And, while its position on such forms of birth control as RU-486 (the so-called "morning after" abortifacient pill) is so-well known, why do supposed "civil rights" groups like the NAACP refuse to take an official position on the most savage form of birth control imaginable, abortion? Let us go, then, where the facts lead us and let the chips fall where they may. We won't like what we find, but we owe it to ourselves to discover and face the ugly truth.

Planned Parenthood likes to portray itself as merely a "women's health" organization that provides a full range of services, such as pap smears, mammograms, and breast cancer screenings, and that it only "refers" women to abortion providers. Yet, the facts show that this is far from the case. Further, it paints itself as an organization that depends in large measure on private and charitable donations. But, in actuality, Planned Parenthood receives the bulk of its funding from the federal government, which means that the U.S. taxpayer is bankrolling its activities to a very large degree, often with little to no say in the matter. Consider this: Planned Parenthood received over $350 million of tax money in 2006, over $360 million in 2009, over $500 million in 2012, and over $540 million in 2013. Now, that's a lot of mammograms, pap smears, and breast cancer exams, to say the least! And, while the abortionists tell us that the practice must be kept "safe, legal, and rare," our examination of this issue will clearly demonstrate that while the practice may well be legal, it most certainly cannot be called "safe" or "rare."

As the facts surrounding the activities of "Doctor" Kermit Gosnell in Philadelphia have come to light, they give the lie to this notion. In May of

2013, Gosnell went on trial for murder in the largest city in Pennsylvania in the deaths of seven infants who survived attempts to abort them, as well as that of Karnamaya Mongar, a 41-year old Virginia woman, who died from a drug overdose on his operating table during her procedure. Some witnesses at trial testified that Gosnell had killed anywhere from 100 to 200 newborns over a 30-year span. Stunningly, charges were brought only after the clinic was cited for not complying with provisions of the city's health code after it was revealed that Gosnell's facility was operating under conditions that would have closed down any restaurant or meat-packing facility.

In the wake of these nauseating developments, Planned Parenthood immediately went into damage-control mode, calling his actions an "aberration," and not indicative of a more sinister, deadlier agenda. But, as the saying goes, "facts are stubborn things." So let us examine a few facts about abortion and Planned Parenthood's transformation from a supposed "women's health" organization whose founder publicly opposed abortion into the nation's largest private abortion provider, which enabled Gosnell, to whom we shall return shortly, to run his house of horrors in the "City of Brotherly Love" for so many years, almost without detection.

It has been well-documented in these pages that Margaret Sanger began her crusade with the stated goal of providing women with reliable information on birth control. It has also been well-documented that this search soon led her into her disastrous involvement with the eugenics movement. She stated that she opposed abortion because it was, in her words, "the taking of a life." Let the reader be reminded that she did not have to favor abortion as she was an advocate of sterilizing those whom she and her fellow-travelers decided were "unfit" or "inferior" for any number of reasons and should, therefore, be kept from bringing any more of their progeny into the world. Sanger continued to publicly oppose abortion for more than 20 years after the BCFA changed its name to Planned Parenthood Federation of America in 1942. And, in fact, there was a time when its official position on abortion was quite different from what it is today. As late as the early 1960s, it made itself quite clear when it issued the following public statement: "An abortion kills the life of the baby after it has begun." [1]

This is surprising, to say the least, especially in light of the fact that PPFA soon began to alter its position on the taking of unborn life, a stance it completely abandoned in 1970 when the State of New York legalized the practice a full three years before the Supreme Court declared abortion on demand to be legal under the Constitution. Sanger's group did not wait very long to start performing abortions, administering the first such procedures in Syracuse on the first day that New York legalized them. [2] PPFA soon dropped all pretense of opposing abortion in December 1971, when George Langmyhr, the chair of the group's medical committee, wrote an article that was published in that month's issue of *Clinical Obstetrics and Gynecology.*

In a chilling foreshadowing of things to come, Langmyhr wrote, "We support the view that when an unwanted pregnancy has occurred, abortion services should be available, with the decision essentially being made by the patient and her doctor...In summary," Langmyhr concluded, "Planned Parenthood hopes that abortion will become *even more available* and supports the efforts of others seeking reform and repeal of outdated laws (author's emphasis added)." [3] Let us pause for a moment to examine the gravity of this statement. First, Langmyhr states that the decision to abort an unborn child, which PPFA rejected in 1963, should now be left in the hands of the mother and her doctor, with no mention at all being made that the father's wishes should be taken into consideration. This is a stance Planned Parenthood holds to this day, although now proponents of abortion have added the words "and her God" to their statements on the issue. How gracious of them.

Secondly, Langmyhr's article calls the laws that were in place at that time to protect unborn life "outdated." It is nothing short of frightening to contemplate that this or any member of the medical profession would refer to these laws in such a way. Sentiments like Langmyhr's bring to mind the statements of one Barack Hussein Obama, President of the United States, who as an Illinois State Senator opposed passage of that state's version of the federal Born Alive Infant Protection Act. As the reader will recall, this law would protect survivors of failed abortions by providing them with basic medical services that any patient in any hospital would come to expect, even if they only survived outside their mother's wombs for even a few minutes. But Obama opposed this law because, as he put it, it would have "violated the wishes" of the mother to terminate her pregnancy and the life that would have resulted from it. It is most telling, indeed, that Obama was the *only* senator in the Land of Lincoln who voted against this law not once, but twice.

Planned Parenthood believed so strongly in the New York decision to liberalize its "outdated" abortion law that it filed an *amicus curare* ("friend of the court") brief with the Supreme Court urging that abortion be made legal across the country with absolutely no restrictions whatsoever. Furthermore, it was so confident of its position that it began to offer abortions in New York City in January of 1973. [4] The rest, as they say, is history, and a tragic one at that. Reliable estimates show that Planned Parenthood performed at least 2,000 abortions from 1970-72, but once the Supreme Court issued its ruling in *Roe vs. Wade* in 1973, all bets were now off. Planned Parenthood performed an estimated 5,000 abortions in 1973, 58,770 in 1977, 104,000 in 1987, 213,026 in 2001, 329,445 in 2009, [5] and 333,964 in 2011. [6] These were not "referrals" to other abortion providers as Planned Parenthood claims, but operations that were performed at the group's *own clinics*! And, remember that most of these procedures were carried out on black women. Considering these numbers, can the "pro-choice" movement seriously claim to have achieved its goal of making abortion a "rare" occurrence?

Now, let us turn to the "pro-choice" argument that abortions must be conducted safely, i.e., that the woman suffer no ill effects from the procedure. It makes no mention in this argument of the fact that the baby growing in her womb is a human being as well, and that, except in those cases where the child is born despite the attempts to abort it, the baby is almost always killed, which hardly makes abortion "safe" for the child in question. But then, Planned Parenthood, NARAL Pro-Choice America and other pro-abortion groups cannot honestly deal with this rather inconvenient truth (to borrow a phrase made popular by former Vice President Al Gore) without exposing their real agenda.

Every now and then, though, the mask slips and we get a glimpse of what lies at the heart of the "pro-choice" movement. This brings us back to the aforementioned "Doctor" Gosnell, who received his comeuppance when he was convicted on three counts of murder in May 2013 in the deaths of children who were born alive, despite his attempts to kill them in the womb. He also was convicted in the drug overdose death of Karnamaya Mongar, who succumbed on his operating table during the course of her surgery. As the trial unfolded, grisly details emerged about the manner in which the remains of the butchered children were handled, the conditions present in Gosnell's chamber of horrors, and disgustingly, his attitude toward both his patients and the children whose lives he snuffed out before they ever had a chance to be born.

Needless to say, the story made national headlines and raised a firestorm of outrage across the country. While NARAL, to its credit, issued a statement condemning Gosnell's actions, Planned Parenthood circled the wagons and pooh-poohed his activities as merely an "aberration'" and not at all typical of what regularly takes place inside an abortion "clinic." This statement is laughable on its face for the simple reason that PPFA unabashedly supports the despicable and barbaric practice known as late-term, or "partial-birth," abortion. So, it is inconceivable that any rational-thinking person could come to such a conclusion.

Then, amazingly, the group blamed Gosnell's actions on its favorite target, the *pro-life* movement, and followed up by calling for *fewer* regulations on abortion. It did not call for cleaner conditions at its clinics; it did not even call for such facilities to be placed under the same set of health regulations which any other type of clinic or hospital would be required to observe. It called for *none* of these things, only that abortion services be made more readily available, no strings attached, no questions asked.

Planned Parenthood is infamous for its opposition to parental notification laws, the use of technologies such as sonograms and ultrasounds that show the woman the life growing inside her body, and it staunchly defends the use of such chemically-induced forms of abortion as RU-486 and the "morning after" abortion pill that the Food and Drug Administration authorized for sale in 2013 to girls as young as 15 years of age without a prescription or their parents' knowledge or consent. But on the other hand, it says nothing about the value of the lives taken by abortion since 1973 (57 million unborn children, by most estimates), nor does it acknowledge the physical and psychological damage done to women who undergo these procedures.

Increased rates of breast cancer and sterility, or the tremendous grief and guilt that so often accompany an abortion sadly are far too commonplace among the overwhelming number of women who undergo such a procedure. Many women who have had even one abortion have also displayed symptoms of Post Traumatic Stress Disorder (PTSD) after having had their operations. We will examine some of the consequences of abortion more in our next chapter. But, suffice it to say, despite its best efforts to desensitize women to the fact that they are killing an unborn child, the abortion industry has not yet won its war on the human conscience. If they are given the correct information about the risks of abortion to both their physical and psychological health, there is still at least a glimmer of hope that many women will make the right choice and decide to let their baby live after all.

But, to abortion advocates, life really has nothing to do with it, at least not the life of the child. All that matters is "a woman's right to choose." Remember what Barack Obama said in defending the two "no" votes he cast as a state senator in Illinois before he went on to bigger and (at least for him) better things. And, do not forget the tortured answer he gave in 2008 when asked when life begins, that it was "above my pay grade." But again, life has nothing to do with it, only the "right to choose," even though the father is often completely shut out, and the unborn child has absolutely no say in the matter, even apparently as in the Gosnell case, after it is born.

A revealing example of the latter came to light in March of 2013, when Alicia Lapolt Snow, a lobbyist for Florida's Alliance of Planned Parenthood Affiliates, testified before a State House committee that was debating the treatment of survivors of failed abortions, in this case, whether to pass a state law much like the federal Born Alive Infant Protection Act. In response to questioning about whether the baby should be allowed to live or die, Snow stated that "any decision that's made should be left up to the woman, her family, and the physician." [7] The reaction of many lawmakers, to put it mildly, was one of stunned incredulity.

Representative Daniel Davis pressed Snow on this point, asking, "What happens in a situation where a baby is alive, breathing on a table, moving? What do your physicians do at that point?" Snow pleaded ignorance, saying, "I'm not a doctor. I'm not an abortion provider. So, I do not have that information."

The hearing continued with Snow being queried by Representative Jose Oliva, who asked, "You stated that a baby born alive on a table as a result of a botched abortion, that that decision should be left to the doctor and the family. Is that what you're saying?" Snow held firm, stating again that "That decision should be made by the patient and the health care provider." Oliva continued to press her on this point, asking Snow, "I think that at that point, the patient would be the child struggling on the table, wouldn't you agree?" Snow seemed to be genuinely taken aback by this rather simple exercise in logic and admitted, "That's a very good question." Of course it was! But, Snow neither could, nor would deal with it, adding, "I really don't have the answer to that. I would be glad to have some conversations with you about this." Evidently this was "above" her "pay grade" as well.

But, it was Snow's answer to another question that was truly jaw-dropping. When asked, "What objection could you possibly have to obligate a doctor to transport a child born alive to a hospital where it seems to me that they would most likely be able to survive?" she replied that Planned Parenthood was supposedly concerned about "those situations where it is in a rural health care setting, the hospital is forty-five minutes or an hour away, that's the closest trauma center or emergency room. You know there's just some logistical issues involved that we have some concerns about." So *that* was what lay at the heart of the matter, according to the nation's largest abortion provider: that there wouldn't be enough time or that it was just too hard to reach a hospital where the child could receive even the most basic medical treatment or care. This obscures the obvious legal ramifications that attach to Planned Parenthood's position, that those who allow or enable the baby to die after it has been born alive are guilty of manslaughter at the very least, and murder at the very worst.

Snow's candor in her testimony and Planned Parenthood's complicity in the deaths of children whose only crime is that they survived attempts to kill them before being born is and should be shocking to any truly compassionate person. Sadly, though, this sentiment isn't nearly as rare as one might think. Many so-called "intellectuals" have no problem at all with what is increasingly referred to as "post-birth" abortion. The case of Peter Singer, an Australian professor of bioethics at Princeton University in Princeton, New Jersey, is particularly insightful.

Singer first gained notoriety in the 1990s for his involvement in the animal "rights" movement. His book *Animal Liberation* argued that animals should have the same rights as human beings and is widely regarded as the "bible" of the movement. Singer, like a lot of animal "rights" advocates, is decidedly "pro-choice," but he takes his position to a much higher level with his outspoken support for "post-birth" abortion. Professor Singer's views hark back to the rationale the German Nazis used to justify the atrocities they committed under the *T-4* forced euthanasia program we examined in Chapter 3 of this work.

As the reader will recall, the program started out with children who were severely disabled or handicapped, but was soon expanded to anyone, adults included, whom the regime considered "unworthy of life." Singer has gone on record as saying that parents should have the right to kill their disabled children up to the age of two years. Further, this man, who believes that animals are at least equal and some cases superior to humans, holds the view that life does not begin at the moment of conception, and that a child does not possess rights until the age of four months, because that is the age at which he holds that "personhood" begins.

To call this statement breathtaking is an understatement of the first magnitude, and it says a great deal about the administration at Princeton. That it would even consider hiring a man who holds such anti-human views, let alone make him a tenured professor in charge of shaping impressionable young minds, is beyond the realm of human comprehension. But, it is just as mind-boggling that any parent who cares about human life would pay good money, in Princeton's case tens of thousands of dollars in tuition, to have him teach this intellectual dreck to their child.

It also speaks volumes another Ivy League school, Yale University in New Haven, Connecticut, not only endorses his position, but hosted a conference on "non-human personhood" featuring Singer and other like-minded academics in December of 2013. The university's own article about the conference, which was titled "Personhood Beyond the Human," [8] and which was co-sponsored by something called the Nonhuman Rights Project, sought to lend legitimacy to the chilling proposition that rights are somehow granted by people and not by God. If such is true, then can it not, therefore, be said that in the case of those who survive failed abortions, that it is perfectly permissible to deprive them of their right to live? And, if it is true that rights are not granted by God as stated in the *Declaration of Independence,* but by Man, does it not then follow that we *have* no rights, unalienable or otherwise, and that those rights that we do possess can be taken away from us at any moment and for any reason?

These would seem to be rather simple questions, almost no-brainers, in fact, to sane, rational people, but not to Peter Singer and those of like mind. But, one would do well to remember that positions held by Singer and his ilk (e.g. eugenics, population control, post-birth abortion, animal "rights," "non-human personhood," and anthropogenic, or human-induced climate change, just to name a few), are almost without exception, based on little more than pure gut feeling and raw emotion with almost no evidence, scientific or otherwise, to support their views. In fact, when such evidence to the contrary is proffered, those presenting it are savaged as being "anti-choice," "flat-Earthers," "enemies of the planet," "animal haters," etc. What is worse, they are often singled out for harassment or humiliation in any number of ways.

A particularly ugly example of the Liberal/Progressive assault which was unleashed on those who believe in the sanctity of unborn human life was the infamous and non-existent "War on Women," which commenced at the height of the 2012 Presidential campaign. Sandra Fluke, a female Georgetown University graduate student, testified that she had been discriminated against by the Catholic school because it would not pay for her use of birth-control pills. The Georgetown administration based its decision on its long-standing opposition to the use of birth-control by its students, a policy which was under attack by the Obama Administration, which sought to force religious institutions to violate their own core beliefs as part of the Affordable Care Act, otherwise known as "Obamacare." It was this policy that Ms. Fluke found to be "oppressive" and "misogynistic," even though she had known about it from the first day she set foot on campus and yet chose not to broach the subject until this particular moment. Hmm. How curious.

Although she could have obtained birth-control pills at any pharmacy in Washington for about $9.00 per month, an amount she could have easily paid out of her own pocket, Fluke argued that this represented an unfair "hardship" and demanded that Georgetown pay up. This story made national headlines when syndicated radio host Rush Limbaugh called her a "slut" by asking his audience what someone who demanded that somebody else pay for her sex should be called. Limbaugh realized he had used language that was, to put it mildly, inelegant and apologized for his remarks, but the damage was already done.

Fluke was now a victim of the "misogynistic" Far Right who was canonized in Liberal/Progressive circles as the new patron saint of the "pro-choice" cause. Planned Parenthood, NARAL, and other pro-abortion and far-left women's groups circled the wagons around her, and she was even accorded the honor of a telephone call from President Obama himself, who praised her for her "courage." But, that was just the opening salvo in what was soon to become the Right's "War on Women." Limbaugh's remarks about Ms. Fluke and his subsequent apology were followed by another gaffe, this time by pro-life Missouri Republican Congressman Todd Aiken, who was running for the U.S. Senate seat held by Democrat incumbent Claire McCaskill, an abortion supporter.

In a debate with McCaskill, Aiken, who was leading her in early polling among the state's voters, was asked about his position regarding abortion in cases of sexual assaults, such as rape or incest. In his answer, he alluded to what he called "legitimate rape" and said that he had been told by doctors (whom he later had to admit he had not consulted) that in such cases, a woman's body "shuts down" and prevents her from getting pregnant. As a result of these remarks, Aiken came off as someone who was not only clueless about female anatomy, but a stereotypical knuckle-dragging buffoon who was dangerously out of touch with the women voters of Missouri.

Although Aiken realized how what he said sounded and ardently apologized for his language, it was too late for him to correct the damage he had inflicted on himself. What he should have said, and what he eventually did say, was that victims of rape or incest are especially vulnerable and should be shown all the love and compassion that can be given, but that the baby, who had no choice in the way it was conceived, should not be killed.

However, by now, he was unmercifully caricatured in the media as incredibly insensitive, and this charge would dog him all the way through to his defeat in November.

Aiken's remarks and his refusal to withdraw from a winnable Senate race guaranteed that McCaskill would serve at least another six years and that millions of unborn children in the future would never draw their first breaths, see their first sunrises or sunsets, take their first steps, say their first words, or start their first days of school. McCaskill was re-elected, and thanks to her and her pro-abortion allies, these children would now join the tens of millions who have been denied that first and most critical unalienable right of all, the right to life.

Each of these incidents by itself provided the enemies of the unborn with plenty of ammunition to attack their opponents, but taken together, the Fluke controversy and the Aiken incident of "foot in mouth" became the perfect storm that the political Left had hoped would erupt. Never mind that Sandra Fluke could have walked into any drug store she wanted and gotten her birth-control pills at any time, with no questions asked. She knew full well that the Supreme Court had ruled decades ago that women had the right to obtain contraceptive devices. But that wasn't the point; the point was to demonize anyone who believes in the sanctity of unborn human life, even to the extent that it was perfectly permissible to lie that conservatives were seeking to deny women access to such pills and devices. In the same way the Left distorted Aiken's remarks about "legitimate rape" to make him appear dangerously naïve at the very least, and misogynistic at the very worst. From their perspective, it worked even better than they themselves could have hoped.

The Left's strategy served the dual purpose of slandering those who seek nothing more than to save the innocent unborn and preserving the political power of those who want to destroy them. It is of critical importance to remember that Margaret Sanger, who was raised in a Catholic family, later became one of the Church's most vicious attackers. The assault mounted on organized religion, in general, and against the Catholic Church, in particular, by the Obama Administration in the summer of 2012 would have made her exceedingly proud, as would have Aiken's politically-suicidal remarks during the 2012 Missouri Senatorial campaign. Both cases gave the Left the chance to paint conservatives, in general, and pro-life advocates, in particular, as the worst kinds of human beings who yearned to turn back the clock and take women back to the "bad old days" when they were kept "barefoot, pregnant and in the kitchen" and subject to dangerous back-alley abortions. Of course, as the Gosnell case so graphically illustrates, the Left has virtually nothing to say about the dangerous and often deadly consequences women face from the legalized abortions that take place every day on the operating tables in the very clinics that Sanger's organization oversees.

The tactics employed by the pro-abortion crowd against Christians and conservatives during the 2012 campaign came right out of the late Saul Alinsky's seminal work *Rules for Radicals*. Published in 1971, this book advised American leftists and their fellow-travelers on how to destroy America from within by attacking its institutions and its democratic ideals. Dedicated to "the first radical, Lucifer," *Rules for Radicals* is a book that operates from the premise that the world must not be taken the way it is, but rather on "how it should be" (a subjective appraisal to say the least), and lays out the tactics that are to be employed to bring about such a change. Rule #13, for example, is quite enlightening on this point: "Pick the target, freeze the target, personalize the target and polarize it" [9]

The importance of this tactic must not be underestimated, particularly in regard to abortion. As we have seen, the Left immediately picked the target (organized religion and pro-life supporters), froze the target through ridicule, lies, and deception (the "War on Women" and a return to the "bad old days"), personalized the target (again, those who believe in the sanctity of unborn human life, even that which was conceived through rape or incest), and polarized that target (pro-life supporters are extremists who want to deny women the "right to choose"). Obviously, the Left learned all too well what Alinsky taught, especially where the life issue is concerned.

When the likes of Sandra Fluke, Nancy Pelosi, Jesse Jackson, Barack Obama, Carl Levin, Barbara Boxer, Diane Feinstein *et al* seized on the birth-control issue in the 2012 campaign to demonize conservatives, Christians, and others who believe that the unborn should not be butchered in their mothers' wombs, they accused them of waging a "War on Women." But what they were actually doing was using this patently false narrative as cover for the real war the Left has been conducting for nearly a hundred years—a war on the *womb itself*. For nearly 50 years it has glossed over Margaret Sanger's racist past and the fact that she was hell-bent on exterminating as many minorities as possible through any means necessary. It is strangely silent about the clear evidence of the physical, psychological, and emotional damage suffered by millions of women from legalized abortion since 1973.

And, it certainly does not want to discuss the atrocities that have been committed at abortion mills across the country by the likes of Kermit Gosnell, George Tiller, and Heaven only knows how many other of these so-called "doctors" who have forsaken their sacred oaths to "first, do no harm." Reverend Levon R. Yuille, Pastor of the Bible Church in Ypsilanti, Michigan, and Director of the National Black Pro-Life Congress (NBPLC), estimates that for every Gosnell or Tiller about whom we know, there are likely thousands of others who are operating under the radar screen and are doing exactly the same thing. Further, abortion supporters almost completely ignore the holocaust that is being perpetrated on black America by Planned Parenthood, NARAL, and other like-minded groups, but they proudly point to the fact that the Reverend Martin Luther King, Jr., who gave his life fighting to secure full citizenship for black Americans, was the first recipient of the Margaret Sanger Award in 1966, when Planned Parenthood's official position on abortion was quite different from what it is today. They use his acceptance of this award as some sort of validation of abortion, but his niece, Dr. Alveda King, has quite a different view of the matter.

A Pastoral Associate of Priests for Life, based in Staten Island, New York, Dr. King has this to say about the nation's largest private abortion provider's use of her uncle's name and image on its website: "Planned Parenthood is no stranger to deception." Dr. King, who experienced abortion herself, continues, "I know this first hand, because prior to my abortion a Planned Parenthood doctor told me that my baby was 'just a blob of tissue.' Now," Dr. King says, "Planned Parenthood is trying to imply that my uncle, Dr. Martin Luther King, Jr., would somehow endorse the organization today. He most certainly would not." [10]

King adds, "Uncle Martin accepted an award from Planned Parenthood in 1966, when abortion was illegal in every state and before Planned Parenthood started publicly advocating for it. In Planned Parenthood's own citation for Uncle Martin's prize," Dr. King elaborates, "not only is no mention of abortion made, it states that 'human life and progress are indeed indivisible.' In 1966, neither the general public nor my uncle was aware of the true agenda of Planned Parenthood, an agenda of death that has become painfully obvious as the years have unfolded. [11] Dr. Martin Luther King, Jr. said, 'The Negro cannot win if he is willing to sacrifice the future of his children for personal comfort and safety,' and 'Injustice anywhere is a threat to justice everywhere.' There is no way he would want his name or image associated today with Planned Parenthood, the group most responsible for denying civil rights to the over 45 million babies killed by abortion, one-third of them African-American. There is no way my uncle would condone the violence of abortion, violence that Planned Parenthood has always tried to mask, which brings painful death to babies, and can result in torn wombs, serious infections and emotional devastation for their mothers. Let me be clear," Dr. King concludes, "Planned Parenthood must stop lying to my family and the entire community of humanity." [12]

The heartfelt and sincere sentiments expressed by Dr. King in exposing the agenda of the nation's largest private abortion provider were presaged by the Reverend Johnny Lee Hunter on Columbus Day in 1999 when he led a march to the steps of the U.S. Capitol to protest two Supreme Court decisions, the 1954 ruling in *Brown vs. Board of Education* and *Roe vs. Wade* nearly 20 years later. Reverend Hunter, the national director of the Life, Education and Resource Network (LEARN), organized the march and issued a blunt and scathing statement about abortion and the damage it has wreaked on the black community for more than forty years.

"Civil rights," Reverend Hunter declared, "doesn't mean a thing without a right to life!" [13] Dedicated and truly compassionate black leaders like Dr. King and Reverends Yuille and Hunter have seen through the smokescreens of lies and obfuscation about the reality of abortion that are all too often utilized by the "pro-choice" movement to advance its agenda, and they have brought the ugly truth to light, a truth which is borne out by these two facts alone, from Planned Parenthood itself:

- In 1992 alone, according to its own records, 23.2% of women who underwent abortions at Planned Parenthood affiliates were black, even though they only comprised 13% of the total female population of the United States, [14], and

- Four years later, the group's research arm revealed that 31% of all abortions these affiliates performed were on black women, even though they made up only 14% of all women of childbearing age. [15]

Calling it "the number one killer of blacks in America," Hunter decries the damage abortion has done. "We're losing our people at the rate of 1,452 *a day*. That's just pure genocide. There's no other word for it." Hunter further condemns the nearly wholesale embrace of abortion by black Americans: "Sanger's influence and the whole mindset that Planned Parenthood has brought into the black community...say it's okay to destroy your people. We bought into the lie; we bought into the propaganda." [16] Addressing the loss of generations of potential future black leaders through abortion, Hunter goes further. "We're destroying the destiny and purpose of others who should be here," he laments. "Who knows the musicians we've lost?" he asks. "Who knows the great leaders the black community has really lost? Who knows what great minds of economic power people have lost? What great teachers?" [17] Who, indeed? But Hunter draws from his own personal experience in his travels across America to show how Planned Parenthood places as many of its abortion mills as possible in black inner city neighborhoods.

"When I travel around the country," Hunter relates, "I can think of only one abortion clinic [I've seen] in a predominantly white neighborhood. The majority of clinics are in black neighborhoods." [18] To bear this out, he cites PPFA's infiltration of black schools with materials that promote abortion as just another form of "birth control," a strategy that sadly has duped so many black Americans into believing that there is no other way to deal with an unplanned pregnancy than to snuff out the life that is growing inside the mother's body. For example, Hunter cites a 1999 case from Baton Rouge, Louisiana, in which officials of the city's school district attempted to distribute birth control and pro-abortion materials in health clinics in the city's high schools.

Hunter smelled a rat, and when he delved into the issue, he found that such materials were to be handed out *only* in the city's black high schools and nowhere else. He brought the matter to the attention of Louisiana State Representative Sharon Weston Broome, who had at first endorsed the idea, although she had reservations about such a scheme, adding that these clinics should be teaching abstinence. Hunter urged Broome to suggest that the materials be distributed in Baton Rouge's white high schools, as well, with the predictable results. The idea was dropped by the school district like a hot potato. [19]

This was not the first time that abortion supporters attempted to infiltrate America's government schools, in particular the black schools, and that Planned Parenthood was leading this assault. George Grant, author of *Killer Angel,* a biography of PPFA founder Margaret Sanger, points out that the group had been at it for at least two decades prior to the Baton Rouge incident. In *Grand Illusions: The Legacy of Planned Parenthood,* Grant gives us a chilling insight into the cynical and calculated strategy embarked upon by the nation's largest private abortion provider and precisely who the target was. "During the 1980s when Planned Parenthood shifted its focus from community-based clinics to school-based clinics," Grant tells us, it again targeted inner-city neighborhoods. "Of the more than 100 school-based clinics that have opened nation-wide in the last decade (the 1980s), *none* has been at substantially all-white schools. All," Grant writes, "have been at black, minority or ethnic schools." [20]

Such a trend has long been the dream of the Liberal/Progressive Left in this country, beginning with the successful takeover of education by the federal government and its enablers at such teacher unions as the National Education Association and the American Federation of Teachers. When the Carter Administration spun off the Department of Education from the Department of Health, Education, and Welfare in an unprecedented political payoff to these unions for their support in the 1976 Presidential Election, it blatantly ignored the fact that *there is no role in education that is reserved to the federal government anywhere in the United States Constitution!* If there were, would it not have made sense to the framers to include one in this magnificent document? But, of course, they didn't, because they knew that educating children is their *parents*' responsibility.

Parents, working in concert with the local school boards in their respective districts, have always known and been able to assess and address the educational requirements of their children far better than legions of nameless, faceless bureaucrats who inhabit a monstrous federal educational apparatus that is often thousands of miles away. Because the 10th Amendment to the Constitution guarantees that the rights *"not reserved to* the *United States by the Constitution, nor prohibited to it by the States, are reserved to the States respectively, or the people,"* the federal government is *explicitly* prohibited from playing any role at all in education. Now, this would seem to be rather obvious to any student of the Constitution, but it is of little import in the ever-growing and burgeoning federal power-grab in Washington.

And, the nation's schools are the poorer for it. The institution of school-based health clinics that offer birth-control pills and abortion counseling to girls and condoms to boys, often without the parents' knowledge and/or consent, makes it crystal-clear that while the teacher unions talk a good game about parental involvement in their children's education, they are really at the forefront of propagandizing and indoctrinating them into accepting whatever values the liberal and progressives hold dear, values that too often are *directly* contradictory to those the parents have spent their children's formative years instilling. Such values as patriotism, delayed gratification, and hard work are belittled by too many teachers, union officials, and school administrators in favor of pacifism, victim hood, and political correctness.

Discipline in the classroom is now a thing of the past, endangering both student and teacher in the process.

All sex-education classes in today's government schools teach students "how to do it," but very few, if any of them, teach students about the importance of responsibility for one's actions. History classes are often taught in such a way that gives the student little or no grounding in our republican form of government and why we have it, our long struggle to secure our freedom from England, or that our nation's founders created an exceptional nation based on the idea that we are all equal in God's sight. No, to the modern "progressive" education establishment, what seems to matter more to them is not the fact that George Washington, the Father of our country, was a courageous soldier who held together the Continental Army in the dark days of 1776, that he was an accomplished farmer who successfully experimented with new strains of plants, or that he was possessed of an amazing intellect, which served him well as our first president.

And it matters little to today's "enlightened" progressive educators that Thomas Jefferson, who wrote our nation's birth certificate, the *Declaration of Independence*, also was an accomplished farmer, a brilliant inventor, President of the University of Virginia, fought the country's first war on terror against the Barbary pirates as our third president, and sent Lewis and Clark west to explore our vast, new, uncharted lands following the Louisiana Purchase, just to name a few of his many achievements. No, indeed. Good luck opening any history textbook used in today's government schools and finding any mention at all of either these extraordinary men or any of our founders. Alas, the only reference to them that you are likely to find is that they held *slaves*.

It would be bad enough if we only had to deal with the politicization of our history texts and classes. If that was the only thing that concerned us, we would have a much better idea about how to correct such a blatant and obvious distortion of our nation's history. However, this politicization does not end there. A great number of science classes in today's government schools are taught from the leftist political perspective that human beings are a viral cancer on the planet, and that their activities are responsible for everything from ozone depletion (heard anything about *that* lately?) to "global climate change," both of which have proved scientifically to be monumental hoaxes. Therefore, in the view of leftist elites, they must be eliminated from the natural equation as quickly as possible to stave off environmental Armageddon. It is this population-control component that is the driving force behind the United Nations' *Agenda 21* worldwide power-grab, which we will explore further in Chapter 7.

Another example of how the Left has damaged America's system of public education is the terrible job that government schools have done in teaching our children how to read. Abandoning phonics in favor of failed methods like whole language (or the "look-say" approach to reading) has resulted in generations of students who are so functionally illiterate that they cannot read, let alone understand, what is written on their diplomas when they graduate. As a result, these students leave school not only ill-prepared to make their own way in the world, but many of them have to *return* to the same failed government schools to take remedial courses to repair the damage that was done to them in the first place!

Nevertheless, the proponents of the "progressive" approach to education that emerged in the late 1960s do not see themselves as bearing any responsibility for the wasteland that has become the American system of government schools, a system that supplanted the proven and time-honored system of true public education. Instead, they have doubled down on failure and offered more of the same approaches to education that they originally created. Albert Einstein once defined the word "insanity" in this way: "doing the same thing over and over and expecting a different result." Nowhere is this adage truer than in America's failed experiment with "progressive" education.

Meanwhile, the federal government, which as we showed, has no Constitutional role in the business of educating our children, demonstrates the truth of Einstein's definition of insanity by showering this failed school system with billions upon billions of dollars in taxpayer money *per year* trying to correct a problem which never should have arisen in the first place. America's teacher unions compound the problem by giving millions of dollars in dues money each election cycle to politicians who to a very great extent owe them their jobs, which consist largely of advancing their interests in Congress and the Senate. Teacher unions like the National Education Association (NEA) and the American Federation of Teachers (AFT) are in the forefront of short-changing our elementary, high school, and college students, robbing them not only of a decent, well-rounded education, but ultimately of cheating them out of a real chance to achieve the American dream. These people should be ashamed of themselves. But, according to at least one higher-up in the teacher union establishment, helping excellence in education is the *last* thing that concerns them.

For instance, Albert Shanker, one-time head of the American Federation of Teachers, was once asked what his union was doing to provide a better education for our children. The AFT President replied that this was not the point: "When they start paying union dues," he replied stunningly, "we'll start representing them." While not often expressed with this level of honesty from a union official, let alone the leader of one of the country's leading teacher unions, such sentiments are eye-opening at the very least, and alarming at the very worst. What's more, this attitude is not unique to Mr. Shanker. It is standard operating procedure among officials at every level of the union establishment. This should give great pause to any parent who is thinking of entrusting their most precious assets, their children, to those who have such a view of things. No wonder more and more parents are in favor of school vouchers to rescue their children from failing government schools, or are opting to teach them at home. But, again, Shanker was not alone. He had plenty of help.

When people think of modern public education, the name of John Dewey usually comes to mind. And, while it is true that Dewey had much to do with the decline of our public schools, there were others who did plenty of damage as well, in particular Chester M. Pierce. Pierce, who, like Lothrop Stoddard, was educated at Harvard, is openly disdainful of the role parents play in teaching their children the values and traditions that made America not only a great nation, but an *exceptional* one, as well. It is a role he considers quite dangerous, indeed. In *Educating for the New World Order,* Pierce makes clear his utter contempt for parents in no uncertain terms by writing, "Every child in America who enters school with an allegiance to our elected officials, toward our Founding Fathers, toward our institutions, toward the preservation of this form of government, all of this proves *the children are sick* (author's emphasis added)." [21]

If the chutzpah of this statement seems breathtaking, to say the least, just wait; there's more. Pierce expands further and lets us know what the remedy is for this form of "mental illness," as he puts it, on the part of both the parents and their children: "because the truly well individual is one who has *rejected* all those things and is what I would call the true international child of the future (again, author's emphasis added)." [22]

So, as Pierce and his contemporaries in the educational bureaucracy see it, it is not their role to help these children lay a solid foundation for success in life. It is not even their job to reinforce the values which set us apart from every other nation on earth, values like the intrinsic worth of the individual, the importance of our system of constitutionally-limited government, and the absolute necessity of allowing people to pursue their own dreams so that they can become the best they can be.

No, to Pierce and his ilk, all these things, including the most important right we have, the right to life, are outdated, old-fashioned, quaint, or simply dangerous, and must be expunged from what our children are learning in the classroom. Not only do they see it as their job to do this, they consider it a sacred trust. Such ideas as those expressed by Pierce represent both a clear and direct threat to our children and the future of our nation, but they are certainly nothing new, not by any stretch of the imagination.

We have seen them before in places like the old Soviet Union where Lenin openly bragged how the State would take the place of parents in educating (or more precisely, in indoctrinating) their young; in National Socialist Germany where Hitler spoke of creating "a nation without a conscience;" and more recently in mainland China, in Cuba, and in North Korea, countries that continue to enslave their own people under the iron fist of murderous, oppressive totalitarian rule. The very idea that a place like Harvard, founded by men of deep religious conviction long before this country won its independence, could turn out someone so openly hostile to its own founding principles, should have them spinning in their graves.

However, this is the crisis that confronts our educational institutions and poses a dire threat to the very future of our republic. If we truly care about the future, we must confront the Peter Singers, the John Deweys, and the Chester Pierces of this world and reject their ideas entirely. Instead of granting such people legitimacy through the system of tenured professorships, we need to expel them and their ideas forthwith from every college and university campus in the country.

Even more to the point, with so many of these places depending so heavily on the donations from alumni that total in the hundreds of millions of dollars each year, we must make it crystal-clear to our university presidents and boards of regents that these people and their ideas are no longer welcome in our institutions of higher learning and that they will receive no further funding from those who have graduated from them until this situation changes. And, if that isn't enough, we must hold them to account by depriving not only these professors, but these administrators of their jobs, as well.

Unfortunately, this is not likely to happen anytime soon, if it ever does. We have reached a point where the inmates truly are running the asylum, and it is highly open to question whether we have the guts to rip out the dry-rot that passes for education in our institutions of higher learning, a dry-rot that began to set in nearly fifty years ago during the turbulent period of campus unrest at places like Berkeley, Brown University, the University of Michigan, and Kent State. For the first time in our history, those who not only questioned the school's authority, but acted violently on that principle were not only not dealt with as the thugs that they were, they were actually *rewarded* for their criminal actions by these administrations. The results were not pretty, and the consequences of this disastrous policy are plain for all to see even today, more than four decades later.

Speech codes were enacted, *de facto* self-segregation was established through separate student unions, and various black, female, Hispanic and gender-specific "studies" courses meant to remedy the perceived "inequities" and "injustices" that were supposedly running rampant on campus. Perhaps most the chilling of all, we now witnessing the logical conclusion of such campus madness as those with opposing views are intimidated into silence lest they be dragged in front of the aforementioned student "courts" which we examined earlier in this work, star chambers that have been set up by the same people who are now being taught ideas that run directly counter to the time-honored principles that made the United States the greatest nation on God's green earth. We see the results even now with alarming regularity as conservative speakers like David Horowitz and Ann Coulter, who stand for the sanctity of unborn human life, are routinely subjected to all forms of threats and abuse by students who come from the so-called "enlightened" and "tolerant" Left.

Appallingly, we have seen it in the abject surrender of the University of Notre Dame in South Bend, Indiana, which caved in to the demands of a sitting President of the United States, Barack Obama, that the school drape its religious statuary in shrouds before he addressed its graduating class of 2009. But, the Left's assault on our religious liberty did not stop there, for in 2012, the administration went to war against religious freedom on campus by requiring Georgetown and other Catholic universities to violate their own most deeply-held religious principles by forcing them to comply with the provisions of the so-called Affordable Care Act and pay for their female students' birth control pills and devices.

By the actions of so many of our colleges and universities, it has become very clear that the most basic principle on which our republic was founded, the right to life, has come under increasing attack by the secular/progressive Left. However, people like Sandra Fluke are merely a symptom of this ever-growing animus toward mainstream organized religion, And Planned Parenthood and the bloody legacy it has bequeathed from the very beginning under its founder, Margaret Sanger, lie directly at the heart of this issue. The true history of the birth-control movement has been muddled to such a great extent by those who call themselves "pro-choice" that its racist nature has been all-but forgotten, especially in our black colleges and universities.

All across the nation, from Morehouse and Bethune-Cookman Colleges to Tuskegee Institute and Grambling University, the racism of Margaret Sanger and her cohorts like Lothrop Stoddard, Harry Laughlin, and Madison Grant has been deliberately papered over by groups like Planned Parenthood and NARAL, and they wouldn't have it any other way. They have a vested interest in propounding and disseminating the image of Sanger and her ilk as only being concerned with "women's health," "family planning," or "child spacing," not that their true intention was to eliminate "inferiors" by any means they had at their disposal, including abortion. They would, indeed, have much for which to answer if the real truth ever came out, and they know it. That is why they fight so ferociously to conceal it, and that is why they will descend to whatever depths they feel they need to in order to assure that it never sees the light of day.

Why else would the "pro-choice" movement use the benign-sounding euphemisms mentioned above if not to mask its bloody agenda? Why else would its leaders find it so necessary to hide its real history, a history that long ago targeted minorities, in particular black Americans, for extinction? Why did its founder eagerly embrace the New Jersey branch of the Ku Klux Klan that infamous night in 1926? And why does it today feel it so necessary to tar anyone of good conscience who opposes abortion as "misogynistic," "anti-choice," engaged in a "War on Women," or any other negative adjective it can muster?

Further, why does the "pro-choice" movement deny the simple biological fact that life does, indeed, begin at the moment of conception, characterizing the human fetus, an entity that is alive from that moment on, as merely "a mass of cells" or just "a blob of protoplasm?" Why does it fear, almost to the point of hysteria, the use of modern medical technology such as sonograms and ultrasounds that show a woman who is contemplating abortion that she is, indeed, killing another human being, namely her own unborn child?

Why will the movement not admit what former United States Surgeon General C. Everett Koop once famously noted, that with the technological advances that have been made in the last several years, that "abortion is almost never medically necessary?" The truth can be inconvenient at times, and can sometimes even painful to admit. Nonetheless, these are questions that must be answered, if we are ever to have an honest dialogue on this issue.

We must also examine why the supporters of abortion, such as Planned Parenthood, find it necessary to lie to and intimidate other groups, as it did in the case of the Susan G. Komen Foundation in 2012. In her *New York Times* best-seller *Planned Bullyhood: The Truth about the Planned Parenthood Funding Battle with Susan G. Komen for the Cure,* author Karen Handel gives a first-hand account of how the nation's largest private abortion provider resorts to lies and character assassination to intimidate others into silence, all while keeping the dollars flowing into its coffers. Mrs. Handel should know; as Senior Vice President of Public Policy for Komen, she oversaw the awarding of grants to organizations that are dedicated to helping women overcome one of the most devastating forms of cancer known to Mankind—-breast cancer.

At issue was Komen's awarding of grant money to Planned Parenthood, which as we have previously seen, likes to promote itself as providing such health services to women as mammograms, the most popular and critical form of detection and prevention of breast cancer in women. For nearly two decades, the Komen Foundation had been raising money through its "Race for the Cure" events and had been awarding grants to Planned Parenthood, but that was beginning to change when Handel, a former candidate for the office of Lieutenant Governor of Georgia, joined the Foundation in 2011. By that time, thanks to the heroic efforts of James O'Keefe and Lila Rose of the pro-life group Live Action, the racist aspects of Planned Parenthood been exposed through undercover phone calls to its clinics asking that money be spent specifically to abort unborn black children.

This, however, was only the tip of the iceberg. O'Keefe's and Rose's undercover videos also brought to light Planned Parenthood's attempts to cover up its role in sex-selection abortions, and, incredibly, its involvement in encouraging child sexual abuse. Because of O'Keefe and Rose, people were finally starting to learn the truth, and Planned Parenthood suddenly found its gravy train in mortal danger of finally being derailed. The ensuing public outcry eventually resulted in the United States Congress' decision to cut off the flow of taxpayer dollars into the organization's bank account, a situation which would seriously hamstring it, if not ultimately drive it into bankruptcy.

Handel's job was to eliminate what she called "crappy grants," or those that proved to be ineffective in achieving Komen's goals, and to redirect that money into providing better services to women who were suffering from breast cancer, and more importantly, to better measure their success. This would allow Komen to get a "bigger bang" for its buck, so to speak. As Congress proceeded to end Planned Parenthood's access to the taxpayers' wallets, Komen began to reassess its support for the organization, as well. The negative publicity surrounding O'Keefe's and Rose's revelations was beginning to affect Komen in a big way. A number of Catholic charities began to withdraw from Race for the Cure events, and a number of corporate sponsors followed suit, as well.

According to Handel, in its attempts to avoid a political firestorm on the Left, a firestorm which would come to include charges that the charity had "abandoned women" by no longer funding Planned Parenthood, Komen committed a number of incredible strategic blunders, first by hiring Brendan Daly, a former communications director for Representative Nancy Pelosi (D-CA) as a consultant. The group then compounded this error by taking Democrat National Committee Operative Hillary Rosen, who also served as an advisor to President Obama, on board. Rosen, the reader will recall, ridiculed Ann Romney, the wife of Republican Presidential nominee Mitt Romney, for "never having worked a day in her life" during the 2012 campaign. Rosen also mocked Mrs. Romney, who suffers from multiple sclerosis, for competing in equestrian events as a form of physical therapy. Rosen was eventually made to apologize for both incidents, but her remarks illustrate clearly the hypocrisy of those on the "compassionate" and "tolerant" Left. In addition to working at the White House, Rosen also toiled at the public relations firm SKD Knickerbocker and was a member of the DNC. She, in turn, hired Emily Lezner as one of her key advisors at Komen. Lezner, it so happened, handled Planned Parenthood's account at SKDK.

Handel had seen the dangers of such "foxes guarding the henhouse" and warned both Nancy Brinker, Komen's founder, and Liz Thompson, its CEO, that having such people so high up in the organization would mean nothing but trouble, but to no avail. Neither listened and it didn't take long for things to unravel at Komen. Planned Parenthood had agreed previously to respect Komen's decision to end its grants to the group, which had not amounted to a particularly large sum, but as the old saying goes, "it's not the money, it's the principle of the thing." After Daly, Rosen, and Lezner had finished doing their dirty work, Komen was forced to capitulate with barely a whimper, a mere *three days* after its decision to discontinue its financial support for Planned Parenthood.

Predictably, the media was ready to pounce, and pounce it did when MSNBC's Andrea Mitchell grilled Brinker about Komen's decision on the February 2, 2012 telecast of *Meet the Press.* Handel had warned Brinker about Mitchell, whose outspoken support for abortion, in general, and Planned Parenthood, in particular, made it clear that she could not have approached the interview with even so much as a modicum of objectivity. This was precisely what Handel had feared would happen; that despite Brinker's plea that "this is not our fight," and while trying to avoid a political controversy over what Komen thought was a "funding dispute," it now found itself embroiled in what Brinker had called a "culture war that is not ours." Too late. The damage had been done. Its reputation all but destroyed, this worthy charity was now forced to backtrack after a mere 72 hours and resume its grants to Planned Parenthood.

Not long after, Handel, whose reputation had been badly damaged, resigned from the Board of the Susan G. Komen Foundation. She had endured incredible abuse at the hands of the abortionists and their willing accomplices in both the media and the Democrat Party (people like Florida Congresswoman and DNC Chair Debbie Wasserman Schultz, for example), abuse that included charges that she was some kind of "Trojan Horse" who had come aboard to sabotage the Foundation, when nothing could have been further from the truth.

This good and decent woman, who had a long and distinguished record of service in both the public and private sectors, had committed no offense other than trying to help an honorable organization with a proven track record of helping women who suffered from a horrible disease get better treatment. Now, because of the political machinations that had permeated the Komen Foundation, Karen Handel was paying a price that no one should have to pay. To call the shameful goings-on at Komen because of this whole sorry, sordid episode a "shake-down" on Planned Parenthood's part would be an understatement, to put it mildly. Far more apropos would be to call the entire business odious, disgusting, thuggish, and brutal. If we were looking for a prime example of the saying that "no good deed ever goes unpunished," one would be hard-pressed to find a better one than this.

But this is, after all, the track record of the Left, in general, and Planned Parenthood, in particular. We have seen, time and again, especially when it comes to the "pro-choice" movement, that no one who opposes its agenda is safe from being vilified, demonized, and slandered. The Left has no logical or rational arguments for any of its policies. Therefore, it relies so heavily on lies, distortions of fact, and character assassination to carry out its program.

Recall Rule #13 in Saul Alinsky's *Rules for Radicals:* "Pick the target, freeze the target, personalize the target, and polarize the target." The Left has learned this lesson well and has used it to great advantage. We would do well to learn from this as well, for if we are to have any hope of keeping even a smidgen of our freedoms, we must realize who it is who is trying to destroy us.

Leftists love to accuse Americans who base their belief in the sanctity of unborn life on religious teachings of "shoving their beliefs down everyone else's throats." However. when one considers that leftism itself is a religion, it doesn't take a lot of digging to realize just how hypocritical these people really are. As Ann Coulter points out in the beginning of *Godless: The Church of Liberalism,* "Of course, liberalism is a religion. It has its own cosmology, its own miracles, its own beliefs in the supernatural, its own churches, its own high priests, its own saints, its own total worldview, and its own explanation of the existence of the universe. In other words, liberalism contains all the attributes of what is generally known as 'religion.'" [23] Coulter explains how abortion is a key sacrament of the religion of liberalism, and that Margaret Sanger has become one of its patron saints: "Margaret Sanger, the founder of Planned Parenthood and an early proponent of 'positive eugenics'...cited Darwinism to promote her 'religion' of birth control. She believed the theory of evolution provided the grounds for eliminating the 'unfit.'" [24]

Coulter also points out how successful Sanger's work was, especially in regard to blacks and other minorities: "Undoubtedly," she writes, Sanger "would be delighted to know that today: (1) Planned Parenthood is the leading provider of abortions in the United States, and (2) that about 36% of our aborted babies are black, about three times their percentage in the American population. Mission accomplished, Margaret!" [25] Given Sanger's racist associations, especially with members of the Klan, it wouldn't be much of a stretch to say that the abortionists are finishing the job that the KKK started.

Elsewhere in *Godless,* Coulter gives us additional horrifying insights into the views of Peter Singer, tenured professor of Bioethics at Princeton's laughably misnamed "Center for Human Values" and an outspoken advocate of abortion. We have already seen that Singer believes that parents should have the right to kill their severely handicapped children up to and including the age of two, but as Coulter tells us, there is more, far more, to the thought processes that have shaped this man's worldview. "In his book *Practical*

Ethics," Coulter writes, "Singer explains that 'the life of the fetus is of no greater value than the life of a non-human animal at a similar level of rationality, self-consciousness, awareness, capacity to feel, etc., and since no fetus is a person, no fetus has the same claim to life as a person.'"

Worse, just when we thought that we no longer had Hitler, the Nazis, and their *T-4* euthanasia program to worry about, along comes this "distinguished" member of academe at a prestigious Ivy League university promoting the very same thing in twenty-first century America. Coulter alerts us to more of the blood-curdling views of this "eminent" scholar who is making a generous salary indoctrinating impressionable minds with all manner of anti-human bilge: "Embracing a survival-of-the-fittest ethic," Coulter writes," Singer says parents should have the right to kill babies with birth defects such as Down syndrome and hemophilia, because killing a disabled child, the Princeton professor says, 'is not morally equivalent to killing a person.'" [26]

Wow! It is a sad commentary, indeed, that a place like Princeton would consider infanticide a "human value." And, it is even sadder that the University would hire a known supporter of such a practice. Yet, such a view should hardly be surprising since this is evidently what passes for "education" these days at far too many of our institutions of higher learning. Apparently, no longer is the idea taught at these places that human beings have an inherent right to life. In fact, many members of the American Left, including Ingrid Newkirk, founder and President of People for the Ethical Treatment of Animals (PeTA), unapologetically reject this viewpoint, in her case with the infamous remarks that "when it comes to feeling pain, we're all the same. A rat is a pig is a dog is a boy," and more to the point, "I believe that human beings have no inherent 'right' to life."

Such sentiments are odious and highly offensive because they attack the very basis on which our society, or any just society, is supposed to function. A healthy respect for the most defenseless among us, including the unborn, is absolutely necessary to its continued survival. To deny this in such a cavalier fashion as Singer, Newkirk, and those who run the abortion industry in this country do, is to destroy the very underpinnings of that society. Because of people like Singer, Newkirk, and Sanger, we are locked in an argument centering around when life begins vs. when "personhood" begins. Those who established this nation did not need to have such a debate. Due to their deep religious convictions, as well as simple common sense, they knew almost instinctively that life begins *at conception*. Consequently, since logic dictates that simple fact, they listed the right to life as the first unalienable right bestowed on us by God in the *Declaration of Independence.* Let us remember what Johnny Hunter declared so famously on that Columbus Day in 1999: "Civil Rights doesn't mean a thing without a right to life."

Leftists are so irretrievably weeded to the culture of death that has pervaded America in the last forty years that they cannot bring themselves to admit what is so blatantly obvious to even the most casual observer, that yes, life does begin at conception, and that it is every bit as wrong to destroy that life in the womb as it would be to snuff it out after it has entered this world. To these people the sacrament of abortion is essential to the "religion" of modern liberalism, and it must be protected at all costs, by any and every means necessary. Even when the truth about this barbaric practice is staring them in the face, they bend over backwards defending abortion as an absolute "right" that cannot be touched, either now or in the future.

The truth *is* out there, despite the "pro-choice" movement's attempts to ignore it or wish it away. That truth is embodied in the nearly 44,000 human beings who have survived despite their birth mothers' attempts to kill them before they ever saw the light of day. We can see that truth thanks to the work of the Abortion Survivors Network, [27] a support group founded by Melissa Ohden in 2012. In her case, Miss Ohden survived a saline abortion, a particularly gruesome procedure in which a salt solution is pumped into the woman's uterus and left there for up to 24 hours. The liquid burns the baby alive and induces the body to expel the now-deceased child. Melissa's story is especially compelling because of the fear and isolation she needlessly experienced until she underwent a sudden and profound revelation in 1997.

"After I found out at the age of 14 about surviving my birth mother's abortion," Melissa says, "I spent the next five years feeling terribly alone and afraid. Then," she adds, "I discovered Gianna Jessen's story online, and it changed my life." [28] Up to that point, Melissa continues, she felt as if she were the only one who had escaped the deadly grasp of the abortionist. But Jenna's revelations were, she tells us, "...life-changing for me. To read about how Gianna was using her survival to make a difference additionally provided me with the encouragement and strength I needed to prepare myself for coming forward publicly as a survivor."

The case of Gianna Jessen is especially poignant and compelling. On April 22, 1996, she told her story publicly for the first time in testimony before the Constitution Subcommittee of the U.S. House Judiciary Committee. [29] Gianna revealed the circumstances surrounding the attempt to take her life at a Planned Parenthood clinic in Los Angeles at 6 o'clock on the morning of April 6, 1977. At the time, Gianna told the subcommittee, her mother "was 17 years old and seven-and-a-half months pregnant." Gianna's mother was administered a dose of saline solution, which Gianna told the Subcommittee, remained in her body for 18 hours. It was only because "I was early," she revealed, that she exited the womb before the scheduled 9 a.m. arrival of the abortionist and was spared a ghastly fate. Her unexpected arrival sent the operating room into an uproar. "There were many witnesses to my entry into this world," Gianna recounted. "My biological mother and other young girls, who also awaited the deaths of their babies, were there to greet me."

"I am told this was a hysterical moment," Gianna related to the subcommittee and added, "Next was a staff nurse, who apparently called emergency medical services and had me transferred to a hospital." Gianna's experience once she was placed under the hospital's care was hardly a pleasant one, for a number of reasons, as she explained to the subcommittee. "I remained in the hospital for three months," Gianna said. "There was not much hope for me in the beginning. I weighed only two pounds. Today, babies smaller than I was have survived."

But there were other complications involved, ones that remain with Gianna to this very day. Because she suffers from cerebral palsy as a result of the attempted abortion, "My foster mother," Gianna testified, "said it was doubtful I would ever walk or crawl. I could not sit up independently. I have continued physical therapy for my disability, and after a total of four surgeries, I can now walk without assistance." [30] But, despite all that happened to her, Gianna displayed a remarkable sense of courage and self-deprecation in her testimony when she told the subcommittee, "Sometimes I fall, but I have learned to fall gracefully after falling for 19 years." [31] Gianna also displayed a deep gratitude and insight into the value of human life when she revealed, "I am happy to be alive. Every day I thank God for life." Then, in a direct challenge to the "pro-choice" movement's contention that a fetus is not a living human being, she delivered this rejoinder: "I do not consider myself a byproduct of conception, a clump of tissue, or any of the other titles given to a child in the womb. I do not consider any person conceived to be any of those things."

Gianna concluded her testimony by telling the assembled lawmakers, "I have met other survivors of saline abortions. They are all thankful for life. Only a few months ago, I met another saline abortion survivor. Her name is Sarah. She is only two years old. Sarah also has cerebral palsy, but her diagnosis is not good. She is blind and also has severe seizures. The abortionist, besides injecting her mother, also injects the baby victim. Sarah was injected in the head. I saw the place on her head where this was done. When I speak, I speak not only for myself, but for the other survivors, and also for those who cannot yet speak."

"Today," Gianna told the assembly, "a baby is a baby when convenient. It is tissue or otherwise when the time is not right. A baby is a baby when miscarriage takes place at two, three, four months. A baby is called a tissue or clump of cells when an abortion takes place at two, three, four months. Why is that? I see no difference. What are you seeing? Many close their eyes. The best thing I can show you to defend life," she said, "is my life. It has been a great gift. Killing is not the answer to any question or situation. Show me," she challenged, "how it is the answer. There is a quote," she told the lawmakers, "which is etched into the high ceilings of one of our state's capitol buildings. The quote says, 'Whatever is morally wrong is not politically correct.' Abortion is morally wrong. Our country is shedding the blood of the innocent. America is killing its future. All life is a gift from our Creator," she reminded those in attendance. "We must receive and cherish the gifts we have been given. We must honor the right to life."

One is tempted to wonder what exactly went through the minds of the members of the subcommittee that day in 1996 when Gianna was giving her sincere and heartfelt testimony, especially those who believe that it is a woman's "right" to snuff out the precious life that is growing inside her. What did these people think about having a "blob of tissue" or a "mass of cells" look them squarely in the eye and address them so frankly and openly? And Gianna Jessen and Melissa Ohden are not alone. Tens of thousands of survivors of the gruesome practice of abortion are out there among us, each with their own unique story to tell.

People like Sarah Smith, who says that "my mother's choice was my death sentence."

According to Sarah, her mother had an abortion and thought that the "problem" had been solved until she discovered that she had been pregnant with twins instead of just the one child she had killed in her womb. [32] "My mother, Betty," Sarah says, "had an abortion...a few weeks after that she was sitting at home reading when the book on her stomach began to bounce up and down. That's when she knew she was pregnant...with ME!" Sarah's mother returned to her doctor who apologized, saying, "I'm so sorry. You were carrying twins." Was the doctor expressing sorrow that Sarah's brother had been aborted, or was he sorry that Sarah had not been killed, as well? Sarah does not say, but she has found it in her heart to forgive her mother, who refused the second procedure and brought her to term. Sarah's life has not been without complications, as she reveals, "I was born with bilateral congenital dislocated hips, a condition for which I've had dozens of operations." However, Sarah has not let this misfortune stand in her way. "It hasn't stopped me from pursuing my medical studies, though," she says, "or from speaking out wherever I can for the right to life."

Or, take the case of Rebekah Forney, who discovered quite by happenstance what occurred when her mother was 16. "When I was eight," she recalls, "I was snooping around my mom's Bible while she wasn't home and found four pieces of paper that were folded up and stuffed between the pages. I unfolded them," she says, "and read the first sentence: 'I was sixteen years old when I was pregnant with Elizabeth and I had no idea what to do.' Not knowing what I had found," Rebekah relates, "I shoved the papers back into the Bible and tried to forget about it." [33] However, Rebekah could not just "forget" and decided to confront her mother about what had happened.

"Two nights later. it was still bothering me," she says. "My mom, dad, and I were out to dinner, and in the middle of their conversation I blurted out, 'Mom, were you pregnant when you were sixteen?' She just looked at me with tears filling her eyes. She explained to me how she had an abortion; and, as an eight-year old, I could only imagine what it was. She said something about my sister, whom she had named Elizabeth, being in Heaven. At that moment, it clicked for me that I had lost my sister." Rebekah tried a number of ways to deal with what she had discovered, including starting entries in her diary with "Dear Elizabeth," and trying to locate her sister's birth father. She tells us that it took years to come to terms with the revelation and that this had led to a great deal of alienation from and anger toward her mother for "being so selfish and taking the life of her own child just so she wouldn't have to bear the weight of having a kid at 16."

Over the years, however, Rebekah has been able to come to grips with what her mother had done. She no longer blames her and has forgiven her for her actions. She also credits her aunt for helping to heal the relationship, and given the fact that she lost so much, it is not surprising that Rebekah is an ardent supporter of the right to life. She is far too busy to be bitter or angry, and has decided to direct her energies in a positive direction. She advises those who have lost a sibling through abortion not to remain silent. "You have to let your feelings out," she says. "Don't keep them bottled up inside you because you will drive yourself crazy. Tell your parents what you're thinking so that they know what you're dealing with; and," she adds, "try not to be mad at them for taking the life of someone who could have been in your life." And most importantly," Rebekah concludes, "building a relationship with Christ is the best way to let go of your pain." [34]

Some abortion survivors, like Alex, prefer not to give their last names. Alex recalls how, "When I was 3 years old, I saw my mom on TV. She was speaking to a man about how she killed her baby and regretted it. My grandma didn't think I was old enough to understand." [35] How wrong Alex's grandma was, as it turned out. Alex *did* understand, and pressed her mother on the issue. "When my mom picked me up that night," Alex says, "I asked her why she killed my brother and sister and didn't kill me. My mom said she was in a state of shock that her 3-year old would ask these questions. She answered them the best she could for me, and as I got older I learned more."

"Now, my mom and I are pro-life speakers," Alex tells us. "She has been one for almost 15 years, and I just started last year. My mom was 18 when she had the abortion, and I'm now 17. I thank God I am alive. I'm still sad to know I have an older brother or sister who was denied the chance to live, something we all take for granted. I hope someday we will meet. That's why I do what I do."

The courage, honesty and willingness of these survivors of abortion to forgive stand in stark contrast to the actions of the "pro-choice" movement. Their very presence among us forces groups like Planned Parenthood and NARAL, which deal in butchery on a daily basis, to confront their bloody past, one which has seen nearly 57 million human lives destroyed with thousands adding to the body count every 24 hours. Melissa Ohden, Gianna Jessen, Sarah Smith, Rebekah Forney, the young lady named Alex, and tens of thousands of other abortion survivors are an inconvenient truth of the first magnitude for the "pro-choice" movement, for they are living proof that every abortion stops a beating heart and denies humanity the chance for advancement. For as Johnny Hunter reminds us, especially those in the black community, which has been so ravaged and devastated by the inordinate number of abortions that take place within it, "...we're destroying the destiny and purpose of those who should be here."

It's well past time we heeded Reverend Hunter's clarion call and stand once more for the sanctity of unborn human life. Let us firmly and resolutely reject, once and for all, the gruesome, bloody, and deadly practice of abortion.

If we truly care about "human rights," then we have no business denying such rights to those who are the most vulnerable—-the unborn. We owe them more, far more, than that.

We certainly owe them more than the incoherent musings of Peter Singer, whose position on when "personhood" begins we have explored in this chapter; we surely owe them more than the cynical rants of Texas State Senator Wendy Davis, who in June of 2013, filibustered that body's deliberations on passage of a law that would outlaw late-term abortions past twenty weeks. [36] And we most assuredly owe them more than a gruesome death through the practice of partial-birth abortion, which is clearly the most barbaric and despicable form of the procedure.

Partial-birth abortion involves inducing labor to speed the exit of the child from the birth canal. The attending physician then uses a pair of surgical scissors to punch a hole in the skull of the baby, who is now a mere six inches away from being fully born. The dead child's brain matter is then removed via suction and discarded along with other forms of medical "waste." It is this procedure of which Senator Davis approved, and which several hundred of her supporters cheered on the night she filibustered the proposed Texas bill, which not only would have banned abortions after 20 weeks, it also would require that abortionists provide a clean environment in their facilities. And lastly, it would have mandated the admission of patients to hospitals within a reasonable distance from these facilities.

Senator Davis' filibuster was initially successful, and she was widely hailed in the mainstream media for her "heroism" and "courage." But, her victory was short-lived as Rick Perry, the Lone Star State's governor, vowed to sign the new restrictions, which he did on July 20, 2013. [37] He did so in spite of threats from Davis' supporters, threats that included jars full of human waste, which some apparently intended to throw on the lawmakers who voted for the bill and a seamstress from Houston who decided to make and sell voodoo dolls of Governor Perry, the proceeds from said sales going to support Planned Parenthood. [38] He also displayed great courage despite additional threats that the new law would be challenged in court. Perry was confident that it would withstand Constitutional muster and expressed deep sorrow that Davis, a single mother, would support the practice of killing children who are completely formed just before they are dispatched by a set of surgical scissors and a glorified vacuum cleaner.

Let the reader remember that this nation was founded on clearly defined, immutable principles that were laid down and set forth in the *Declaration of Independence*. Our Founders wrote clearly and unmistakably that *"all men are created equal; that they are endowed by their Creator with certain unalienable rights,"* and that among these God-given rights are *"life, liberty and the pursuit of happiness."* If we fail to acknowledge that the most defenseless among us, the unborn, are deserving of even the most basic human right, that of life, we cannot legitimately claim to be the greatest nation on earth, a nation that recognizes and stands for the intrinsic worth of the individual. We have seen far too many times down through history what happens when a nation considers anyone to be "inconvenient" and, therefore, unworthy of living and defending. It has never ended well.

What does it say about a nation whose chief executive officer not only believed as a state senator (and still believes as President) that children who are born despite attempts to kill them in their mothers' wombs are not deserving of even the most basic of medical services, but sought God's blessing on the organization that performs more abortions than anyone else in the country? What does it say about any nation that countenances such a barbaric practice as partial-birth abortion and tacitly approves through its silence the activities of a George Tiller or a Kermit Gosnell? Did anyone ever think to point out to Senator Davis that, by her actions, she has put herself squarely in the camp of those who support such a ghastly form of infanticide?

And, what about the National Association for the Advancement of Colored People?

Incredibly, the NAACP, the nation's largest civil rights organization, a group whose leaders should be speaking out against what can only be described as a holocaust being waged by Planned Parenthood, NARAL and other "pro-choice" groups, has stated that it has no "official" policy regarding the activities of the organization that was founded by Margaret Sanger, one of the most notorious racists in American history? But, Planned Parenthood has an official policy regarding the NAACP; it lists itself on its website as one of its most enthusiastic supporters. Perhaps, that's why Nancy Pelosi, House Minority Leader and outspoken advocate of abortion at any time and under any circumstances, was the keynote speaker at the group's annual "Freedom Dinner" at Detroit's Cobo Center on April 28, 2013. At this point, it would be helpful to ask just what kind of "freedom" was the NAACP celebrating? The "freedom" to abandon responsibility for one's actions? The "freedom" to snuff out a life because it has become "inconvenient?" Or, more ominously, the "freedom" to destroy your posterity? Because, and make no mistake about it, the skyrocketing abortion rate among black Americans will rob them of their future in a way that is far deadlier than any means the Ku Klux Klan or any other racist group could ever devise.

And, the so-called black "leadership," people like Jesse Jackson (who used to be pro-life, by the way), Al Sharpton, and all those ministers, politicians, educators, and others who should know better are strangely silent about the destruction that is raining down on the heads of their own people. And, just why is that? It is because of the lie that has been propounded for decades among black Americans that the killing of unborn children in the womb is a necessary and oftentimes even desirable pursuit. Clearly, this must stop before America's black demographic is utterly annihilated. Any people that seek economic and political empowerment cannot hope to achieve either if it is willing to kill off one-third of itself. Nor can it withstand the kind of "leadership" that not only stands back and watches it happen, it openly and actively cheers it on.

This is what everyone, regardless of skin color, must recognize: If this can happen to black Americans, it can happen to all of us. And, it *is* already happening. The year 2012 marked the first time that America's overall birth rate dropped below replacement level, due in large part to the inordinate number of black abortions. Is that enough of a warning, or do we need something else to wake us up? More than 17 million black babies have died since 1973 because of abortion; yet, the black leadership will not explain why it supports it so blindly. And, yet, we seek God's blessing despite this? In just what kind of a fool's paradise are we living, anyway?

NOTES

1. Planned Parenthood pamphlet, 1963. *40 Years: Planned Parenthood Becomes an Abortion Empire*, O'Bannon, Randall K., MD, *National Right-to-Life News*, Winter 2013, Vol. 40, Issue 1, p.8.
2. Ibid, p.8.
3 O'Bannon, Randall K, MD, *40 Years: Planned Parenthood Becomes an Abortion Empire*. From *Right-to-Life News*, Winter 2013, Vol. 40, Issue 1, p 8.
4. O'Bannon, Randall K, MD, *40 Years: Planned Parenthood Becomes an Abortion Empire*. From *Right-to-Life News*, Winter 2013, Vol. 40, Issue 1, p.8.
5. O'Bannon, Randall K, MD., *40 Years: Planned Parenthood Becomes an Abortion Empire*. From *Right-to-Life News*, Winter 2013, Vol. 40, Issue 1, p.8.
6. Ertelt, Steven, *Poll: 55% of Americans Don't Know Planned Parenthood Does Abortions*. From *Life News.com*, April 29, 2013
7. Snow, Alicia Lapolt, lobbyist, Florida Alliance of Planned Parenthood Affiliates, *Video: Planned Parenthood Lobbyist Argues for Post-Birth Abortion*. From *The Weekly Standard Blog*, March 29, 2013. Posted by John McCormack.

8. Warhawk, Jennifer, *Yale Conference to Promote "Non-Human" Personhood: Will Feature Infanticide Advocate Peter Singer.* April 17, 2013, www.conservativesacttoday.org/blogs/abortion-blog.
9. Alinsky, Saul, *Rules for Radicals.* c. 1971, p. 130
10. King, Dr. Alveda, *Dr. King to Planned Parenthood: Stop Using My Family, Black Voice Blogs,* March 4, 2008, p. 4.
11. Ibid.
12. King, Dr. Alveda, *Dr. King to Planned Parenthood: Stop Using My Family, Black Voice Blogs,* March 4, 2008, p. 4.
13. Hunter, Reverend Johnny Lee. From *The Negro Project: Margaret Sanger's Eugenic Plan for Black Americans,* by Tanya L. Green, May 10, 2001.
14. Planned Parenthood Federation of America Service Report, *Characteristics of Abortion Patients,* p.12.
15. U.S. News and World Report article *"Who Has Abortions?" Survey by the Alan Guttmacher Institute Contradicts Popular Notions about the Kinds of Women Who Receive Abortions,* August 19, 1996, p.8.
16. Hunter, Reverend Johnny Lee, November 14, 2000 interview with Tanya L. Green. From *The Negro Project: Margaret Sanger's Eugenic Plan for Black Americans,* May 10, 2001, p.13.
17. Hunter, Reverend Johnny Lee., November 14, 2000 interview with Tanya L. Green. From *The Negro Project: Margaret Sanger's Eugenic Plan for Black Americans,* May 10, 2001, p.13.
18. Ibid.
19. Broome, Sharon Weston, Louisiana State Representative, November 16, 2000 interview with Tanya L. Green. *From The Negro Project: Margaret Sanger's Eugenic Plan for Black Americans,* May 10, 2001, p. 13.
20. Grant, George, *Grand Illusions: The Legacy of Planned Parenthood,* c. 1992, p. 98.
21. Pierce, Chester M., *Educating for the New World Order,* by Beverly K. Eakman, c. 1991, p. 130.
22. Ibid.
23. Coulter, Ann, *Godless: The Church of Liberalism,* c. 2006, p. 1.
24. Ibid, p. 271.
25. Ibid.
26. Coulter, Ann, *Godless: The Church of Liberalism,* c. 2006, p.274.
27. Ohden, Melissa, *I Am a Survivor of Abortion, Here is My Story. Lifenews.com,* June 2, 2013.
28. Ibid.
29. Ohden, Melissa, *I Am a Survivor of Abortion, Here is My Story. Lifenews.com,* June 2, 2013.
30. Jessen, Gianna. Testimony before the Constitution Subcommitee of the U.S. House Judiciary Committee, April 22, 1996.
31. Ibid.
32. www.teenbreaks.com., *Abortion Survivor Stories: Who Are Abortion Survivors?*
33. Ibid.
34. www.teenbreaks.com, *Abortion Survivor Stories: Who Are Abortion Survivors?*
35. www.teenbreaks.com, *Abortion Survivor Stories: Who Are Abortion Survivors?*
36. *Long Filibuster against Texas abortion limits suspended, CBS News,* June 26, 2013.
37. *Texas Governor Signs Strict Abortion Law that Sparked Protests, Reuters,* July 18, 2013.
38. Rick Perry *Voodoo Dolls Are Being Sold to Protest Texas Abortion Law---and Guess Where the Proceeds Will Go?* From *The Blaze,* July 18, 2013.

Chapter 6:

Crime, Illiteracy, Drug Abuse, Unemployment, and Abortion in Black America - An Extinction-Level Event

> *Extinction-level Event:* An event where all species on the planet can become extinct."
>
> — *Rational Wiki* Website, February 11, 2013

Many of us are familiar with the term "extinction-level event," or ELE., which is used mostly by geologists and archaeologists to describe the wholesale disappearance of a vast number of life forms down through the Earth's history, usually in the blink of an eye in geologic time. The two most well-known of these events are the Cambrian Ordovician Extinction Event, which occurred 488 million years ago and resulted in an estimated loss of 90% of the planet's life forms up to that time, and the more recent incident that took place 65 million years ago in which an asteroid struck Mexico's Yucatan Peninsula and destroyed the dinosaurs. Both events gave rise to creatures that then dominated the earth for eons, the first mass extinction allowing the "terrible lizards" to ultimately hold sway, the second enabling mammals, including Man, to take over.

But, such events do not take place overnight, as is so often portrayed in such movies as 1997's *Armageddon* and *Deep Impact,* or in 2004's *The Day After Tomorrow*, or even in 2012's appropriately-titled *2012*. While these films dealt with natural disasters, others such as *War of the Worlds* (1953), *Independence Day* (1998), and *Battleship* (2012), to name a few, had to do with invasions by creatures from across the galaxy who were bent on conquering the earth. It is important to bear in mind that we are dealing with science fiction in each case, but ELE's have occurred throughout history that were anything but the products of such sci-fi writers as H..G. Wells, Ray Bradbury, Issac Asimov, or Arthur C. Clark.

Such naturally-occurring extinctions take place over tens of thousands or millions of years, as is the case with the two examples given above. However, they can also happen in a relatively short time-frame and need not be confined to the geological or archaeological realms. An extinction-level event can also be examined anthropologically, as well, as in the case of the Inca, Mayan, and Aztec tribes in Mexico and South American, who were subdued by the Spanish *conquistadors* in the sixteenth century. In this instance, one society (the indigenous tribes) came into contact with another (the more technologically-advanced Spaniards), was unable to defend itself, and was consequently wiped out.

The Y2K scare at the end of the twentieth century and the controversy surrounding the Mayan calendar's prediction that the world would end on December 21, 2012, are both prime examples of extinction-level events that never took place. Even today, we read and hear stories about comets and asteroids that are large enough to cause great destruction and even the end of all life on earth, if they ever strike us. And, we are still waiting for events such as a massive earthquake ("The Big One") that will cause California to sink into the Pacific Ocean, or a gigantic volcanic eruption in Yellowstone National Park on the order of one that occurred there 600,000 years ago. These disasters, however, have nothing on an ELE that is taking place right here, right now, that is every bit as horrific and devastating—the alarming number of abortions taking place among black Americans.

The problems that have plagued this group throughout our history have been well-documented and debated almost to a fare-thee-well. Books on this subject have been written (e.g. Charles Murray's *Losing Ground*), discussions have been held, arguments have raged, and government policy-makers have scrambled for reasons as to why this minority, in particular, has become so devastated since the vile and disgusting institution of slavery was done away with after a long and bloody Civil War that cost the lives of 600,000 Americans. All kinds of rationales and theories for the plight of these people have been offered, as have a myriad of government programs designed to assuage the crisis that faces black Americans today.

In this chapter, we will examine the many causes of what can only be described as an extinction-level event that faces this particular group of

Americans. It is nothing short of inhuman that a people could suffer so much over the last three centuries, enduring a heinous form of bondage until only 150 years ago. And, it is a tribute to the triumph of the human spirit that once they had emerged from that horrible experience, they were able to overcome such monstrous and unspeakable evils as the segregation and lynchings that followed their emancipation. However, blacks were not yet full citizens, despite the many attempts by Republicans to correct that injustice. Democrats, especially those from the South, fought tooth and nail at every turn to deny them any form of citizenship, even after President Abraham Lincoln issued the Emancipation Proclamation. Democrats opposed passage of the 13th, 14th , and 15th Amendments. They rolled back the rights of blacks in the South after Reconstruction, and they shamelessly unleashed their paramilitary arm, the Ku Klux Klan, to undermine the new rights guaranteed to former slaves and their descendants.

At the dawn of the twentieth century, Democrats, led by the segregationist President Woodrow Wilson, continued to stand against full citizenship for black Americans. The early 1900s saw blacks continued to be denied their basic rights as Americans by people like Sherriff William ("Bull") Connor, Governors George C. Wallace, Orval Faubus, and J. William Fulbright, and Senators Albert Gore, Sr., James Eastland, and Sam Ervin. Those who are old enough will remember that Ervin chaired the Senate committee that was charged with impeaching Richard Nixon until the president resigned in disgrace in the wake of the Watergate scandal in 1974. Even as late as 1957, when President Dwight Eisenhower attempted to get civil rights legislation passed, it was Democrats who bitterly opposed it, including Texas Senator and future President Lyndon B. Johnson.

Democrats fought passage of the Civil Rights Act in 1964 and the Voting Rights Act a year later. President Johnson finally supported the legislation, but for purely cynical and nakedly political reasons. President John F. Kennedy had been murdered in 1963, and he had favored passage of civil rights legislation before his death. Because JFK had gotten tremendous support from blacks in the 1960 election, his assassination hit them probably harder than any other group of Americans. They recalled how he had called the Reverend Martin Luther King, Jr. after the civil rights icon had been jailed for his activities while Kennedy's opponent, Richard Nixon, had not. King backed Kennedy for president and JFK, in turn, backed civil rights legislation in return for that support. However, it languished in the House and Senate until Kennedy's death on November 22, 1963.

It wasn't until Johnson received support from the Republicans in the Senate and not the Democrats, that the Civil Rights Act of 1964 finally became law. In fact, Republican support was crucial in securing the rights of black Americans after centuries of lynching, oppression, and discrimination of all kinds. More work still remained to secure their right to vote, a battle which was finally won when the Voting Rights Act of 1965 was passed, again with little thanks to Senate Democrats like Gore, Eastland, and Ervin. And, we must not forget another Southern Democrat, Robert Byrd of West Virginia. Byrd, it should be noted, was a former "*kleagle*," or recruiter, for the West Virginia branch of the Ku Klux Klan before he came to the Senate where he would one day be revered in Progressive circles as "the conscience" of that body. None of these Southern lawmakers had anything to do with securing either the civil rights or voting rights of black Americans. Rather, it was the Republicans once more, living up to their heritage as the party that was founded to end slavery, who got the job done. And, although Johnson had portrayed himself as a champion of the cause of civil rights, he was later shown to have done this, not out of any sense of justice for millions of Americans of black descent, but out of nothing more than pure pragmatism and political expediency. In his book *Inside the White House* (1995), author Ronald Kessler reveals the blatant cynicism President Johnson expressed to two governors while traveling on Air Force One at the height of the civil rights debate. Johnson, Kessler wrote, openly stated that, if the 1965 bill passed, "I'll have them niggers voting Democratic for 200 years."

LBJ was cynical, pragmatic, and opportunistic, but he was also prophetic. For as time went on, more and more black voters abandoned the party that had freed their forebears for the party that had enslaved them. As more and more blacks left the Republican Party, their support for Democrats increased almost exponentially, even as the social programs that would soon prove so devastating to them were put into place. As the decades passed, black support for the party of slavery, "Bull" Connor, Jim Crow, the Klan, and abortion grew so dramatically that by the turn of the twenty-first century, Democrat presidents received almost monolithic support from black Americans.

In the 2008 election, Barack Obama was elected with a jaw-dropping 96% of the black vote! That is the kind of support Americans would expect a tyrant in a banana republic or a dictator in a communist regime to receive. To be sure, many Americans wanted to be a part of history and vote for the first "black" president. Never mind the fact that his mother was white; in politics image is, after all, everything. However, the facts surrounding

Obama's past were never seriously examined, save for a few brave souls in the conservative media who warned that Obama was not what he seemed to be. Had his dealings with terrorists like former Weather Underground members William Ayers and Bernadine Dohrn been more widely publicized, had his decades-long association with the radical Reverend Jeremiah Wright gotten more than passing scrutiny, and had more people taken a long, hard look at his views on terrorism, economics, race, and, yes, abortion, we might have been spared the disaster his administration soon became. Yet, as the economy began to tank early in his tenure as president; as energy costs continued to skyrocket; as the world's best health care system was deliberately dismantled; as America, once again, came under attack from devout muslim terrorists; as our world standing took a nosedive; as race relations continued to deteriorate and more black babies fell to the tender mercies of the abortion industry, Mr. Obama was *still* able to enjoy near-unanimous support from black voters.

Although fewer blacks supported him in 2012, they showed that they were still the one bloc of Democrat voters on which he could rely by casting 94% of their ballots for four more years of the same. Whether it was due to the mainstream media carrying his water and ignoring, if not covering up, his misdeeds in a way it would not have done if a Republican president were in office, the effects of years of brainwashing by black clergy, politicians, educators, and community organizers, whatever the reason, black Americans found themselves worse off under Barack Obama by nearly every educational, economic, and cultural indicator, than nearly any other demographic group in this county. And, make no mistake—-this was no accident.

Take your pick. The crime rate is higher among black Americans, especially black-on-black crime. This is particularly true in the outrageous number of murders of blacks by other blacks in cities like Detroit, Washington, D.C., and Chicago. Consider this jarring statistic: From early 2012 through the summer of 2013 alone, more than *11,000 blacks* were murdered by other blacks. Consequently, blacks are incarcerated at a higher rate than other demographic groups. More black families are headed by single parents, the vast majority of whom are female, than any other group of Americans. The rate of drug abuse is higher among blacks, more blacks drop out of high school than in any other segment of society, and more blacks are unemployed than any other group of Americans.

Because of the disastrous government approach to public education, more blacks are functionally illiterate than any other group of Americans.

More black families are now on some form of government assistance, including food stamps, than any other group of Americans. The out-of-wedlock birth rate is higher among blacks than it is in any other demographic group, and as of 2013 stood at an astounding 74% of all babies born to this segment. And, as has been so often pointed out in these pages, the abortion rate is higher among black Americans than in any other demographic group. Two stunning examples of this madness come from New York State, where over 70% of all black babies were aborted in 2013, and in Mississippi, where more than 71% of all black babies met the same fate. Let us be clear: if a foreign power were targeting any group of Americans for annihilation in the same way black Americans are being singled out for extermination by the abortion industry, would this nation not rightfully be going to war to defend them in the same way it did to free the slaves 150 years ago?

We have previously touched on some of the many government entitlement schemes that have brought black America so low, from the "War on Poverty" that began in the mid-1960s to the affirmative action programs that followed a few years later. We have seen how welfare "reform" destroyed so many black families by forcing fathers from the home to be replaced with an uncle—-Uncle Sam. And, now we see the horrific effects of the most savage and brutal form of "entitlement" of all—-the legalized murder of more than 1.5 million unborn children a year since 1973, one-third of whom are black. If all of this is not an extinction-level event, one would be hard-pressed, indeed, to find a better example. Yet, in spite of all that is taking place around them, despite the horrifying numbers we have cited above, and seemingly against all odds, blacks still consider themselves among the most religious of all Americans. We can only pray that this continues to hold true, because it may be their only hope of eventual salvation.

Unfortunately, there are far too many blacks who seem to suffer from some form of mass amnesia about who it was who held their ancestors in bondage and who it was who liberated them. It is truly astounding in this day and age, with so much information that is readily available at the mere touch of a computer key, where anyone can access the proper website, that black America remains so ignorant about its past. There are a number of explanations for this, from the dumbing down of our government school students to the need to foster a continuing attitude of victim hood by politicians and social activists to serve their own purposes. It is deceitful, dishonest, and only serves to further divide us as a people and a nation. This is why demographics are so important, so crucial, in studying what is happening to black America.

"Demography" is defined as "the statistical study of human populations." [1] The field of demographics uses a number of tools to analyze population trends, such as economic status, cultural factors, crime rate statistics and population shifts to better understand and explain what is taking place in the general population or in a particular segment of that population. Demographic data are used by a host of government and private entities and for a variety of purposes. For example, census figures are used to distribute hundreds of billions of dollars every year in federal government benefits. Businesses analyze reams of demographic data to determine market trends. Pollsters use demographic information in taking surveys that cover a wide variety of issues to aid political candidates when they run for election or to remain in office. And, educators study demographic trends to track the progress of students as they navigate their way through the government and private school systems. Demographics are increasingly ubiquitous and are seemingly used to measure nearly every aspect of our lives.

Demographics can be used to track both positive and negative population trends. We see this at work economically in tracking the growth in our nation's GDP (Goss Domestic Product). We use demographics in gauging progress in student test scores. On the other hand, we see demographics at play in determining why economic contractions occur or in determining why so many government school students fail to complete their educations. And, sadly, we see demographics at work when discussing the mountains of negative data on black Americans, from the alarming rate of crime, how many blacks are behind bars, the rate of drug abuse, dependency on government programs, the out-of-wedlock birth rate, the incidence of single-family households headed by black females, the illiteracy rate, all the way down to the one category that dwarfs all others—the mind-boggling abortion rate among black women.

While black Americans have faced a number of crises that would have destroyed other demographic segments of our society, their troubles are almost completely self-inflicted as a result of their support of the terribly misguided policies of both federal and state governments over the past 50 or so years. Nowhere is this more evident than in the black community, which has been ravaged more by the breakup of the nuclear family than any other demographic group. Single-parent families are more the rule rather than the exception. The absence of strong fathers from black households has robbed children of proper role models and made the task of the mother infinitely more difficult in raising her children.

Remember, as well, that the feminist movement bears a large part of the blame for bringing this about. Far too many women, especially black women, bought into the seductive allure of the feminist line that they could "have it all." Feminist dogma also taught far too many women, black women included, that motherhood was "outdated," "old-fashioned," and "oppressive," and would somehow leave them "unfulfilled." People like Betty Friedan, Germaine Greer, and Gloria Steinhem regarded the traditional family as a relic of a patriarchal society, in which the woman was expected to "know her place." The natural role of the female as both the nurturing and moderating influence in the family was belittled and condemned by feminists, whose ranks even include former First Lady, New York Senator, and former U.S. Secretary of State Hillary Clinton. It was Clinton, who as a student at Wellesley College in the late 1960s, infamously compared marriage and the family to "slavery" or "life on an Indian reservation."

Recall also that Margaret Sanger was exceedingly critical of large families and used her hatred of them to justify and further her campaign of extermination. And, from what we have seen so far, we have a pretty good idea of whom she had in mind, do we not? It is by no means a stretch to assert that the combination of failed government social policy toward black Americans from roughly 1965 onward and feminist influence that infected college and university campuses during the late 1960s and early '70s proved to be more profoundly devastating to them than it did to any other group of Americans.

The decline of the black family unit in the last few decades has been astonishing and stunning. Consider again the following for a moment: in the years leading up to the advent of the so-called "Great Society" in the mid-1960s, black families were more intact than those in other demographic groups. Black students graduated from high school in greater numbers than their white counterparts. The crime rate was lower among blacks than it was among whites. More black women bore their children within the bounds of wedlock than white women. Fewer blacks were in jail than members of other demographic groups. The rate of drug abuse was lower among blacks than it was among whites, and, it must be pointed out, so was the abortion rate. This may be old ground that we have covered, but the importance of it cannot be overstated, nor must it ever be forgotten.

It is critical to bear in mind that all this was occurring despite the incredible amount of discrimination and segregation that blacks were enduring in the South, which, we must never forget, was home to segregated lunch counters and drinking fountains, Jim Crow laws, Sherriff "Bull" Connor,

George Wallace, lynchings, and the Ku Klux Klan. It is also crucial to remember that the South was heavily controlled by Democrats, who fought so ferociously to defend the vile institution of slavery and later battled just as desperately to deny black Americans the selfsame rights that their fellow citizens enjoyed as a matter of course. It was a Democrat, U.S. Supreme Court Chief Justice Roger B. Taney, who wrote the majority opinion in the infamous *Dred Scott* decision in 1854, a decision which many historians call a turning point on the road to the Civil War. One truly has to marvel at the success of Democrats in sanitizing their racist past to the point that so many blacks buy into the notion that it was they, and not the Republicans, who not only set their ancestors free, but later secured their civil rights and their right to participate in the political process.

Too many Americans, especially black Americans, either have forgotten or were never properly taught that it was the Republican Party that was founded to end slavery; that it was a Republican, Abraham Lincoln, who issued the Emancipation Proclamation; and that it was Republicans who introduced the first civil rights legislation in 1867. They are also dangerously ignorant of the fact that it was Republicans who authored the 13th, 14th , and 15th Amendments to the Constitution; that public schools in the South were desegregated in 1957 by President Dwight D. Eisenhower, a Republican, and that the GOP introduced civil rights legislation that same year. It wasn't a Republican governor who stood in the schoolhouse door in Little Rock, Arkansas, in 1957, attempting to deny black children a chance at a good education. It was Orval Faubus, a Democrat and a committed segregationist who did that. It was not a Republican governor who declared his undying devotion to the racial status quo when he defiantly endorsed "segregation now, segregation forever!" That was Alabama Governor George C. Wallace, a Democrat.

Too many Americans, including black Americans, also do not know or were never taught that it was not Harry S. Truman, a Democrat, who actually desegregated the country's armed forces. It was his successor, Republican President Eisenhower, who finally sealed that deal. They evidently do not know, either, that President Woodrow Wilson, a Democrat, refused to open up the armed forces to full participation by black soldiers and sailors in World War I. Wilson was an unabashed segregationist who not only threw in with racist Southern Democrats, he refused to back anti-lynching laws and, worse, openly courted the paramilitary arm of the Democrat Party, the Ku Klux Klan.

Far too many blacks have been kept blissfully unaware of the real history of the party that held their forebears in bondage for nearly 300 years and was literally dragged kicking and screaming into finally acknowledging their rights, the unalienable rights that the rest of their fellow citizens take for granted. And, it wasn't the Republicans. This is not an exercise in political partisanship; far from it. This book is about getting at the truth, and the truth, as painful as it may be to some, is that it was Democrats who fought tooth and nail at every turn, first against freeing the slaves. When that failed, they fought just as hard against securing their rights and those of their descendants. But, despite these defeats, the Democrats, through decades of sanitizing their image and purging the ugly truth, have largely succeeded in brainwashing black Americans, to the point that blacks in the present day vote in nearly monolithic numbers for the political party that fought so hard to keep their ancestors in chains, the Democrat Party.

Consider this: 96% of blacks voted Democrat in the 2008 presidential election, and 94% voted the same way again in 2012, despite the fact that the man they helped elect, Barack Obama, instituted economic and social policies that were an unmitigated disaster for those who helped to put him office. As we have seen, the black unemployment rate skyrocketed. Food stamp dependency increased almost exponentially. More blacks were senselessly murdered at the hands of other blacks. The out-of-wedlock birth rate in the black community rose to such a point that in 2012, nearly three-quarters of all babies born to black females were to those who were not married, nearly a tenfold *increase* over what it was in the early 1900s. And, tragically, more unborn black babies were aborted in Obama's first term as president than those in any other demographic category.

What can explain all this? Why are blacks, historically among the most religious and socially conservative of all Americans, and who should be so in tune with the horrors their ancestors experienced, so blithe and blasé about the extinction-level event that is staring them in the face at this very moment, an event which is largely due to policies enacted under the Democrats? Because of them, millions of blacks have been deceived into accepting a new kind of slavery on a new kind of plantation, a slavery on a plantation that is every bit as insidious, as vile, and as oppressive as anything anyone in the Antebellum South could ever have devised—the slavery of dependence on government.

The crisis that is facing America's black citizens is one that never should have taken place, but with the expansion of the welfare state in the 1960s, the crisis was on. Fathers were expelled from the black home, denying their children a strong male role model. The weekly paycheck was replaced with a monthly stipend, making the recipient dependent not on their own drive or initiative to make a living, but on politicians in Washington for their sustenance.

Educational choice was taken out of the hands of parents and local school boards, thereby signaling the death knell of the greatest system of public education the world has ever seen. The rates of functional illiteracy and absence of discipline in the government school classrooms of today are painful and depressing for all to see, most strikingly in relation to black students, who continue to drop out of school in alarming numbers, numbers that are far higher than among their peers in other demographic groups. Today, where once black students exceeded their white counterparts in academic achievement, they are among the most illiterate of all Americans when they graduate from school.

Drug abuse began to increase dramatically among black Americans in the new "Great Society," and has skyrocketed to epidemic proportions nearly 50 years later. Relaxation of sexual morals and rules of social behavior and comportment resulted in what some have called the "hookup culture," one in which long-term male-female relationships become more the exception than the rule. All of these demographic factors, combined with the unemployment crisis among black Americans (and, especially, among those in the nation's inner cities), have converged over the last half-century to wreak enormous havoc on an entire segment of our population. But, as depressing as this is, there is more—-far, far more.

Crime rates, which were on the decline throughout the late 1950s, suddenly began to increase sharply in all categories, from petty theft to grand larceny, from rape to murder, in particular among blacks. Before the shift in focus from punishment to "rehabilitation" in the criminal justice and court system that occurred in the 1960s, the black crime rate, including black-on-black crime, was lower than it was among white Americans. As a result, it was often safer to walk about in a black neighborhood than it was in other parts of town. It was not uncommon, for example, to leave one's front door unlocked at night, and a person could be reasonably certain when they went to bed that their car would still be in the same place where they parked it the night before. Not so, today, sad to say. For today, this level of confidence no longer exists because of the decline in all standards of decency and respect for our fellow man that has taken place under the liberal/Progressive policies that were enacted in the 1960s. And, no policy has been more destructive to the black population than abortion.

The numbers are telling and damning. Since abortion on demand was declared to be a right under the Constitution in the landmark *Roe vs. Wade* decision in 1973, more than 57 million of these procedures have taken place over more than 40 years. That breaks down to nearly 1.5 million abortions annually, or roughly 20,000 a week. Of those abortions, more than 1,000 a day are performed on black women. Abortion alone dwarfs all other causes of death among black Americans. For example, 11,000 blacks were killed in violent crimes from February of 2012 through July of 2013, an average of less than 1,000 such fatalities per month. Yet, in that same time-frame, more than 500,000 black children were butchered in their mothers' wombs. These children committed no crime other than the offense of being "unplanned" or "inconvenient." Yet, they met the same fate as their adult counterparts because a handful of unelected and unaccountable judges decided that women have some sort of "right" to end their children's lives before they have even begun.

It isn't even close. When all causes of death among black Americans are put together (crime, drug abuse, diseases such as sickle-cell anemia and AIDS, etc.), they don't even *approach* a fraction of the deaths caused by a procedure that has been codified into American law as a "right." We already know that for any society to survive, thrive, let alone prosper, it must have a minimum replacement level of at least 2.1 live births per female. Yet, because of the high premature death toll among black Americans, one where abortion plays such a disproportionate role, the replacement level of this particular demographic group is alarmingly low, a staggering 0.7 live births per black female! Such a trend cannot be sustained for more than even one generation without real and long-term damage.

The numbers that bear this out come not from some figment of a troubled mind or from a fevered imagination. They are borne out by decades of data from the U.S. Census Bureau. From 1900 to 1970, the last census year before abortion on demand became law, the black population in America increased from approximately 9 million (8,883,994) to slightly over 22.5 million (22,580, 289). [2] This represents a nearly three-fold increase in native black population over that time. Yet, Census Bureau figures show that from 1980 to 1990, it only increased from slightly below 26.5 million (26,495,025) to just under 30 million ten years later (29,986,060). [3] These figures demonstrate that the native black population had already begun a slow, steady decline due to the many negative societal factors that were already ravaging the black demographic, factors that include the high number of abortions that are performed every day on black females. And, as we have seen thus far, abortion dwarfs all other causes of premature death among black Americans.

Further, when one examines the census data from 2000 to 2010, it shows that native black population ("Black or African-American Alone") rose by only a bit more than 4 million, from 34,658,190 in 2000 to 38,929,319 a decade later. While this might not appear too alarming in terms of sheer numbers, the really striking thing is that this represents an increase of *less* than 1%, from 12.9 to 13.6%, of total U.S. population from 2000-2010. [4]

Now, compare the census numbers for white Americans from 1790 to 1970, again the last census year before *Roe vs. Wade* became law. From the first U.S. census, taken in 1790, the white population grew from 3,172,006 to 177,748,795. After *Roe,* it grew from 188,371,622 in 1980 and to 199,686,070 by 1990. [5] Abortion had already begun to lead to a decline in native-born white population by the first census taken after *Roe vs. Wade,* but it hit the black population in far greater ways than it has affected Americans of any other demographic group. Now, there are many who scoff at the idea that a decline in native-born population is of any great concern. So what? we are told. We can always allow more immigrants into the country to make up any shortfall. There are at least two things wrong with this line of reasoning.

First, it is important to recognize that allowing more immigrants into the United States is not necessarily a bad thing; after all, we are, as the saying goes, a "nation of immigrants." Many people have come to the U.S. over our long and proud history and have enriched our unique culture almost beyond measure. We will always need and can always use the talents and abilities of those who have something to offer and are willing to do things the right way, that is, to do them legally. This is the key word—*legally.* That means waiting one's turn, filing the proper documents, and obtaining the necessary papers with the clear intent of becoming a citizen of this great republic. That also means learning English, having marketable skills that an employer can utilize, a willingness to learn about our history, our system of laws, and our form of government, and most of all, being willing to assimilate into American society. If one is not willing to do these things, what is the point of coming here in the first place? But, if one is willing to do these things, America will always have a place for people like these, who often prove themselves to be better citizens than many of those who were born here.

But, as we have seen by the debate raging over "comprehensive" immigration reform, there is now a movement afoot to legalize anyone who breaks our laws in order to enter this country. Often these so-called "undocumented immigrants," who are actually illegal aliens, are either low-skilled people, or worse still, are those who have no skills at all to offer. As so many news stories have demonstrated, a large number of these individuals not only have no intention of contributing to our culture, they have *no* interest *at all* in becoming citizens. Statistics from the U.S. Department of Justice, the FBI, and other law-enforcement agencies belie the argument from "open borders" advocates that those who break our immigration laws only "want a better life" for themselves and their families.

Far from it. In fact, hundreds of thousands of illegal aliens are involved in any number of serious crimes that range from drunk driving to grand theft, drug trafficking to rape, and even murder. For example, at this very moment the violent drug gang MS-13 is not only operating in dozens of American cities from San Francisco to New York and seemingly everywhere in between, it is doing so with arrogance and impunity, literally daring law enforcement to do something about it. Drug abuse happens to be one of the leading causes of death, along with murder and abortion, of black Americans. It is a demographic nightmare of monumental proportions, and the body count that has resulted from this plague keeps on rising each and every year.

To make matters worse, compounding the problem is the policy of a number of cities across the country that refuse to help federal authorities enforce immigration law. These so-called "sanctuary cities—-places like San Francisco, Detroit, and New York City, to name but a few—-are not only thwarting efforts to protect our borders by failing to round up illegal aliens and incarcerate or deport them, they are, in the name of some misplaced attempt to show how "compassionate" they are, in reality posing a dire threat to their own citizens.

However, just as is the case with abortion, this type of "compassion" has cost, and will continue to cost, untold thousands of lives, all so the Left can "feel good" about itself. Our federal prison system is crammed to bursting with thousands of people who not only entered this country with no intention of "making a better life" or taking the necessary steps to become citizens, they compounded the act of entering the country illegally with far more serious crimes. If these people went through the proper channels in the first place, they would not now be "hiding in the shadows," they, in all likelihood, would never have been allowed to enter the country in the first place.

However, politics makes for strange bedfellows, and immigration "reform" has it supporters on both sides of the aisle. Of course, the "reform" of which they speak is not reform at all, but just another round of *de facto* amnesty on the order of those which were granted to illegals in 1965 and again in 1986.

Senators from both parties, like Charles Schumer (D-NY), Carl Levin and Debbie Stabenow (D-MI), Susan Collins (R-ME), Lindsey Graham (R-SC), John McCain (R-AZ), and Marco Rubio (R-FL) are enthusiastic supporters of "comprehensive immigration reform" that would legalize millions of people who broke U.S. law to come here, issue them papers that will permit them to work here, in many instances with no questions asked, and avail themselves of tens of billions of dollars in government benefits to which they are not entitled (Social Security, welfare payments, food stamps, and guaranteed student loans among them). One would do well to ask just why are they doing this when our borders, especially our southern border, are little more than sieves? Why are these people embarking on such a disastrous course when our own U.S. Department of Justice has refused to discharge its responsibilities under the Constitution to "protect each" state "against invasion" (Article 4, Section 4) and, instead, sues states like Arizona, which has found it necessary to do the job the government will not do in enforcing immigration law? The answer would seem to be quite simple: Democrats want more votes, and establishment Republicans want more cheap labor.

Government attempts to "regularize" illegal aliens failed in 1965 and again in 1986 because it refused to enforce the law. In 1965, the late Senator Ted Kennedy (D-MA) assured the country that if the law was changed, there would be no abuses in which immigrants would come here without sponsors. He was wrong. Millions came here *en masse* without anyone to vouch for them. He also promised that they would be ready to pull their own weight and contribute to American society and culture. That didn't happen, either. People came here and were immediately eligible for a whole range of government programs and benefits without paying a dime into the system. Welfare, food stamps, Section 8 housing, and more were all available almost immediately to immigrants and their families, many of whom never got off the public dole and who have raised at least two generations of offspring, who have never worked for anything in their lives.

But, why work? Why should they have to earn their keep when welfare made it more profitable to wait for a handout from Uncle Sam than going out and earning a weekly paycheck? Kennedy was wrong, spectacularly wrong, in 1965. Unfortunately, we seemed to have learned nothing from this fiasco by the time Ronald Reagan signed another round of immigration "reform" in 1986. In this case, millions of illegal aliens were granted actual amnesty, and once again, the government failed to enforce the law. It no longer kept proper track of those who were here without authorization, including those who entered the country on visas, which they overstayed. The resulting chaos has overwhelmed federal, state, and local law enforcement, the delivery of public services, our retirement and education systems, and our health care system.

For instance, state hospitals from Texas to California have had to close their doors because of the crush of illegal aliens without insurance who have used the emergency rooms not just for emergencies, but for all of their health care needs. And, there is nothing these facilities can do about it since they are required by federal law to treat anyone who comes through their doors, regardless of the ailment or their ability to pay. As 2014 unfolded, the rush to legalize those who have broken immigration law at the expense of the millions of people who have gone through the proper channels may have slowed a tick due to pressure on lawmakers from their constituents, but it did not come to a halt. If "comprehensive immigration reform" is ever enacted, it will bode ill, ill indeed, for America as a nation and as a culture. Amnesty did not work in 1986, when there were far fewer illegal aliens in the United States, and it will fail just as miserably this time around, if it ever becomes the law. And remember that in December of 2014, President Obama, after stating on 22 separate occasions that he did not have the Constitutional authority to do so, acted unilaterally by executive order to grant working papers to nearly 4.5 million illegal aliens. The President's action in the aftermath of the 2014 mid-term elections touched off a Constitutional crisis of unprecedented proportions that leaders in the newly-minted Republican House and Senate vowed would not stand as 2015 dawned. Only time will tell if these lawmakers have the intestinal fortitude to truly hold the President's feet to the fire.

The second thing to remember about immigration, either legal or illegal, is that it does nothing to reverse the decline in the native-born population of our country from a demographic perspective. It only stands to reason that if fewer than two children are born to a couple, regardless of their race, color, economic standing, or any other demographic category to which they belong, that society will begin a slow, steady decline into national oblivion. And, it is very doubtful if, let alone when, that trend can be reversed. We see it unfolding right before our very eyes in the extinction-level replacement rate among black Americans, but we are also seeing it begin to emerge in other demographic groups, in particular among white Americans. Because the feminist line that children are largely an impediment to a woman's success has worked so well, especially when it comes to white females, an increasing number of women have either deferred having children into their late 30s or have chosen not to have *any* children at all.

This situation is alarming, to say the least, and would be bad enough when taken by itself. But, combine that fact with the stupefying decline in black childbirth because of the inordinate number of abortions among these women, and this demographic group faces an unmitigated disaster. The warning must be sounded again and again until we finally get the message: if this situation does not soon reverse itself, black Americans will, for all intents and purposes, become virtually extinct in less than one hundred years. Make no mistake, this narrative is already playing out in every corner of this nation, and it is nothing short of shocking that those who should be the angriest and most alarmed about this, black Americans themselves, are not more vocal or active in bringing this crisis, yes, this *holocaust*, to the country's attention.

Why are so-called "civil rights leaders," people like Jesse Jackson and Al Sharpton for example, not seizing on this extinction-level event and condemning the practice of abortion at every turn? Why have they not mounted their pulpits and denounced this clearly racist practice, which takes the lives of more than 1,000 black babies every day? Why are not Messrs. Jackson and Sharpton exposing at every turn the cruel and barbaric agenda of Margaret Sanger and her Negro Project in the same way that they have condemned the Tuskegee Experiment's deliberate denial for decades of medical attention to unsuspecting blacks who were suffering from venereal disease? Why have they not even the slightest criticism, let alone the strongest condemnation, of the NAACP's "unofficial" policy in regard to Planned Parenthood, the leading abortion provider in this country and, in turn, the number one killer of black people in this country? Where are Jesse Jackson's and Al Sharpton's fellow clergymen on this subject? Why have their flocks not demanded an explanation for this outrage from these individuals? And, these "men of the cloth" are not alone in all this. Where, too, are the black athletes, entertainers, and educators? And, where, oh where, are the members of the Congressional Black Caucus, people like Sheila Jackson Lee, Maxine Waters, John Lewis, and Elijah Cummings?

Since these people are so well-respected in the black community, one would think that they would be just a bit more vocal, but for some reason, all we hear is a deafening silence from these "leaders" when it comes to the most critical issue facing black people today—-the life issue. In fact, they seem to have lost the ability to speak out at all against a practice that kills more blacks in *one week* than all the incidents of lynching that took place in the South from 1870 to 1940, and surpasses in little more than seven days the number of blacks who die from gun violence, drug abuse, sickle-cell anemia, or AIDS in one year. Why? Why is the only response that seems to come from the so-called "leaders" and "role models" in the black community the sound of crickets chirping in an open field? Why is silence the only reply that comes from those who are being victimized, devastated, and driven to the brink of extinction —-black Americans?

Perhaps, it is because of the culture of disrespect for life that has arisen around us for the past half-century, a culture that is 180 degrees out-of-phase with what was the societal norm for the first 160 to 170 years of our existence. This *avant-garde* worldview, which arose in Europe following the end of World War I and which took root in America in the early 1920s, scoffed at the existing norms of behavior and comportment and sought to undermine them at every turn. It took some time, but by the 1960s, it began to achieve its full impact. Feminism attacked traditional male-female relationships. Federal government interference signaled the onset of an all-out assault on the nuclear family, a relentless attack that continues even down to the present day. Drug abuse exploded. A deep and lasting mistrust of "anyone over 30" became the rule rather than the exception. The genie had been let out of the bottle and no one knew how to get him back in. And, the case is no different when it comes to abortion, especially among black Americans. These people have been sold a bill of goods, often with the full, complete, and willing participation of those to whom they turn for guidance, and it has been nothing short of disastrous. But, what else is one to expect when one examines the reasons why women have abortions in the first place?

A survey conducted by the Alan Guttmacher Institute in September of 2005 revealed some facts which are very interesting, to put it mildly. Given that Guttmacher actively gathers data on abortion from providers for Planned Parenthood, it cannot, therefore, be said that this is propaganda emanating from the pro-life movement. It is critical to bear in mind that this data is provided voluntarily and it is not a legal requirement to give out such information.

Among the responses the Guttmacher Institute received were the following, and they clearly showed that abortions were not always a matter of medical necessity. This is what the Institute found:

- 74% of women replied that having a baby would interfere with work, school, or other responsibilities;
- 73% said they could not afford to have a child;
- 48% said they did not want to be a single parent or had relationship problems with their husband or partner, and
- 2% said they had become pregnant as a result of rape or incest. [6]

It is extremely important to remember that these figures do not come from any pro-life organization, but *directly* from the data-gathering arm of the nation's largest abortion provider. It is also highly informative to see that three out of four of the reasons cited by respondents actually belie the claim made by "pro-choice" advocates that abortion is a matter of necessity. Quite to the contrary, they show that the vast majority of these procedures are performed for *convenience's* sake.

Interestingly, there is one category which was not addressed in the survey, and that is the percentage of women who underwent abortions because their lives or health were in danger by carrying their pregnancies to term. It is unclear why this question wasn't asked, but that is probably because such procedures are extremely rare when compared to those that are performed for the reasons cited above. In any case, as former Surgeon General C. Everett Koop famously observed and we have pointed out earlier in these pages, with the medical advances that have taken place in the four decades since *Roe vs. Wade* became the law of the land, abortions are "almost never medically necessary."

Abortion advocates have long demanded that these procedures must remain available in order to "protect the life and health of the mother, and many reasonable folks can sympathize with this position, at least insofar as the first part of that statement goes. But, what about the second part, that part which deals with the "health" issue? What does the word "health" mean? Physical, emotional, or psychological health? Such a word carries a wide range of meanings, and the "pro-choice" movement recognizes and has used this to advance its genocidal agenda. However, as the facts about abortion show, this argument begins to fall apart, and fall apart quickly. In fact, if we dissect it piece by piece, we can show quite clearly that there is no good reason for keeping abortion legal in the twenty-first century.

Let us start with the "pro-choice" contention that abortion must remain available to protect the physical health of the mother. As we have seen from the examples of George Tiller in Kansas and Kermit Gosnell in Philadelphia, women literally take their lives into their own hands when they enter an abortion clinic. Any surgical procedure is extremely risky, even one as routine as a tonsillectomy or having one's appendix removed. Having an abortion is far riskier for a woman, and we know that, except in certain rare instances in which the abortionist fails to terminate the pregnancy and the baby is born anyway, the procedure is always a death sentence for at least one of the two (or more) people involved. We have seen the statistics on the physical effects, both near and long-term, of abortion on the female body, and they are not pretty. Such effects include internal bleeding from lacerations to the cervix and uterus (near-term) to increased incidences of breast cancer in women who have had even one abortion in their lives (long-term).

In a paper titled "The long-term effects of abortion on women," Sarah Barnes, RN, writes: "Pregnancies carried through to completion lower the risk of a woman getting breast cancer more than if she had never gotten pregnant." [7] "This is because," Barnes points out, "the termination of a pregnancy causes a significant drop in the amount of estrogen secreted in a woman's body. This drop causes a rapid growth in the number of cells in the breast tissue. This cell multiplication greatly increases the risk of getting breast cancer." [8] Barnes continues in this sobering vein, adding that "according to the United States National Cancer Institute, women who have had an induced abortion have a 50% greater risk of getting breast cancer by age 45." Moreover, she concludes, "The risk is higher for women who have had an abortion before the age of 18." [9] Does Susan G. Komen for the Cure know this? If not, maybe someone should tell them ?

Barnes also examines other risks to women's health from abortion, risks which include infertility, post-abortion syndrome, and sexual dysfunction. However, Barnes is by no means the only one sounding the alarm. The Elliot Institute, in a fact sheet titled "Life-threatening risks of abortion," points out that women who have abortions are more likely to experience the following as opposed to those who bring their pregnancies to term. The findings are shocking and sobering, and point out how dangerously wrong those are who deny that women who abort suffer no ill effects from having had the procedure. They also illustrate how abortion needlessly endangers tens of millions of women. Compared to pregnant women who had their babies, those who aborted were:

- 3.5 times more likely to die in the following year;
- 6 times more likely to die of suicide;
- 4 times more likely to die of accidents;

- 1.6 times more likely to die from natural causes, and
- 14 times more likely to die from homicide. [10]

Other negative and deadly effects of abortion include, but are not limited to menstrual disturbance, inflammation of the reproductive organs, bladder or bowel perforation, and serious infection. [11] National Right-to Life cites a number of studies from prestigious medical journals that point out other far-reaching physical complications from abortion, which can and do include the following: damage to the uterus from overzealous cutterage leading to permanent infertility, [12] increased risk of ectopic or tubal pregnancy, [13] more than a double risk of future sterility, [14] and the risk of future miscarriage in women who have additional abortions. [15] And let the reader not forget the worst negative effect of abortion, the death of the mother either during or subsequent to the procedure itself. In fact, several hundred women (411 through 2009) who had abortions since they became legal across the country found out far too late that their "reproductive freedom" carried a heavy price indeed. [16]

All of this and more has led at least one prominent physician to weigh in on this deadly serious issue. Dr. Daniel J. Martin, Clinical Instructor at St. Louis University Medical School, states, "The impact of abortion on the body of a woman who chooses abortion is great and always negative. I can think of no beneficial effect of a social abortion on a body." [17] Now, one would think that this in itself would be enough to deter any woman from risking such tremendous damage to her body and life. Yet, in spite of this, many women, including black women, have had multiple abortions and remain among the most ardent and steadfast champions of this barbaric practice, even as their own demographic group continues to be ravaged by the most destructive aspect of the extinction-level event that is staring it squarely in the face.

Moreover, this seemingly mindless acceptance of and almost hysterical defense of abortion on the part of so many black Americans is a stunning testament to the success of the Left and its campaign of extermination against an entire group of people, a campaign that began in the fevered imagination of a racial eugenicist, Margaret Sanger, and which continues to this very day. It is also a testament to the cowardice of so many black clergy, in particular, who refuse to speak out against this monstrous evil. These "men of God" should be ashamed of themselves, not only for their deafening silence, but also for the willing complicity many of them have exhibited in contributing to the deaths of so many innocent unborn black babies. Tragically, inexplicably, they are not. How sad this all is, how very, very sad, indeed. However, our examination of this subject is far from finished. We still have a long way to go.

Now, what about the mental, psychological, and emotional components that come into play in the "pro-choice" argument surrounding the so-called "health" of women in the abortion debate? We are lectured almost *ad nauseum* by Planned Parenthood, NARAL Pro-Choice America, and other abortion advocacy groups that women will somehow become resentful or mentally unbalanced if they are denied the "right" to destroy the life that is growing inside them.

The facts, however, show almost the exact *opposite,* that a huge number of women who have had abortions have experienced a whole range of negative mental, emotional, and psychological effects precisely because they had these procedures. These effects include feelings of guilt, isolation, worthlessness, betrayal, declining self-esteem, helplessness, symptoms of Post-Traumatic Stress Disorder, and even suicidal tendencies in women who have undergone so much as even one abortion in their lives.

The evidence, gleaned from multiple sources over the years, clearly shows this and it continues to mount with each passing day. Consider the following for a moment. A recent study of 56,741 Medicaid patients in California revealed that women who aborted were 160% *more likely* to be hospitalized for psychiatric treatment in the first ninety days following their procedure than those who carried their pregnancies to term. [18] In another study, which tracked post-abortion patients after their procedures, researchers discovered that:

- 44% complained of nervous disorders;
- 36% experienced sleep disturbances;
- 31% had regrets about their decision, and
- 11% required treatment with psychotropic drugs. [19]

But, tragically, it doesn't stop there. In another study, researchers in Canada who conducted a 5-year retroactive study in two provinces found that women who had a history of abortion made *significantly higher use* of medical and psychiatric services than those who did not. The most striking aspect of this study was the finding that 25% of women who aborted spent time on the psychiatrist's couch compared to only 3% of those who carried their pregnancies to term. [20] If this weren't bad enough, the study found that women who aborted were significantly more likely to require admission to a psychiatric hospital as a result of having had the procedure. At especially high risk, the study also found, are teenagers, separated or divorced women, and women who have had multiple abortions. It further stated that since many post-abortive women use repression as a coping mechanism (a clear indication that they experience tremendous feelings of guilt from their decision to terminate the life growing inside them), "...there may be a long time before a woman seeks psychiatric care."

"These repressed feelings," the researchers continued, "may cause psychosomatic illnesses and psychiatric or behavioral problems in other areas of life." [21] And, small wonder. The decision to abort, whether coerced or freely taken, is literally a matter of life and death for both mother and child. One is truly left to marvel that, given the staggering risks to life, limb, and sanity that are attached to abortion, there has been even so much as a *single* medical procedure of this kind at any time in our history, let alone nearly 57 million of them since the whole bloody business became a Constitutionally-protected "right" in January of 1973.

But this, sadly, is the world in which we live. Despite all the warning signs, physical, mental, emotional, and psychological, about abortion; despite the evidence that belies overwhelmingly the claim that abortion is a "safe" procedure (safe for just whom, one might well ask); despite all this and more, we see politicians, women's rights advocates, and the abortion industry itself lobbying for *wider* access to the procedure, in complete denial of facts such as those contained in a 2008 report by the American Psychological Association's Task Force on Mental Health and Abortion. Among the risk factors, both physical and psychological, that the task force identified were:

- terminating a wanted or meaningful pregnancy;
- feelings of stigma;
- various personality traits (such as low self-esteem, pessimistic outlook, low-perceived outlook on life);
- perceived need for secrecy;
- late-term (or partial-birth) abortion;
- perceived pressure from others to terminate pregnancy, and
- use of avoidance and denial coping strategies. [22]

This is, of course, a partial list, and one would think that each factor taken by itself would be enough to deter any woman, even one who has been raped or victimized by incest, from going down such a disastrous and destructive path. Taken together, however, these risks pose nothing less than an existential threat to the lives and well-being of tens of millions of women from all across the demographic spectrum, to say nothing of the tens of millions of children who have been butchered in their mothers' wombs for more than 40 years. But, it gets worse, far, far worse for the mother, who has to live with the aftermath of her "choice" for the rest of her life. Two other consequences of abortion involve Post-Traumatic Stress Disorder and suicidal tendencies in women who have aborted at least once in their lives. Several studies of PTSD in post-abortive women have been conducted in recent years, one which concluded that at least 600,000 women have been diagnosed with this disease. [23]

In another study, researchers found that fully 14% of all American women who had abortions have all the symptoms of PTSD and attribute them to these procedures. [24] The study revealed the stunning fact that 65% of the women surveyed reported some, but not all of the symptoms associated with PTSD. [25] If this isn't alarming enough, consider the findings of, yet, another survey of post-abortive women. In this survey, albeit a random one, 19% of post-abortive women suffered from diagnosable PTSD. Roughly half those women had many, but not all symptoms of PTSD, and 20-40% showed "moderate to high stress levels of avoidance and behavior" relative to their abortion experiences. [26]

PTSD is defined as "a psychological dysfunction, which results from a traumatic experience, which overwhelms a person's normal defense mechanisms" that results in "intense fear, feelings of helplessness or being trapped, or loss of control." The risk that an experience will be traumatic is increased when the traumatizing event is "perceived as including threats of physical injury, sexual violation, or the witnessing of or participation in a violent death." [27] PTSD occurs when the traumatic event causes the hyper arousal of what psychiatrists refer to as "fight or flight" defense mechanisms. These mechanisms become "disorganized, disconnected from present circumstances, and take on a life of their own resulting in abnormal behavior and major personality disorders." [28] Given that so many women undergo as invasive and violent procedure as abortion is, it is a miracle that more of them do not display the symptoms of Post Traumatic Stress Disorder, some of which include fear, anxiety, pain, and guilt, as a result of their experiences.

However, as painful and debilitating as PTSD is, the deadliest psychological effect of abortion is the taking of a woman's life by her own hand.

An alarming number of women who have aborted their unborn children have entertained suicidal thoughts at various points in time after having had their procedures. In fact, according to one study, "suicidal ideation," or the contemplation of ending one's own life, has been reported in nearly 60% of women who experience post-abortion sequelae, and that of those, 28% actually attempt to take their own lives. [29] To illustrate how demographics can show the dire nature of post-abortion suicide ideation, let us look at what researchers in Finland have discovered.

In a records-based study, they found a strong statistical (or demographic) link between abortion and suicide in post-abortive women. What they found is, quite simply, jarring. They found that while the mean annual suicide rate for all women was 11.3 per 100,000, the rate for women following their abortions was 34.7 per 100,000, or a staggering three-fold *increase* in the number of women who took their own lives! [30]

Now, granted, this study was conducted in Finland, which has far fewer people than the U.S. But, it would then stand to reason, would it not, that since we have a much larger population the crisis is that much more acute? Common sense would seem to indicate that this is the case. Yet, aside from the occasional stories that find their way into print or onto the airwaves, the general public remains almost totally ignorant about this alarming trend. And, that is how the "pro-choice" movement seems to want it. In fact, anyone on the pro-life side who raises this issue is ridiculed, belittled, and excoriated as being someone who wants to "set back the cause of women's rights," deny women their "freedom to choose," keep women "barefoot and pregnant," and so on. Yet, in spite of the abortionists' claims that having the procedure is a matter of "choice," there is frightening evidence that for many women, abortion is not a decision that is freely taken, but a matter in which they are often pressured to participate against their will.

In a fact sheet titled "Forced Abortion in America," the Elliot Institute shows how, contrary to the claims of abortion-rights supporters that the procedure is a matter of their "freedom of choice," many women who find themselves pregnant actually have very little say in the matter at all. Often, the Institute found, women who are in a "family way" come under intense pressure from family, friends, spouses, boyfriends, and abortion providers to embark on what has been proven to be a path that is anything but "safe" or "rare."

"Sixty-four percent of women," the Institute says, "felt pressured by others to abort." [31] The woman's "choice," it goes on to state, "can include the loss of home, income and family, or violence, and even murder." [32]

Moreover, pressure to abort can be brought to bear on the woman from a number of different sides, and can be based on "disinformation from credentialed experts, negligent counselors, or even trusted pastors." [33] "Trusted pastors." Now where have we heard *that* one before?

Pressure to abort can take many forms, from the subtle variety listed above, to hostile and sometimes even fatal coercion. "Intense pressure to abort," the Institute found, "can come from husbands, parents, doctors, partners, counselors, or even close family and friends." [34] To illustrate how abortion many times is not a matter of "freedom of choice" but one of intense physical and psychological coercion, the Institute presents a chilling number of incidents that bear this out:

- In one case, a husband jumped on his wife's stomach to force her to abort;
- In another, a woman forced her pregnant daughter *at gunpoint* to visit an abortion mill; and
- In a third instance, a woman was forcibly injected by the baby's father with an abortifacient drug.

We have already listed many of the "reasons" that women give for killing their babies in the womb, and they have nothing to do with coercion (for example, financial distress, loss of support from family or society, etc.). But as the Elliot Institute points out, on far too many occasions, women are often placed in jeopardy of life, limb, and psyche when they make their decision. Some examples of the pressure brought on the woman by others include the following:

- In 95% of all cases, the male partner played a central role in the woman's decision to abort her unborn child; [35]
- 45% of men interviewed at abortion clinics recalled urging the woman to abort, including 73% of married men; [36]
- In the same study, men justified being the primary decision-maker regarding the abortion, [37] and
- 5% of women who aborted felt pressured by others. [38]

These findings reflect what happens before the woman goes to see the abortionist, but what happens when she arrives at her destination? According to the Institute, not a lot of a positive nature. While we hear the almost hysterical hue and cry that goes up from the "pro-choice" movement that women need "protection" from those who silently pray and minister to pregnant women in the hope that they will decide to keep their babies, we seldom if ever hear about the tactics that the *clinics themselves* employ to deceive or force these women into having abortions.

Such tactics include deliberately withholding information about alternatives to abortion and pressure from staffs that are financially rewarded for having women go through with the procedure. The information compiled by the Institute revealed that:

- 54% of women were unsure of their decision to abort, but 67% received no counseling beforehand; [39]
- 84% received inadequate counseling beforehand, and 79% were not told about alternatives; [40]
- Many women were misinformed by experts about fetal development, abortion alternatives, and risks; [41] and
- Many were denied essential personal, family, social, or economic support. [42]

It is astounding, in light of the physical, mental, emotional, and psychological dangers that attach to abortion, that any woman, regardless of the circumstances surrounding her pregnancy, would even consider setting foot inside an abortion clinic. And, it is even more astounding that so many millions of women, especially black women, have been so thoroughly indoctrinated, conned, bamboozled, and lied to by the abortion industry, which receives hundreds of millions of dollars in private and taxpayer funding each year, into entrusting their physical and mental health, and even their very lives, to such a clear and present danger. Yet, this is exactly what has occurred for more than forty years and is taking place every day in this country, 3,000 times a day, in fact, with more than 1,000 of these operations targeting black females.

Most of them survive the abortion procedure and wind up paying a terrible price on so many levels, as we have just seen. Nevertheless, we must remember that hundreds never made it out of the abortion mill, women like Karnamaya Mongar, who perished in "Doctor" Kermit Gosnell's Philadelphia abortion mill, and 24 year old Tonya Reaves, a Chicago woman who died in a Planned Parenthood Clinic in Chicago on July 20, 2012. Ms. Reaves expired after three unsuccessful surgeries were performed following her botched second-trimester abortion. The incident sparked a firestorm of outrage and a wrongful death lawsuit against the abortion provider, which was forced to pay a sum of two million dollars to the victim's family in February of 2014.

Did Gosnell or Planned Parenthood inform either Ms. Mongar or Ms. Reaves that there are alternatives to abortion? Did they provide counseling, sonograms, or ultrasounds in either case or to the hundreds of women who died in abortion clinics before them? In view of what we have learned thus far, the answer must be a resounding, unequivocal "no!" Yet this is how the abortion industry operates, and millions of American women, most notably black women, are sitting ducks as a result. There is nothing it fears more than the idea that the women who have died in its clinics actually had names and were not just mere statistics. Moreover, the abortion industry cannot afford to have anyone start asking questions lest their financial pipeline be shut off, for there's a lot of money to be made in killing unborn children...gobs and gobs of it.

And, speaking of money, it is important to remember the enormous negative economic impact of the low replacement level America is experiencing. This is due to many factors, but especially because we are killing so many of our children before they are even born. It is precisely because we are not producing enough children to replace ourselves that we are not producing enough people who will grow into productive citizens who will work, innovate, consume, save for the future, and pay taxes. They will also not be contributing to retirement programs like Social Security, which, in turn, will put an even greater strain on the system than has previously been the case.

Abortion on demand has been a Constitutionally-protected "right" since 1973. If those who had been killed prior to birth had been allowed to live, many of them would now be entering their prime earning years. They would be working, saving, spending, having and providing for families of their own, and who knows what they might have accomplished with their lives? We will never know, for instance, if one of them might have discovered a cure for cancer.

Likewise, we will never know if one of them might have become the first person to set foot on another planet, grow up to be a great artist, inventor, musician, or statesman. This is especially true for the black community. Who would be the next Frederick Douglass? The next Harriet Tubman? The next George Washington Carver, Condoleeza Rice, Ben Carson, or Clarence Thomas? We will never know just how many of them would have accomplished some great thing to enrich our society because these people are not around.

Where will the next Martin Luther King, Jr. originate? The next Jackie Robinson? The next Louis Armstrong or Count Basie? Again, we will never know because so many black babies are being killed to fulfill the warped dream of a racial eugenicist. Remember, once more, the Reverend Johnny Hunter's anguished lament on the steps of the United States Capitol on Columbus Day 1999: "We are killing our future...Civil rights doesn't mean a thing without a right to life!" Yes, Reverend Hunter, we are killing our future because we have listened for far too long to feminists, abortionists, and population-control advocates. And, because we have bought their bill of goods, because we have swallowed their intellectual snake oil, we are now producing fewer and fewer children to take our places and secure the future of our unique and exceptional nation.

Lest this warning be dismissed as little more than just another nativist rant, we would do well to examine the evidence, evidence that is all too plain to see, if we only take the time. This evidence comes from economists, demographers, and social scientists. It has been compiled painstakingly over a number of years and even decades. It has been thoroughly and exhaustively examined and published in a number of scholarly journals and in newspapers from *USA Today* to The *Wall Street Journal*. Let us now see this evidence for ourselves.

Even a cursory look at data from the U.S. Census Bureau shows that our birth rate has been in decline since the turn of the nineteenth century. In 1800, the number of live births per female ("replacement" or "total fertility" rate) stood at roughly seven. [43] This high birth rate was understandable since the U.S. was largely an agrarian society, so it needed people to work the farms, and several more decades would pass before the advent of the Industrial Revolution and the onset of the demographic shift to the nation's growing cities. While it is true that we have always allowed a large number of immigrants, as well (including Margaret Sanger's father Michael), the vast majority of Americans were born on these shores.

Times, however, change. Circumstances also change, and as our nation became more and more industrialized and peoples' lives improved as a result of a steadily growing economy, advances in health care, technology, and the overall standard of living, fewer children were being born. By 1900, the replacement rate stood at roughly 3.5 live births per female, still well above the 2.1 live births per female that demographers deem to be the absolute minimum for societal survival. [44] By 1940, the number had dipped roughly to replacement level, then spiked upward to slightly around 4 children per couple by the onset of the 1950s (the time of the so-called postwar "Baby Boom") This trend held steady for roughly the next 10-20 years before reversing itself in the mid-1970s.

Bear in mind that it was during this time that feminism emerged, and the population-control movement began to gain new life. By the turn of the twenty-first century, America's population decline had resumed in full force, and by 2010, the U.S. began to experience a sustained drop in live births per female in the non-immigrant population, bottoming out at a replacement rate of just 1.93. A number of factors contributed to this decline, especially among black Americans, not the least of these factors being the inordinate number of abortions that were being performed on black women. As we have seen throughout these pages, because of a number of negative factors that affect the black community, the replacement rate for this particular demographic group now stands at 0.7 live births per female. Unless something happens to dramatically reverse this trend, it is not out of the realm of possibility that this number will decline even further before all is said and done. To make matters worse, there are ominous signs that other demographic groups are being adversely affected, as well, including whites and Americans of Asian descent.

This decline has become so serious that it could not long escape the notice of other publications such as *USA Today,* which ran a copyrighted story early in 2013 titled "As U.S. birth rate drops, concern for the future mounts." The article sounded an ominous tone, couched in dire economic terms that stated, "The drop in U.S. births to their lowest level since 1920 is sounding alarms about the nation's ability to support its fast-growing elderly population." [45] The *USA Today* piece referenced the 2013 book *What To Expect When No One's Expecting: America's Coming Demographic Disaster* by Jonathan Last. In the book, Last takes a sobering look at the precipitous drop-off in births in California and warns of "significant challenges" to the state's economic future.

The seriousness of the situation is not lost on demographers like Dowell Myers, the Director of the Population Dynamics Research Group at the University of Southern California. Referring to the number of retiring baby boomers and the shrinking number of children being born in the Golden State, Myers says, "These are two trends that are going in the opposite direction. We will be increasingly dependent economically and socially on a smaller number of children." [46] Myers says that due to this widening gulf between retirees and young earners who pay into programs like Social Security and Medicare, the economic burden on a child born in 2015 will be twice that of a child born in 1965. The *USA Today* article reveals that in 1970 there were 22.2 people age 65 and over for every 100 working adults age 25-64. Forty years later, in 2010, that number had grown to 24.6, which at first blush does not seem so dramatic. But, Myers points out, by 2030, that number will have increased to 40 people age 65 and over for every 100 workers age 25-64. [47] Last adds that the decline in births bodes especially ill for society, and not just economically. "All of the energy goes out of society when fertility gets low," he says. [48] Myers thinks we can overcome the crisis, saying "We can survive with fewer kids, but we need to bring them along. At the end of the decade, when 'Baby Boomer' retirement hits us really hard, at that point we'll be begging for workers."

Yet, a new Baby Boom is exactly what America needs, one lasting for the next 40 to 50 years, according to Dennis Howard of Movement for a New America. Howard has done extensive research into the impact on the nation's economy that nearly 57 million abortions since 1973 has had, and none of it, he says, is anything good. In fact, Howard has pegged the economic cost of abortion at between 35 and 70 *trillion* dollars in lost Gross Domestic Product. [49] "No matter how you slice it," Howard says, "aggressive population control exacts a huge price in future economic growth that can never be recovered. Indeed, it reverberates through all future generations. Without an enormous new Baby Boom lasting another 40-50 years, that growth is lost forever. We don't have a debt crisis; we have a death crisis." Citing a 1997 report titled *The Abortion Bomb: America's Demographic Disaster*, Howard laments, "I see little hope that we can avoid an eventual crash on Wall Street that will make the 1930s look like cashing in your cards after a bad game of Monopoly."

The Abortion Bomb sounds a grim alarm about our future if we do not reverse the number of these procedures and begin to bring the replacement rate back into line with what is was in decades past. The report states (and remember, this was in 1997) that "the estimated loss in U.S. GDP already exceeds 38 trillion dollars, more than twice our current national debt. That's why, even if abortion ends tomorrow, it will still take more than a generation to recover." [50]

The Abortion Bomb also points out that the toll taken by abortion "adds up to a 30% loss in the younger generation under age 45. The toll includes some 18 million African-American babies and some 37 million others. That's about 3,535 times as many African-Americans as were lynched in the Civil

War." [51] *The Abortion Bomb* examines as well the dire implications for our education and health care-systems if we continue killing off so many of our young before they ever see the light of day. "If we do," the report states, "we face a looming shortage of 1 million nurses and 2 million teachers." Further, *The Abortion Bomb* warns, "We also face critical shortages in key professions such as science, medicine, and higher education." [52] Nearly everyone on the Left and, sad to say, many on the Right (in other words, people who should know better) like to dismiss those who believe in the sanctity of unborn human life by calling abortion a mere "social issue" and that it's really about "the economy, stupid." In light of what we have just seen, however, can it not credibly be argued that abortion *is,* after all, an economic issue?

The crisis is especially acute in America's black community. Again, we must ask the critical question: if we keep killing so many black babies in the womb, where will the next generation of black leaders come from? Where will we get the next Colin Powell or Clarence Thomas? The next Star Parker of Jesse Lee Peterson? The next Walter Hoye or Alveda King? The next Ben Carson or Herman Cain? Where, indeed? We certainly can't import them from other countries, so what are we to do? Even the most ardent proponents of immigration "reform" admit that this will not solve the problem.

As *The Abortion Bomb* puts it, the bottom line is simple, direct, and succinct: "No kids, no future. It's as simple as that." The highest crime rate (including violent crime) in America. The highest illiteracy rate in the U.S. The highest incidence of drug abuse in America. The highest unemployment rate in the nation, especially among the young. More broken families than any other group in the U.S. The highest rate of welfare dependency. A skyrocketing illegitimacy rate, the highest of any demographic group in America, and sadly, horribly, the highest abortion rate. Which, when put together add up to the *lowest* replacement rate of any demographic group in the United States.

This, then, is the crisis which confronts black America, a crisis that cries out for immediate and decisive action. And the greatest part of the blame for this crisis lies on two fronts: 1) the current generation of black "leaders," the politicians, educators, and men of the cloth who have led their people over a demographic cliff by encouraging them to fulfill the blood-stained legacy of Margaret Sanger, and 2) all of those who have granted them legitimacy. The warning signs are all there, and they are as plain as day. It is high time that people in America's black community begin to wake up, confront this crisis, and demand accountability from those who have led them astray. It has the means to avert the coming disaster at its fingertips, right here, right now. It always has, and it had better start using it and using it soon. Because unless something changes drastically, unless the black population repudiates the culture of death that so many of its "leaders" embrace, a culture that includes abortion, it will not have a bleak future, it will have *no future at all!*

No kids, no future. It's as simple as that.

NOTES

1. *Webster's New World Compact Desk Dictionary and Style Guide*, 2002, p.131.
2. United States-Race and Hispanic Origin, 1790-1990. U.S. Census Bureau, September 13, 2002, Table 1.
3. Ibid.
4. Black or African-American Population: 2000-2010 Black or African-American Alone. U.S. Census Bureau.
5. United States-Race and Hispanic Origin: 1790-1990. U.S. Census Bureau, September 13, 2002, Table 1.
6. Alan Guttmacher Institute, *Perspective on Sexual & Reproductive Health*, September 2005.
7. Barnes, Sarah, RN, *The Long-Term Effects of Abortion on Women.* From www.The Gospel.org, February 10, 2009, p. 3. Updated December 23, 2010.
8. Ibid.
9. Ibid.
10. Elliot Institute, www.AfterAbortion.org.
11. National Right to Life, *Abortion: Some medical facts, physical complications*, p. 5.
12. Danforth, David N., Ph.D. & MD, and Nichols, David H., MD, *Gynecologic and Obstetric Surgery,* 1993, p. 260.
13. Levin, A. et al, "Ectopic Pregnancy and Prior Induced Abortion," *American Journal of Public Health*, Volume 72, No. 3, March 1982, pp. 253-256.
14. Tzonou, Anastasia et al, "Induced Abortions, Miscarriages and Tobacco Smoking as Risk Factors for Secondary Infertility," *Journal of Epidemiology and Community Health*, 1993. Volume 47, p. 6.
15. Levin, A. et al, "Association of Induced Abortion with Subsequent Pregnancy Loss," *Journal of the American Medical Association*, June 27, 1980, Volume 247, pp. 2495-96, 2498-99.
16. www.Abort73.com, *Abortion Fatalities.*
17. Martin, Daniel J., MD. "The Impact of Legal Abortion on Women's Minds and Bodies," a paper presented at the Human Life and Health Care Ethics conference, April 1993.
18. Strahan, Thomas, *Detrimental Effects of Abortion: An Annotated Bibliography with Commentary,* Third Edition.
19. Ashton, *The Psychosocial Outcome of Induced Abortion, British Journal of Obstetrics and Gynecology,* 1980, Volume 87, pp. 1115-1122.
20. Badgley et al, *Report of the Committee on the Operation of the Abortion Law* (Ottawa: Supply and Services), 1977, pp. 313-321.
21. Kent et al, *Bereavement in Post-Abortive Women: A Clinical Report, World Journal of Pscyhosynthesis,* Autumn-Winter 1981, Volume 13, Nos. 3-4.
22. www.afterabortion.org, *Abortion Risks, Abortion Complications, Abortion Dangers, Abortion Side Effects*, 2012, p. 6.

23. Ashton, *The Psychosocial Outcome of Induced Abortion, British Journal of Obstetrics and Gynecology*, 1980, pp. 1115-1122.
24. Ibid.
25. Badgely et al, *Report of the Committee on the Operation of the Abortion Law* (Ottawa: Supply and Services), 1977, pp. 313-321.
26. Barnard, Catherine, RN, *The Long-Term Psychological Effects of Abortion.* Institute for Pregnancy Loss, Portsmouth, NH, 1990.
27. Herman, *Trauma and Recovery*, Basic Books, New York, 1992, p. 4.
28. Ibid.
29. Speckard, *Psychological Loss Following Abortion*, Sheed & Ward, 1987.
30. Gissler, Hemminki, & Longqvist, *Suicides in Finland after Pregnancy, 1987-94*, register linkage study.
31. Rue, V. M. et al, *Induced Abortion and Traumatic Stress: A Preliminary Comparison of American and Russian Women, Medical Science Monitor 10* (10): SR5-16 (2004).
32. www.unchoice.info/resources/html, *Forced Abortion in America.*
33. M. Gissler et al, *Pregnancy Associated Deaths in Finland 1987-94-definition problems and benefits or record linkage, Obstetrica et Gynecologica Scandinavica*, 1997, Volume 76, pp. 651-657.
34. Elliot Institute, *Forced Abortion in America: Coercion Can Lead to Violence, Even Murder.*
35. Zimmerman, Mary K., *Passage through Abortion*, 1977. Prager Publishers.
36. Shostak, Arthur, and McClouth, Gary, *Men and Abortion: Lessons, Losses and Love*, c. 1984, Prager Publishers.
37. Ibid.
38. Rue, V. M. et al, *Induced Abortion and Traumatic Stress: A Preliminary Comparison of American and Russian Women, Medical Science Monitor 10* (10); SR5-16, 2004.
39. Rue, V.M. et al, *Induced Abortion and Traumatic Stress: A Preliminary Comparison of American and Russian Women, Medical Science Monitor 10* (10); SR5-16, 2004.
40. Ibid.
41. Burke, Theresa, *Forbidden Grief: The Unspoken Pain of Abortion*, c. 2000, Alcorn Books.
42. Ibid.
43. *America's Baby Bust, The Wall Street Journal,* February 12, 2012.
44. *America's Baby Bust, The Wall Street Journal,* February 12, 2012.
45. *USA Today*, February 13, 2012.
46. Ibid.
47. *USA Today,* February 13, 2012
48. Ibid.
49. www.Lifesitenews.com., *Researcher: Economic Impact of Abortion in the U.S. Since 1970: $35-70 trillion.*
50. www.movementforabetteramerica.org., *The Abortion Bomb: America's Demographic Disaster,* 1997.
51. Ibid.
52. Ibid.

Chapter 7:

Population Control, Abortion, and the U.N.'s *Agenda 21*

> *"Indeed, it has been concluded that compulsory population-control laws, even including laws requiring compulsory abortion, could be sustained under the existing Constitution if the population crisis became sufficiently severe to endanger the society."*
>
> —John C. Holdren,
> lead Science Advisor to President Barack Hussein Obama
> in *Ecoscience,* 1977, p.837

On June 3, 1992, representatives of more than 178 countries, including the United States of America, gathered in Rio De Janeiro, Brazil, to formulate a strategy to address the perceived threat posed by human beings to the global environment. By the time the United Nations Conference on Sustainable Development (the so-called "Earth Summit") concluded eleven days later, the delegates had hammered out a 300-page document titled *Agenda 21,* billed as "a comprehensive plan of action to be taken globally, nationally, and locally by organizations of the United Nations System, Governments, and Major groups in every area in which humans impact on the environment."

According to the U.N., *Agenda 21* was intended to combat a myriad of problems confronting developing countries, problems ranging from poverty, overpopulation and environmental degradation to women's rights and "social injustice." It would be carried out over a period of several decades and would ostensibly be entered into through the voluntary co-operation of the signatory states. Indeed, the U.N. itself stated that *Agenda 21* was to be "non-binding" and would not carry the force of law. However, over time, it became quite evident that if voluntary co-operation was not enough, the use of force to coerce the compliance of reluctant nations with its provisions would not be ruled out.

A good example of such coercion can be found in a leading environmentalist organ that pushed for the use of force in bringing the provisions of *Agenda 21* about: "*Agenda 21* proposes an array of actions which are intended to be implemented by EVERY person on Earth...it calls for specific changes in the activities of ALL people...Effective execution of *Agenda 21* will REQUIRE a profound reorientation of ALL humans, unlike anything the world has ever experienced." [1] So much for "voluntary" co-operation.

The term "Sustainable Development" first came into vogue in 1987, five years before the Rio gathering, when the U.N. issued a report titled *Our Common Future*. The report was produced by the body's World Commission on Environment and Development and was authored by Norwegian Prime Minister and World Socialist Party Vice President Gro Harlem Bruntland. The stated objective of Sustainable Development is "to integrate economic, social and environmental policies in order to achieve reduced consumption, social equity and the restoration and preservation of biodiversity." High-minded and laudable goals, indeed, at least on their face.

However, looks are often deceiving, and, at least in the United States, some of our elected officials smelled a rat, a big rat, and despite the fact that President George H.W. Bush made the U.S. a signatory to the agreement, *Agenda 21*was not a treaty, and the U.S. Senate refused to ratify it after closer examination.

This was probably the smartest thing the Senate ever did in recent memory, but that didn't stop Bush's successor Bill Clinton from doing an end run around that august body by issuing Executive Order #12858 after taking office on January 20, 1993. With the stroke of a pen (which had Clinton adviser Paul Begala all atwitter, no doubt), the 42nd President effectively inflicted *Agenda 21* on the American people with no debate or input whatsoever. This, despite the admission by its *own supporters* that they didn't know what was in it or how it would ever be fully implemented. Sound familiar? Does the Patient Protection and Affordable Care Act ("Obamacare") ring a bell? Remember Nancy Pelosi's infamous comment that the bill had to be passed so that we "could find out what's in it?" So too, it seems, with the provisions of *Agenda 21*.

So, what did *Agenda 21's* own backers say about it? If some of their comments are any indication, there is little cause for optimism or confidence among the masses. Take this quote, for example. The International Council for Local Environmental Initiatives (whatever *that* is) stated as far back as 1996, "The realities of life on our planet *dictate* that continued economic development as we know it cannot be sustained (author's emphasis added)... Sustainable development, therefore, is a program of action for local and global reform—-a program that has *yet to be fully defined*" [2] (Again, author's emphasis added).

Elsewhere in the ICLEI's Local *Agenda 21* Planning Guide we find this statement: "No one fully understands how, or even if, sustainable development can be achieved; however, there is growing consensus that it must be accomplished at the local level if it is ever to be achieved on a global basis."[3] Well. Quite an indictment, wouldn't it be fair to say? But little niceties like details or cause and effect never seem to be taken into account where bureaucrats and elitists are concerned. To the contrary, these people inflict policies on the rest of humanity that are neither well-thought out nor even remotely beneficial to the very people about whom they profess to care so much.

The goal of *Agenda 21* is nothing short of an international power grab that will affect how each and every person conducts their life in the future. Even a cursory glance at the document demonstrates the danger inherent in such a breathtakingly huge attempt on the part of a very tiny minority of international social planners to dictate what the vast, vast majority of the world's citizens will do in their daily lives. Every decision we make in the future will be shaped by what a handful of international bureaucrats in New York and their fellow-travelers in every world capital will dictate.

And, while the provisions of *Agenda 21* pose a dire threat to private property rights, individual freedom, and national sovereignty, they bode especially ill for those who are the most defenseless among us—-the aged, and the infirm, and, especially, the unborn. As we will see, population control lies directly at the heart of this ominous program. The international Left believes that human beings pose such an existential threat to the survival of the planet that their numbers must be severely limited through various means that include eugenics, euthanasia, and abortion. The means by which this is to be accomplished should send chills down the spines of every person on earth.

So, now, let us embark on a closer examination of *Agenda 21's* anti-human and even murderous aspects, aspects which will hardly come as a surprise to anyone who cares to pay attention. Sadly, alarmingly, most people are not paying attention and they do so at their dire peril. What we will discover along the way is odious, astounding, horrifying, and repellent, and should serve as a clear and unmistakable warning about what is in store not only for the United States, but the world as a whole if this program ever takes full effect.

The notion of population control goes back a long way, at least to the end of the eighteenth century. It was at that time that the world became acquainted with the theories of Thomas Malthus (1766-1834). Malthus was an economist and clergyman in the Church of England who laid out his case in his 1798 treatise *An Essay on the Principle of Population*. In it, Malthus posited that human population, while increasing geometrically (that is, from 2 to 4, to 8 to 16, and so on), would soon outstrip the ability of food production, which could only increase arithmetically, (or from 2 to 3 to 4 to 5 and so on) to feed enough people to keep most of them from eventually starving to death. [4] Malthus also argued in his *Essay* that because of these inevitable food shortages, certain "positive checks" or mitigating factors would come into play to keep the population more or less in balance. Malthus identified some of these "positive checks" as including "war, famine and disease." [5] It was a bleak outlook for humanity, indeed.

There was, however, one "check" that Malthus did not view in a positive light, and one that would have put him at odds with the modern population control movement. This was the idea of keeping the numbers of humans down by means of contraception. He viewed this method as a "vice" or "improper art" that threatened the moral order of the existing society. To him, the only acceptable method of averting the crisis was to put off marriage and starting a family until one was financially able to do so. This argument was based more on class concerns, and he viewed the poor as being the greatest culprit due to, their lack of self-restraint. To him, they only had themselves to blame for their plight, and for that reason, he opposed the passage of English "Poor Laws" that would aid families in need. Malthus viewed such laws as aggravating the situation because they rewarded the poor for their negative behavior, at least in his view.

"Hard as it may appear in individual instances," Malthus put forth in his *Essay*, "dependent poverty ought to be held disgraceful. Such a stimulus seems to be absolutely necessary to promote the happiness of the great mass of mankind, and every general attempt to weaken this stimulus, however benevolent its apparent intention, will always defeat its own purpose." [6] Malthus condemned those poor who brought children into the world thusly:

"A labourer who marries without being able to support a family may in some respects be considered as an enemy to all his fellow labourers." Because of his self-professed "economic pessimism," Malthus saw no way out, effectively resigning himself to the worldview expressed in Thomas Hobbes' *Leviathan* that, for the vast majority of the world's people, life would remain "poor, nasty, brutish, and short."

As stated above, a bleak outlook, indeed. And, for more than a century afterward, Malthus' theories served to impede necessary economic reforms in Britain, condemning millions to grinding poverty and despair. Thankfully, though, these notions have proved completely without merit due in large part to two crucial events that took place at the latter part of the eighteenth century and the early part of the nineteenth, namely the American Revolution and the Industrial Revolution. The American Revolution showed, for the first time, that a nation could be established based on the idea that ordinary people were able to create a system of self-government based on the principle that Man's rights come from God and that they had no need of monarchs or dictators to rule over them.

Moreover, because of the ideas articulated by Thomas Jefferson in *The Declaration of Independence,* the United States enshrined the concept of private property rights which grew out of the broader rights to "liberty" and "the pursuit of happiness." These rights served to prepare the fertile soil of economic opportunity for millions of Americans who were either born here or who came from other countries seeking a better life, and as the Industrial Revolution dawned in the early 1800s, its effects were felt infinitely more dramatically in the United States than anywhere else on earth. As our level of knowledge increased throughout the nineteenth century and into the twentieth, so, too, did our ability to create new inventions that would save time and money, not to mention lives, and in the bargain people began to live longer and standards of living improved all over the world.

The freedom to create, invent, and to innovate that was embedded in our national DNA permitted entrepreneurs from Andrew Carnegie, John D. Rockefeller, and the Wright Brothers, to Thomas Edison, Henry Ford, and Alexander Graham Bell to make their dreams a reality and, in the process, put what was once seen as only available to the well-off within the reach of the average citizen. Telephones, automobiles, electric lights, air travel, and so much more that were once considered luxuries now became items of everyday use to the common man, and although the Industrial Revolution improved life for millions around the world, nowhere on earth was this development felt more dramatically or profoundly than in it was in the United States.

Improvements in living standards also meant an accompanying improvement in agriculture, again brought about by the freedoms won in the American Revolution, which, in turn, allowed the Industrial Revolution to work its magic in connection with our system of entrepreneurial capitalism. Improved agricultural methods such as crop rotation and the introduction of fertilizers and pesticides meant greater crop yields per acre of land, which, in turn, led to more mouths being fed, and at a lower price. These developments went a long way in discrediting Malthus' contention that human population growth would one day doom us to eventual wholesale starvation.

And as our level of technology increased over the years, so, too, did our level of medical knowledge, leading to better diagnosis and treatment of diseases that used to routinely kill millions of people before they entered their 30s. Our increasing level of knowledge and expertise in all medical disciplines served to further discredit, not only Malthusian theory, but also Hobbes' contention of a "poor, nasty, brutish and short" existence for Mankind. It is by no means a stretch to say that the people of the entire world owe a great debt of gratitude to both the American and Industrial Revolutions.

Given what we know now, more than 200 years following the publication of Malthus' *Essay on the Principle of Population*, one would think it would be easy to dismiss his predictions as quaint, outmoded, and more than a little pessimistic and nonsensical. After all, for all his research, for all the experience he gained in studying the poor classes in Great Britain, he was spectacularly wrong for a very simple reason: Malthus failed to take into account the one thing that would ultimately discredit his theory, the unlimited ability of Man's intellect to allow him to rise like a phoenix above his base and threadbare existence and better his meager station in life. One would also be tempted to think that because he had been shown to be so incredibly wrong, Malthus would be confined to the ranks of those who once believed that the Earth was flat or that the Sun revolved around it. But, one would be almost as wrong as Malthus himself turned out to be.

As it happened, his ideas never really died, and as the twentieth century unfolded, they received new life with the rise of the modern environmental movement that began in the late 1940s and is still with us today. Malthus' notions came back into fashion beginning with the publication of a number of books, most notably William Vogt's *Road to Survival* (1948), Rachel Carson's *Silent Spring* (1962), Paul Erlich's *The Population Bomb* (1968), and

Al Gore's *Earth in the Balance: Ecology and The Human Spirit* (1992). Each work relies heavily on Malthus' ideas, and each in its own way has been a driving force in the implementation of the U.N.'s *Agenda 21* program.

In *Road to Survival*, William Vogt revived the Malthusian contention that human population would, if not held in check, result in poverty, mass starvation, war, the spread of disease, and other forms of human suffering. He looked on in horror as life-saving technologies to fight disease and poverty were introduced in the developing world after the Second World War, especially in such places as China and India. In the introduction to Vogt's book, Bernard Baruch, one of the most influential financiers and government advisors of his time, laid out Vogt's thesis in clear and unmistakable terms.

"Because of the great abundance of the Earth's resources," Baruch wrote, "we have taken them for granted. But now, over most of the globe we are face to face with a serious depletion of 'resource capital.' More than one country is already bankrupt." [7] Baruch charged that mankind had "backed itself into an ecological trap" and was living on what he called "promissory notes" that were now "falling due" [8] and that payment of these "notes" could no longer be put off. In Baruch's view, and therefore Vogt's own, there was an option between "payment and utterly disastrous bankruptcy on a world scale," and that solution, he wrote, involved adapting to "the imperatives posed by the limited resources of the environment." [9] In his book, Vogt laid the blame for the world's ills on one thing above all else: the growth in population, most notably in the developing world. The main culprits in Vogt's view were, not surprisingly, rich countries in general and the United States of America in particular. Such nations, especially the U.S., were in Vogt's estimation simply too big, too rich, and consumed far too many of the world's limited resources while leaving too few of them over for the rest of the world to utilize.

In Vogt's estimation, the U.S. and other "rich" nations weren't doing the world any favors by subsidizing what he called the "unchecked spawning of inhabitants in poorer countries and they should refrain from doing so until they adopted a "rational population policy." [10] Since Vogt was a supporter of the discredited practice of eugenics, it was only natural that he would advocate a high mortality rate in the developing world, and he made no bones about it, writing that this was "one of the greatest national assets" a poor country could possess. [11] But, he was by no means finished, adding that disease-bearing insects like mosquitoes and tsetse flies should be considered as "blessings in disguise" and a "protector of important resources." As remedies to the population crisis, Vogt was in favor of political, economic, and educational approaches, but with this caveat: they would only succeed if "population control and conservation were included."

Vogt's book was widely criticized, but it was also widely read, reaching an estimated 20-30 million people, and it spawned a number of popular catchphrases like "population explosion," "P-bomb," and the most infamous of all, "population bomb." Indeed, it was this term that provided the title for Paul Erlich's book, which followed Vogt's own by 20 years. In fact, Erlich was a devoted follower of Vogt's and the irony of Vogt's death in 1968, the same year *The Population Bomb* first appeared in print, is almost too uncanny to ignore. We'll turn to Erlich's book shortly, but we would be remiss to leave Rachel Carson's *Silent Spring* out of the discussion at this point for a number of reasons, the first being that it was the second of the four books we are examining, second, because it became the top-selling work on the environment since Vogt's book, and third, because its effects are being felt today in ways that no one could have imagined when it came out in 1962.

Carson hit on the title *Silent Spring* to dramatize what she believed would be the deaths of millions of songbirds unless certain man-made chemicals such as DDT were banned from use. Her contention was that, because the use of this chemical, which was invented by German scientists in the late 1800s, had become so widespread, it was causing the shells of birds, especially songbirds, to soften and, thus, kill the chicks that were growing inside them. For the record, there had never been a reported problem of any kind related to the use of DDT when it was properly applied. In fact, not only was the chemical so effective in fighting and preventing the spread of Dutch Elm Disease, it was also a key component in eradicating malaria and sleeping sickness in the developing world.

DDT was also wildly successful in both theatres of combat in the Second World War, as Allied soldiers in Europe used it to delouse the survivors of Hitler's death camps, and American fighting men applied it in the jungles of the South Pacific to kill off and repel the pests that carried the diseases mentioned above. DDT was nothing short of a godsend, and its usage had such dramatically positive effects that malaria had all but been wiped out in the Third World by the time Carson's book was published. Unfortunately, as events unfolded, the final victory against this and other diseases was not to be. The publication of *Silent Spring* saw to that. Carson's hit piece on man-made chemicals, in this case DDT, ushered in the first environmental scare, and it would soon be followed by others.

Carson's book became a best-seller virtually overnight and caught the attention of many scientists and politicians in the process. The impact of *Silent Spring* was so great that it helped lead to the formation of the U.S. Environmental Protection Agency in 1970 during Richard Nixon's first term as president. It also marked the beginning of the end of the use of a whole panoply of man-made chemicals, beginning with DDT and continuing right on through to the present day. The EPA had been in existence for barely a year when its first Administrator, William Ruckelshaus, undertook a unilateral ban on DDT, in spite exhaustive research by the Agency's *own scientists* who analyzed both the chemical and the shells of the eggs in question.

Despite the fact that these researchers found no causal evidence *whatsoever* that linked DDT to the softening of these shells, Ruckelshaus acted alone and banned the substance. This decision, by one individual who was unelected and therefore unaccountable, would have wide-reaching and catastrophic effects across the world as millions of people who once had a fighting chance against terrible diseases like malaria, yellow fever, and sleeping sickness, now began to die by the millions. The DDT ban was not just confined to the U.S., where it had devastating effects on millions of elm trees in cities like Detroit, Michigan, it was soon banned worldwide by the United Nations. Because of the hysterical reaction to DDT by environmentalists in the U.S. and other countries, one of the most effective means of controlling devastating diseases ever to be invented was now unavailable to poor nations, who now had to frantically scramble to find a suitable replacement for the compound.

To this day, no one has been able to do so, and in the meantime, the nations and people of the Third World are condemned to needless and untold suffering and death on a daily basis. Thanks to the totally unnecessary ban on a life-saving chemical, William Vogt's beloved "resource protectors" now breed and fly freely about in the tropical climes of the Third World, spreading diseases that kill millions while the environmentally-correct denizens of the U.N. lecture Third World countries about the need to preserve "biodiversity" and threaten them with a cutoff of aid if they even so much as try to get DDT usage reinstated. Just what is their solution to the crisis? Use *mosquito netting!* How lovely, how very lovely, indeed. May God protect these unfortunates from their "protectors," because it looks as if no one else is willing to do so.

As mentioned earlier, DDT was the first but by no means the last target of what grew to become a new kind of war, a war declared by the political Left against the chemical industry. As the years and decades unfolded, virtually every kind of chemical compound, man-made or not, came under assault by radical environmental groups like Greenpeace, Environmental Defense Fund, Friends of the Earth, etc. The Left's hit list of chemical agents grew almost exponentially and came to include alar, asbestos, benzene, dioxin, PCB's, chlorofluorocarbons (cfc's), and chlorine, just to name a few. And, the growth of regulatory agencies like the EPA went hand-in-hand with this mindless, unnecessary, and dangerously misguided campaign. And the public fell for it hook, line, and sinker. There was even a new word introduced into the American lexicon to describe the blind hysteria, naked fear, and raw emotion that accompanied discussion of the role played by chemicals in our everyday lives—-*chemophobia*.

Thankfully, there were a few scientists who smelled a rat in all this and tried to inject a note of sanity into the discussion, for example, Dixie Lee Ray, a former head of the Nuclear Regulatory Commission. Mrs. Ray, who also served as Governor of the State of Washington, and her associate Lou Guzzo, who served as Managing Editor of the *Seattle Post-Intelligencer,* co-authored a pair of books in the early 1990s, *Trashing the Planet* (1990) and *Environmental Overkill: Whatever Happened to Common Sense?* (1993). In each, they confronted on a case-by-case basis the common misperceptions and outright lies spread by radical environmentalists regarding the chemical industry. But, probably more importantly, they also exposed the Left's hatred of Western industrial civilization and its attempts to destroy it, and warned that the chemical industry was to be but one of many vehicles it would use to achieve its goals.

The expertise in matters of sound science that Ray and Guzzo used to debunk the lies employed in the leftist attack on Western industrial civilization is plain to see, but they also exposed something far more ominous for the future of mankind...that much of its agenda laid at the heart of the *Agenda 21* population-control program. For example, Ray and Guzzo warned in Chapter 12 of *Trashing the Planet* that in order for the world body to achieve its ends, it would be necessary to establish a "green force" equivalent to the blue-helmeted U.N.'s military peacekeeping force." [12] This was the brainchild of, among others, UNESCO General Director Federico Mayor Zaragosa and former Tennessee Senator and, later on, Vice President Al Gore, with whom we shall deal a bit later on in this chapter.

In Chapter 6 of their follow-up book *Environmental Overkill,* Ray and Guzzo cite the shocking views on population of radical environmentalists like Charles Wurster, who served as the chief scientist for the Environmental

Defense Fund. Wurster defended the ban on DDT in testimony before a hearing in House Agricultural Committee in 1971. At the hearing, Dr. Wurster, who was on record as saying that there were already too many people and that banning DDT "is as good a way to get rid of them as any," went farther, a lot farther, in telling what must have been a lot of dumbfounded Congressmen that "it doesn't really make a lot of difference because the organophosphate acts locally and only kills farm workers, and most of them are Mexicans and Negroes." [13] As Ray and Guzzo wrote in what can only be described as a spectacular understatement, "There is no record of any media or public reaction to this shocking statement."

But, what is one to expect from a movement which originated in the ivory towers of Western European academe and later migrated to the shores of the United States to infect not one, but several, generations of impressionable minds? A movement that is so elitist and arrogant in its worldview that it identifies Man, the only creature on Earth with the capacity for rational thought and, therefore, the only creature on this planet possessed of the capability to change his surroundings for the better, as a viral cancer that somehow must, if not eliminated entirely, have his numbers drastically reduced to the point of extinction?

And what, moreover, are we to make of a movement which regards people of color in the developing world as a prime component of that threat, one which requires that they be placed at the head of the line in the plan to reduce human population levels to the point of virtual extinction? And, here we thought that those on the liberal/Progressive Left were so "concerned" about and "compassionate" toward the poor and disadvantaged among them. Well, after reading the sentiments of individuals like Dr. Wurster, wouldn't it be safe to say that with friends like these the poor people of color in the Third World don't need any enemies?

Let us turn now the third book in our examination of population control, *The Population Bomb,* by Paul Erlich. Published in 1968, *The Population Bomb* painted a bleak future for humanity, to say the least. Indeed, Erlich's premise was that humanity had so badly messed things up that it would be virtually impossible to correct the damage unless drastic measures of a draconian, almost totalitarian, nature were implemented on a massive scale to address the situation. And, even then, Erlich charged that it was too late to do anything to turn back from the abyss. As he wrote in the beginning of his book, "The battle to feed all of humanity is over," [14] and there was little that could be done to stave off the massive famines and worldwide starvation that would take place by the 1980s, 1990s and beyond. As Erlich wrote in his work, Mankind was fighting a losing battle against burgeoning populations, especially in the Third World. In fact, he warned that the crisis was much closer at hand than anyone had previously imagined. "In the 1970s," he wrote, "hundreds of millions of people will starve to death in spite of any crash programs embarked upon now. At this late date," he concluded, "nothing can prevent a substantial increase in the world death rate." [14]

As Malthus had done 170 years earlier, Erlich looked at the existing food supply and found it wanting. He believed, as had Malthus, that human population growth was at the heart of the world food shortage. His conclusions, however. left out a key fact of life in the mid-twentieth century that Malthus could not have imagined at the end of the eighteenth, the rise of tyrannical totalitarian regimes in Russia, China, Cuba, and other nations around the world. Dictators such as Stalin, Mao, and Castro imprisoned, starved, and killed tens of millions of their fellow citizens, an enormous number who had been farmers, and expropriated hundreds of millions of acres of farmland to be placed under government control. These "collective farms" proved to be a total disaster and transformed their countries (which in Russia's case had been known as the "breadbasket of Europe" because it exported so much grain to the rest of the continent) into economic basket cases.

Whereas entrepreneurial capitalism with its emphasis on individual liberty and private property rights was the backbone of the American economy and allowed farmers the freedom not only to grow their own food, but to sell their surplus crops on the open market, the planned economies of the new communist nations soon turned vast swaths of prime farmland into virtual deserts. It wasn't long before the "worker's paradises" of Stalin's Russia, Mao's China, and Castro's Cuba were incapable of meeting even the basic nutritional requirements of their own people.

Consequently, it wasn't long before these countries and others that suffered under the yoke of communism found it necessary to reach out to other nations for help in staving off the very thing that Erlich was predicting in his book. To this day, especially in the Third World, repressive, tyrannical, and even murderous regimes in nations like Robert Mugabe's Zimbabwe have killed more people than all the other famines that have occurred through natural causes. But Paul Erlich seems completely tone-deaf to this simple fact. Indeed, in his book he calls for draconian, oppressive, and even murderous measures to solve the world's perceived population "crisis."

And, just what are some of these measures? Well, for one, Erlich proposes adding what he calls "temporary sterilants" to the world's food and water supplies to curb the numbers of people who are being born. [15] He also suggests imposing additional taxes on families who bear more children, as well as luxury taxes on childcare products. Erlich also calls for reduced taxes on men who agree to undergo permanent sterilization before having two children, and he floats the idea of a new federal cabinet agency, to be called the Department of Population and the Environment. According to Erlich, this department would have the power to, as he puts it, "take whatever steps are necessary to establish a reasonable population level in the United States and put an end to the steady deterioration of our environment." [16]

To Erlich, this new agency would have additional responsibilities like supporting research into population control, which would be accomplished through better birth control measures, mass sterilization techniques, and allowing parents to choose the sex of their pending bundles of joy. Erlich bases his reasoning on the notion that people will keep on having children until a male is born; therefore, if they could choose a boy, this would reduce the birth rate. He doesn't say what should happen if a family keeps on having daughters, but there is currently one country, China, that has faithfully observed Erlich's remedy in this regard with its "one child" abortion policy. As we have seen where this policy is concerned, it is almost always the female child that winds up paying the price

Erlich does not stop there. Not surprisingly, he calls for legislation legalizing abortion (which did, indeed, come to pass with *Roe vs. Wade* in 1973, five years after the release of *The Population Bomb*). Sex education programs should also be expanded, and have been, as we have seen in the intervening years, even to include those children in preschool. And, as we have also seen in the quote from his colleague John C. Holdren in their 1977 book *Ecoscience,* even "coerced abortion would be permissible under the existing Constitution if the population crisis became sufficiently severe to endanger the society."

Some of the other "solutions" Erlich proposes include a system of "triage" that would divide the world into groups of nations based on their ability to feed themselves. Under this system, proposed by William and Paul Paddock, those countries that could be seen as being able to achieve self-sufficiency in food production in the future would continue to receive such aid. To those that could not, however, the answer was simple—-their aid would be cut off, or more simply put, " Good luck; you'll need it!"

So much for the "compassion" of Western liberal elites for their fellow human beings, especially those in developing nations like China, India, and Zimbabwe. As noted earlier, what else can one expect when dealing with individuals such as Rachel Carson, William Vogt, and Paul Erlich? It should come as no surprise that *The Population Bomb* sold over two million copies, but what is curious is that Erlich called for his "remedies" to the perceived crisis to be implemented *outside* of the existing United Nations framework, reasoning that it would be necessary to be selective where targeted countries and regions were concerned. In one interesting passage, for instance, he voices support for the Indian government's mandatory sterilization program for men with three or more children: "When he (Indian Prime Minister Sripati Chandrasekhar) suggested sterilizing all Indian males with three or more children, we should have applied more pressure on the Indian government to go ahead with the plan." He wrote, "We should have volunteered logistical support in the form of helicopters, vehicles and surgical instruments. We should have sent doctors to aid in the program by setting up centers for training paramedical personnel to do vasectomies." [17]

If this seems rather extreme, brace yourself. Erlich wasn't finished, not by a long shot. In the same passage he revealed his Malthusian colors for all to see (or, in this case, for all to read), as well as his holier-than-thou, dismissive attitude toward anyone who might suggest that such a scheme smacked of Margaret Sanger, Lothrop Stoddard, or Adolph Hitler: "Coercion?" he asked almost rhetorically. "Perhaps. But coercion in a good cause. I am sometimes astounded by the attitudes of Americans who are horrified at the prospect of our government insisting on population control as the price of food aid."

So, not only was Erich a full-blown elitist who thinks he knows what's best for the rest of us, he also displayed another trait of those who sit in the ivory towers of academe—-an incredible level of insensitivity toward the plight of those for whom they claim to be so concerned. How typical. He ends this part of his book with the following demand: "We must be relentless in pushing for population control around the world." [18] While he did acknowledge that his predictions might be wrong (which, as it turned out, they were in virtually every case), he assured his readers that even then the world would be a far better place if only it followed his course of action. [19]

This attitude, so typical of the true believer, is what is so dangerous when dealing with the liberal/Progressive Left. Those who come from that perspective have always been with us, and we have seen what happens when they accrue even the slightest amount of political power. They know what is best for the rest of society, even when real-world experience proves them to be disastrously wrong, and they will stop at nothing to gain and consolidate even more power over the lives of individual human beings, no matter what the cost to our economy or society. A prime example of this narcissistic pursuit of power would be the furor that arose from the environmental left in the late 1990s over the supposed "hole" in the ozone layer caused by, you guessed it, *Man*. Or to put it more accurately, over Man's attempts to change his environment for the better.

The ozone-depletion scare of the late 1990s illustrated in bold and unmistakable terms just what can happen when raw emotion, half-truths, and outright lies combine with a blatantly leftist political agenda to supplant sound scientific analysis. In this case, the manufactured "crisis" involved the supposed destruction of the earth's ozone layer, which protects us against harmful effects of a particular type of ultraviolet radiation that is generated every day by the sun. According to environmentalists, our reliance on the chlorofluorocarbons (cfc's) in our air-conditioners, freezers, and refrigeration units was responsible for destroying the naturally-occurring protective ozone layer overhead and that we all would someday die from various forms of cancer unless something was done immediately to address this "crisis."

Every day it seemed that some "expert" could be seen on television, heard on radio, or quoted in the newspapers that doomsday was just around the corner, unless we banned the manufacture and sale of cfc's and the equipment in which they were used. Just as was the case with the ban on DDT two decades earlier, these "experts," who often had little if any training in any of the appropriate scientific disciplines, got the majority of print and face time in the media with virtually no countervailing views from those who actually studied the problem, that is the scientists themselves.

No one asked, for example, how cfc's, which had only been in use since the mid-1950s, could do so much damage to something that had been in existence for hundreds of millions, if not billions of years. Nor did anyone ask the environmentalists just how it was that a compound whose molecules were several times heavier that the air molecules surrounding it could be propelled several miles up into the atmosphere by aerosol spray cans to "destroy" the ozone layer. But these and other common-sense questions were not supposed to be asked because they would actually put the onus on those making the accusations to prove their case.

In fact, the environmentalists *were* confronted with evidence to the contrary, a lot of it. Sound scientific analysis showed, for example, that what was being decried as a "hole" in the ozone layer that was created by Man's use of refrigerants was actually a thinning that occurred naturally and had nothing at all to do with Freon usage ("Freon" being the trade name by which the public identified these compounds). Furthermore, such thinning was shown to be most visible in the polar regions, specifically in Antarctica, where less sunlight would reach the earth's surface. Additionally, legitimate scientists have known for years that more atmospheric ozone is destroyed in one volcanic eruption than that which is supposedly destroyed by all the aerosol cans, car and home air conditioning units, freezers, and refrigerators that were ever built or used by Man. But none of that mattered to radical environmentalists like NASA Administrator James Hansen, former Vice President Albert Gore, Jr., or the U.N.'s IPCC (Intergovernmental Panel on Climate Change). They wanted nothing to do with anything that contradicted their well-crafted Chicken Little "sky is falling" scenario, such as the RAND corporation's 1987-88 Annual Report, which began with this cautionary note: "The extent of ozone depletion and the severity of the consequences of emission levels are extremely uncertain." [20]

"Projections of future depletion are based on complex simulation models that have not been reconciled with the limited available measurements," the RAND report went on. "Because of the pervasive uncertainty about the likely extent of future ozone depletion (i.e., thinning, not the apocalyptic "hole" in the ozone layer that had the alarmists all worked up), its relationship to the quantity of potential ozone depleters emitted, its effect on the biosphere, and the appropriate valuation of these consequences, *it is not currently possible* to choose the level of emission-limiting regulations that will maximize welfare by optimally balancing costs of environmental damage against those of emission control (author's emphasis added). Policymakers must act in the face of this uncertainty." [21]

Let us pause for a moment and let this sink in. As far back as 1988, we were being warned not to rely on computer models that did not reflect what was going on in the real world because they were not reliable. And, they were not reliable because scientists simply did not have enough information at the time to render an objective judgment about what means to employ to address a perceived environmental crisis. Moreover, we were being told that we would have to radically alter our way of life to solve a problem about which we were unclear as to its actual causes or its long-term ramifications.

Was the ozone "hole" being caused by our reliance on cfc's in aerosol cans, air conditioners, and refrigeration units, or was it being brought about by factors over which we had no control, such as natural phenomena like volcanic eruptions on Earth or sunspot activity 93 million miles away? We simply did not know enough at the time, although more recent research has indicated that ozone depletion occurs far more because of the latter. However, that did not matter to the radical environmentalists at Greenpeace, Friends of the Earth, the Sierra Club, or the Environmental Defense Fund.

Nor did it matter to them that the ozone "hole" had virtually disappeared on its own in the two decades since the publication of the RAND report. No, what mattered to them (and what still matters to them today) is one thing, and one thing only—*control,* control over the lives of billions of human beings who are mired in grinding poverty and who can only emerge from that state through the freedom to better their lives that capitalism offers them. Capitalism is the engine of upward mobility, the one economic and political system that offers any hope for a better life to those in the developing world. It is critically important to remember that the green agenda is ultimately one of population control, one which condemns untold billions to the slavery of poverty, desperation, hopelessness, and despair, and it is population control that lies at the heart of the U.N.'s *Agenda 21.*

We see this insidious scheme at work in virtually every aspect of the environmental debate the world over, with the same disastrous consequences. We saw it in the mindless headlong rush to ban the use of DDT, a decision that has killed millions of people in the Third World who would otherwise not have died from malaria. We saw it in the attack on numerous industries such as logging, mining, and manufacturing, an all-out assault that has made life more difficult for consumers in terms of lower living standards, especially for the poor. We saw it in the increased mileage standards for cars and trucks that forced auto companies to build these vehicles lighter and less crashworthy, thereby killing tens of thousands of motorists on the world's highways as a result.

We are also, at this very moment, witnessing *Agenda 21* at work in the stampede to reduce the amount of carbon dioxide in the Earth's atmosphere. Co2 is a naturally-occurring trace element without which life as we know it would be impossible. It is a part of what is known as photosynthesis, or the process by which oxygen is produced, and a process which has been in existence for billions of years. Humans and animals exhale carbon dioxide as part of their respiratory cycle. Plants absorb this compound and produce the oxygen which the former inhale, continuing the process. Pretty simple, isn't it? Didn't we learn this way back in elementary school? Not so fast, say the Greens. As always, their default position is that there are too many of us, and they never tire of telling us that.

They tell us that because there are too many people, there is too much Co2 going into the atmosphere. Worse, they lecture us, because industry requires the use of "fossil fuels" such as coal, oil and natural gas, burning these fuels to produce inexpensive, reliable energy releases carbon dioxide into the air, thus, raising the Earth's temperature and thereby creating a runaway "greenhouse effect" that threatens to overheat the planet. The Greens point feverishly to the increased incidence of floods, droughts, blizzards, hurricanes, and any other unusual changes in what they perceive to be the planet's ideal climate as proof that environmental Armageddon is just around the corner, and, they scold us, it is all due to the burgeoning number of people who are doing nothing more than going about their daily lives, breathing the air, and simply working to feed their families.

They tell us that we must "do something" to reverse this disastrous level of "climate change" before it is "too late to turn back the clock." We must, according to the Greens, immediately embark on a "wrenching transformation" of our way of life lest we all burn to death in an inferno of our own making that is due to our incredible short-sightedness. These neo-Malthusians lecture us on our selfishness, proposing cures that are worse than the supposed "disease" they want to cure. We must cut back on our use of "fossil fuels" that are inexpensive and readily abundant in favor of exotic, intermittent, and wildly expensive forms of "green" energy such as wind and solar power, but they fail to ask what happens when the sun goes down and the wind stops blowing.

They also are dead set against the one form of "green" energy that offers a way out, nuclear power. If they gave any thought to the fact that solar power is actually nuclear (or fusion) power, one might be tempted to think that they would support that approach. But one would be wrong now, wouldn't one? Sadly, though, logic is not in the purview of the Green environmental left. No, as at least one environmentalist has declared, where the lack of scientific certitude is concerned, it is necessary to offer up "scary scenarios" to get people to surrender their freedom to pursue their happiness in favor of some amorphous "greater good."

This brings us to former Tennessee Senator and later U.S. Vice President Al Gore and the final book in our discussion, *Earth in the Balance: Ecology and the Human Spirit.* Gore first published his treatise on the environment in1992, in the wake of the Rio Earth Summit, which was attended by Bill Clinton's predecessor in the Oval Office, George H.W. Bush. Early on in his book, Gore excoriated Bush for not rushing to judgment regarding the question of "global warming," referring to a White House memo that was leaked to the press on the eve of Earth Day in 1990.

"The memo," Gore wrote in Chapter 2 of the book, "advised that instead of directly arguing that there is no problem, 'a better approach is to raise the many uncertainties'" about Man's role in the perceived crisis. "So much," Gore lamented, "for the Bush promise to confront the greenhouse effect with the White House effect." [22] And just what "White House effect" on the "global warming" crisis, or "climate change" crisis, or whatever the next crisis *du jour* that the former Vice President and his allies in the population control movement want?

Remember that radical environmentalism is, above all else, about acquiring and wielding the heavy hand of state power over every decision that we make in our day-to-day lives. This is the kind of "White House effect" that Gore seeks. What kind of food shall we eat? How shall we power our homes and businesses? What kind of light bulbs are we going to use? How much water will we be permitted to use? How are we going to keep cool in summer and warm in winter? How will we treat and cure our illnesses? And ultimately, how many children are we going to allow to be brought into the world?

However, we are not to concern ourselves with such questions, because in the eyes of Al Gore, Gro Harlem Bruntland, Maurice Strong, and their allies in the United Nations, the European Union, and other supranational bodies, we are too stupid or unsophisticated to take care of our own problems. Therefore, the international power elites shall decide *for* us. *Earth in the Balance* seeks to create an atmosphere of fear around a whole host of environmental issues from ozone depletion, asbestos, carbon dioxide emissions, and the like, and it proposes a corresponding number of disastrous government policies that will kill the very kind of economic growth the developing world needs to escape its miserable lot in life in order to attain some unrealistic ideal of nature in its "pristine" state. Never mind that that state never really existed at all, except in the minds of the William Vogts, the Rachel Carsons, the Paul Erlichs, and Al Gores of the world and their ilk.

Gore warns in his book that the supposed "crisis" surrounding the environment is far more serious than "any military foe we are ever again likely to confront." Now that's a pretty tall order, considering that we had to defeat not only the Kaiser in World War I, but the Italian fascists, the German Nazis, and the Japanese militarists in World War II. Not only that, but we also had to fight a long and costly Cold War against the Soviets bloc as well as the threat of devout Muslim terrorism in the first two decades of the twenty-first century. But, he believes, we can defeat this enemy as well, if only we apply the solutions he prescribes: carbon taxes, more onerous regulations on business and industry, mandates on new forms of transportation such as electric vehicles, and a firm reliance on exotic and unreliable forms of energy such as wind and solar power. All of this is in addition to another "solution" that Gore prescribes to address the burgeoning world population—-abortion.

Although it only takes up a handful of pages in his book, abortion is a central theme of Chapter 15 of *Earth in the Balance*, which is titled, fittingly enough, "A Global Marshall Plan." Gore offers a 3-pronged approach by which the population should be brought into balance, including point number 3, which reads: "Ensure that birth-control devices are made ubiquitously available along with culturally appropriate instruction." [23]

The arrogance of such a statement is breathtaking. Since developing nations by definition have a high birth rate, they must be shown the error of their ways and get with Gore's program. And, the people that will carry this off are none other than our good friends at the United Nations, aided, of course, by our equally "compassionate" friends at the UN Population Fund, the International Planned Parenthood Federation, and other like-minded entities. It is interesting to note that Gore calls on scientists to step up "research into improved and more easily accepted contraception techniques." [24] Hmm. Could Gore just possibly be referring to Ru486, the so-called "morning after" pill? After all, it would seem that something like that is just what the doctor ordered.

Gore goes on to ridicule those who hold innocent unborn life sacred, painting them as an extremist fringe group that is out of touch with the realities of the modern world. He charges that they are holding the Republican Party hostage in their mindless opposition to birth control. What he does not acknowledge is that while most accept that the Supreme Court ruled long ago that women have a right to contraceptive devices, most abortions that are performed in the United States and around the world are, indeed, done as a means of birth control. And, we have already seen the Guttmacher Institute's own data that show that only two percent of all abortions are performed because of rape or incest.

However, Gore isn't finished. He belittles those who oppose U.S. taxpayer funding of abortion in other countries, the aforementioned "Mexico

City" Policy, which President Clinton repealed as one of his first acts as Chief Executive. The following comment shows just how far Gore is willing to go to marginalize those who stand for life: "While they try to show how our foreign aid might be used for abortions, in reality they are keeping the peace in their own political family by opposing birth control." [25]

So, to Gore, it is just so simple: those Neanderthal Christian Bible-thumpers are the fly in the ointment that is preventing women from experiencing full "reproductive freedom." He also attacks the first President Bush ("Bush 41") by accusing him of cowardice in failing to rein in this handful of "anti-choice" zealots by citing a portion Bush wrote of the foreword to a book on the population "crisis" that was published in 1973. Gore had praised him for the "many eloquent speeches he gave on the need for rigorous U.S. leadership in world family planning programs" as President Nixon's U.N. Ambassador. Somewhere between then and his time as president, Bush "fell off the wagon," so to speak, to the point that Gore cluck-clucks about the "irony" of Bush's changed stance on abortion. "My own first awareness of birth control as a public policy issue came with a jolt in 1950 when my father was running for the Senate in Connecticut," Bush is quoted as writing. "Drew Pearson, on the Sunday before Election Day, 'revealed' that my father was involved with Planned Parenthood," Bush continued before concluding, "My father lost that election by a few hundred out of close to a million votes. Many political observers felt a sufficient number of voters were swayed by his alleged contacts with the birth-controllers to cost him the election." [26] That may or may not be true, as Gore does not reveal precisely what the elder Bush himself thought might have cost him those votes.

After all, there were certainly other issues to concern the voters in Connecticut, like the Korean War, the state of the economy, and so on, and so forth. But, if what George H.W. Bush wrote is correct, if his father's involvement with the group that Margaret Sanger founded to exterminate an entire race of human beings is accurate, the younger Bush learned his lesson and learned it well: always stand for life. The voters of Connecticut did the nation a tremendous favor in denying a Senate seat to someone who would throw in with a group of racial eugenicists led by a woman who believed that black Americans were no more than "human weeds in need of eradication."

And, in the end, if his father's defeat caused the younger Bush to take heed and alter his position on abortion, who is Al Gore to complain? After all, the former Tennessee Senator and two-term Vice President was outspokenly pro-life at one time, wasn't he? But he, like Ted Kennedy and Jesse

Jackson before him, not only became pro-abortion, Gore became *extremely* pro-abortion, so extreme, in fact, as to champion it at any time, any place, and for any reason. Moreover, Gore even came to embrace the barbaric practice of late-term or "partial birth" abortion. It is interesting, indeed, to note that while Gore attacked the 41st president for caving in to the pro-life movement to get their votes, Gore himself seems to have experienced no such qualms about the blatantly cynical political nature of his own conversion to the "pro-choice" side.

To get a better idea of just how hypocritical the man is, let us examine a few of the things Mr. Gore had to say concerning abortion during his time in the U.S. Congress from 1977-1985. On June 26, 1984, Congressman Gore voted to support an amendment that former Representative Mark Siljander (R-MI) proposed to the Civil Rights Act of 1964. The amendment read, rather simply and straightforward in fact, that "for purposes of this Act, the term 'person' shall include unborn children from the moment of conception." [27] The recorded vote to amend read 219 against, 186 in favor. One of those voting "yes" was, indeed, Al Gore, Jr., Congressman from Tennessee.

Less than a week later, in a letter to one of his constituents, Gore sought to burnish his pro-life credentials when he wrote the following: "It is my deep personal conviction that abortion is wrong. It is my hope that someday we will see the outrageously large number of abortions drop sharply." Gore elaborated, "Let me assure you that innocent human life must be protected." He concluded by voicing his belief, "in my opinion, it is wrong to spend federal funds for what is arguably the taking of a human life." [28]

These and other statements on behalf of the unborn helped Gore earn an 84% approval rating from the leading national pro-life organizations, making him one of the leading champions for the rights of the unborn in the U.S. House. For this reason alone, it is mind-numbing that someone who was at one time so passionate about this issue, not only turned his back so completely on those who needed him the most, he went on, less than a decade later, to write a book in which he endorsed worldwide access to abortion as an indispensable tool to fight what he claimed was a population crisis of immense proportions. However, his turnaround did not go unnoticed, as he was called out on it in the run up to the 2000 Presidential election. In fact, it came back to bite him, and bite him hard.

Gore's comeuppance came in the aftermath of a Democrat debate in New Hampshire that pitted him against former Missouri Congressman Richard Gephardt. Several times during the event, Gore emphatically stated that he had always supported both the right of a woman to undergo an abortion and the landmark 1973 *Roe vs. Wade* decision. This was in direct contradiction to his vote to amend the 1964 Civil Rights Act to define life as occurring at the moment of conception. In fact, as far back as 1988, Gore had begun to turn against his pro-life position, one that went back as far as, his first year in the House, 1977. The future VP had already begun to backtrack almost as soon as he had cast his "yes" vote for Rep. Siljander's measure, and in his appearance on NBC's *Meet the Press* on February 21, 1988, he denied that he had cast such a vote. Evidently, Gore forgot the reassurances to which he had taken such great pains to go in the now infamous letter he had written to his constituent in July of '84. One of Gore's advisors explained his boss's strategy this way in an interview with *U.S. News and World Report* on March 7, 1998: "Since there's a record on that vote, we only have one choice. In effect, what we have to do is deny, deny, deny." [29]

So it was that Albert A. Gore, Jr., Vice President of the United States, had now completely abandoned a position that he had held since his first day in the U.S. House of Representatives. He had repudiated the principled stand he had taken on the sanctity of unborn human life, a position he had held so proudly that he even took the time to write a letter to National Right to Life supporting the Hyde Amendment. But by the time he had written *Earth in the Balance*, all that had gone by the wayside. He was now fully and unequivocally in favor of a woman's "right to choose," a position he holds to this day, and a position which is a key component of *Agenda 21*. However, he was caught red-handed by a female caller to a local talk show in the Granite State following his now infamous denial at that 1999 Democrat debate. The woman, who had watched the event, challenged Gore on his denial, telling him, "I understand if you've changed your position during your career. I'm just having a hard...I don't know how I can support your candidacy if you're dishonest about such an important issue and especially on national television." [30] Although Gore did his best to placate the caller, it was clear for all to see just how bald-faced a liar the Vice President turned out to be. Whether his lie cost him any votes among pro-life Democrats is, of course, a matter of conjecture, but it certainly could not have helped him in his ill-fated bid for the White House.

Gore's lies, as we have seen, were not confined just to the abortion debate. Far from it, in fact. *Earth in the Balance* is rife with half-truths and distortions of fact, all designed to frighten people into handing over their freedom and individual sovereignty to an all-encompassing international bureaucracy operating on the banks of the East River in New York City, and the UN will get plenty of help in carrying out its agenda in the persons of non-governmental organizations like the Sierra Club for the environment and the International Planned Parenthood Federation to oversee population control. These entities are the ones who will assist the Al Gores of the world in seeing that their program is fully implemented, and woe to anyone who stands in their way.

Never mind that in the decades since his book was published, Gore's "solutions" have proven to be nowhere near the godsend he had promised they would be. Rather, they have retarded economic growth, both here and abroad. They have stifled innovation and recklessly endangered both life and limb, from the increase in highway deaths from ridiculous mileage requirements to the demise of tens of millions in the Third World from discontinued use of life-saving chemicals such as DDT. But none of that matters, none at all.

Nor, seemingly, does it matter today, more than 20 years since *Earth in the Balance* first appeared in print. It would seem that the former Vice President has been rather busy pushing his "climate change" agenda to any audience that will listen, audiences it seems that are made up of grade school and college students, environmental advocates, and other true believers. But what happened to "global warming?" Wasn't the earth on the verge of the environmental "tipping point" about which we were all being warned in the direst of terms, a point beyond which we would not be able to turn back? Well, in a word, no.

You see, in the two decades since Gore first embarked on his crusade to "save the planet," a few things happened that called his whole thesis into serious question. We were reminded, for example, that the climate does change on its own and always has, in spite of anything we do or do not do. We learned more about such things that influence climate as sunspot activity, cloud formation, and volcanic activity. What we have discovered or learned all over again, thanks to the work of scientists like Dixie Lee Ray and climate scientists like Dr. Roy Spencer at the University of Alabama at Huntsville, is the simple fact that the earth has undergone thousands of climatic cycles in its history that have had *nothing whatsoever* to do with human activity, and this will continue to be the case well after Mankind's time on earth is long over.

We also found out that the computer models on which the whole "climate change' mantra was based were terribly flawed, and were nowhere nearly as accurate as they were advertised to be. They were often constructed to leave out critical data such as an entire period in the earth's history in which an ice age was followed by a period of far more moderate temperatures (i.e., the medieval warm period that followed the last great Ice Age in the early AD 1000s). This reflected a blatant attempt by Dr. Michael Mann at Penn State University, NASA Administrator James Hansen, and Gore himself to "cook the books" as it were, and pin the blame for "global climate change" on the human race.

We also learned a few things about Gore himself. We learned, for example, that while he was out preaching his "climate change' gospel (for environmentalism is a religion, make no mistake), not only had he profited handsomely from his activities since leaving office in 2001, he had constructed a 15,000 square-foot home in suburban Nashville that guzzled immense amounts of carbon-based fossil fuels to power this monument that he had built to himself...all the while lecturing the common man that he was using too many of them himself to try to attain even a fraction of the same level of creature comforts that the 'High Priest of the Environment' himself was enjoying. It also should be noted that Gore's pleasure palace went up across the road from where a number of poor families were living. When queried by the media about this, he tried to weasel his way out of this embarrassing situation by pointing out how "green" some parts of his home actually were, but it was already too late to avoid being shown up for the hypocrite he really was.

This public relations disaster was bad enough for the former VP, but it was nothing compared to the outcry when people learned of his rank hypocrisy in trotting around the globe on Gulf Stream jets that burned thousands of gallons of aviation fuel to spread the alarm about human-caused (anthropogenic) "global climate change." But not to worry, Gore told us, he was using the system of "carbon credits" that he helped create, the very same one that made him a multimillionaire, to offset his profligate use of fossil fuels, the very ones that he lectured and condemned the rest of us for using to go to the store, take the kids to school or maybe go on vacation. But Gore truly saved his worst for last with the release of his book and the documentary it spawned, *An Inconvenient Truth.*

Published in 2006, *An Inconvenient Truth* was premised on the notion that human activity was contributing to a dangerous increase in temperatures around the world that, unless curtailed drastically, would result in environmental catastrophe on a scale of unprecedented magnitude. According to Gore's book, human beings were doing immense harm to the ecology that would result in everything from the increased severity of storms, droughts, forest fires, and famines to a dangerous rise in sea levels, drowning polar bears, and quite possibly the onset of a new ice age. Pretty bad, right? Wrong, wrong, *wrong*!

An Inconvenient Truth was, to put it mildly, a fatally flawed exercise in alarmism on a massive scale. It was so bad that once one got past the use of fear and emotion to make its case, it was obvious to even a casual observer that Gore's work could not stand up to even the most rudimentary type of scientific scrutiny. As it turned out, sound science really had little, if any, place in either the book or the documentary that was shown in theaters around the world four years later. Despite Gore's claims that "climate change" was caused by Man's activities and that it was now "settled science," the fact remains that climate is still a very tricky proposition, whether influenced by humans going about their daily lives or through other causes over which people have no control. Scientists from all disciplines related to this issue are actually nowhere near agreeing on the precise causes of change in the earth's climate, nor are they in agreement as to what the planet's ideal climate should be. Despite Gore's claim of overwhelming "consensus" on the part of the world's scientists that "climate change" is real and is caused by Man, the issue is anything but "settled."

Nevertheless, this did not stop Gore from releasing a book and film that were so far off base in their claims that any scientists who were truly worthy of the title would likely sue the High Priest of the Environment for slandering their profession (and would probably win such a lawsuit). Far from it! Gore's book sold millions of copies, making him extremely wealthy in the process, and his film played in thousands of movie houses around the world, making him even more so. The documentary version of Gore's book was hyped almost to the point of hysteria, and it ultimately won him an Academy Award. Largely due to this, although it was not the sole reason, *An Inconvenient Truth* began to be shown in high school science classes both in the U.S. and abroad. In some cases, parents were "encouraged" to view the documentary with their children, the alternative being that the students might not receive a passing grade if Mom and Dad didn't show up. Gore's book and documentary proved to be just what the population control advocates running *Agenda 21* had always craved in their push for a massive power grab on a worldwide scale.

With so much at stake, it would have been reasonable to presume that all concerned parties would have been consulted for their input on such an important issue. After all, didn't Gore write in *Earth in the Balance* that the environment must be "the central organizing principle of civilization?" Lest the reader forget, he also stated that things were so bad that "a wrenching transformation of society" was necessary to save us all. Therefore, common sense should have dictated that we examine things from every possible angle before embarking on such a radical course. But, that is the *last* thing that Gore or any of his allies on the environmental Left had in mind. Otherwise, he would never have said, either in print or at any of his public appearances, that "the debate is over" surrounding the question of climate change. Neither would he have stated with so much confidence that "the science is settled."

But scientists and climatologists who stand in direct opposition to Gore's position do so not because they are motivated by any sort of political agenda or because they are attempting to line their pockets.

Rather, it is because they are holding true to the principle that science is, above all, a search for the truth, and that is something Gore and his fellow Greens cannot tolerate. The truth is that, thanks to people like Dr. Spencer, meteorologist Joe Bastardi at AccuWeather, and tens of thousands of other scientists, meteorologists, and climatologists around the world, the science is anything but "settled." But that matters not to the environmental Left. They dismiss those who disagree with them as "climate deniers," and place them in the same category as those who believe that the Holocaust never took place.

Some, like Gore's mentor James Hansen, have even called for Nuremburg-style trials to silence and even imprison those who dare to voice any doubts about "man-made" climate change. Moreover, it is those who are engaged in such massive deception and naked fraud about the issue who are really the ones who should be investigated, put on trial, and jailed. For example, in October 2007 the UK High Court ruled against the British government's requirement that *An Inconvenient Truth* be shown to the country's secondary school students as fact. A lawsuit was brought by the father of two school-age students who was extremely concerned that the government was indoctrinating, not educating his children. The Court examined the claims made in the documentary and concluded that it contained at least nine myths ranging from rising sea levels of at least 6 meters (or nearly 20 feet) over the next three decades to the unprecedented loss of ice in the Arctic Ocean during the summer months, all due to the supposed "unprecedented" increase in atmospheric carbon dioxide levels that resulted from human activity. Based on this, the Court ruled that the documentary could not be shown unless it was accompanied by the views of those who dissented on the issue.

However, it was another source, the Science and Public Policy Institute, that found more than *two dozen* additional myths and distortions of fact that were contained in Gore's documentary. SPPI Director Lord Christopher Monckton of Brenchley exhaustively examined the claims made by the former Vice President and found them wanting, to say the least. For example, error number 8, "polar bear dying," is quite illustrative of the way Gore uses emotion and half-truths to flimflam and bamboozle a gullible and unsuspecting public into swallowing the anthropogenic "climate change" sham hook, line, and sinker.

Writes Monckton, "Gore says a scientific study shows that polar bears are being killed swimming long distances to find ice that has melted away because of 'global warming.' They are not." He cites a study conducted in 2005 that found that only four bears had drowned "in an exceptional storm, with high winds and waves in the Beaufort Sea." The SPPI Director points out how the amount of ice in the Beaufort Sea had *increased* over a period of 30 years prior to the study. He then points out how the World Wide Fund for Nature has demonstrated that the number of bears, which are warm-blooded, has actually increased where the temperature has risen and gone down where the temperature has fallen, not died out, which would only seem to make sense. Not that Gore would resort to *that* tactic, mind you.

Monckton points out that the polar bear evolved from the brown bear roughly two hundred thousand years ago, and that the subspecies survived the last interglacial period when temperatures were a full five degrees Celsius warmer than they are today "and there was probably no Arctic Ice Cap at all." Monckton concludes, "The real threat to polar bears is not 'global warming' but hunting." He points out how in 1940 there were a mere 5,000 of these animals around the world, but thanks to controlled hunting the number has increased five-fold, to 25,000. [31]

Monckton relates how Gore's spokeswoman and "environment advisor" Kalee Kreider attempted to counter these points by claiming that the level of sea ice "was the lowest ever measured for minimum extent in 2007." But, he added, "She does not say that the measurements, which are done by satellite, go back only 29 years. She does not say that the North-West Passage, a good proxy for Arctic sea-ice extent, was open to shipping in 1945, or that Norwegian explorer Amundsen passed through in a sailing ship in 1903."

Now, one should reasonably expect that someone who is making such ominous and catastrophic claims as Mr. Gore is doing in his film would at least take some time to research his subject carefully before embarking on producing a film like *An Inconvenient Truth*. Or, at the very least that if he could not he would surround himself with people who would look at the subject in some sort of objective fashion. But in Gore's case, one would be wrong, very wrong, indeed. *An Inconvenient Truth* does not even come close to telling the story in truthful way, and that is a tragedy. Gore and his minions never tire of telling the rest of us that we are "killing the planet" through all kinds of activities, even those as benign and innocuous as the simple act of taking a normal breath. The urge to wield power and control over the masses is so strong that they feel entitled to employ any means they deem necessary to further their anti-capitalist, anti-industrial and, yes, anti-human agenda. They are a glaring example of C.S. Lewis' warning that of all the tyrannies that are inflicted on a people, the most insidious is that which is imposed on them for their own good. They also illustrate clearly and unmistakably the great objectivist philosopher Ayn Rand's admonition that those who follow them are "the ones in need of a *fuhrer*." Although the example we have cited is probably the most glaring, one may find a listing of 35 errors in Gore's film at www.scienceandpublicpolicy.org/monckton/goreerrors.

It was only a matter of time before another scandal broke surrounding the issue of man-made "climate change." In November of 2009, it came to light that the Climate Research Unit at England's East Anglia University had deliberately covered up the concerns of legitimate scientists who deviated from the conventional wisdom and had, at the behest of the CRU's Director Dr. Phil Jones, embarked on a deliberate campaign to smear and destroy anyone who had expressed concerns that the entire story was not being told. Through numerous emails Dr. Jones, who had been at East Anglia for 20 years, was himself found to have taken the lead in this campaign to marginalize those who honestly believe that "global warming" and its metamorphosis into "climate change" was wildly exaggerated at the least and a massive fraud at the very worst.

The release of hacked emails exposing the scandal raised a firestorm of outrage on both sides of the Atlantic. In an article that appeared in *The London Daily Telegraph*, Christopher Booker pointed out that the authors were "not just any old bunch of academics. Their importance cannot be overestimated. What we are looking at here is a small group of scientists who have for years been more influential in driving the worldwide alarm over global warming than any others, not least through the role they play at the heart of the U.N.'s Intergovernmental Panel on Climate Change." [32] Booker pointed out that not only had Dr. Jones been exposed, but also that scientists in the U.S. were now under suspicion, as well, including Dr. Mann at Penn State and Gavin Schmidt, who, Booker noted, was the "right-hand man to Al Gore's ally, Dr. James Hansen." [33]

The 'Climategate' scandal eventually resulted in Jones' resignation, but to date very few, if any, of the other participants in this whole sorry affair have seen fit to follow suit. Al Gore continues to make his millions by lying through his teeth about the factors that influence climate change. He continues to dupe gullible audiences both in this country and abroad in the most shameless and cynical way imaginable, and resorts to his default position by condemning those who do not swallow whole his dire predictions about Co2 levels, the oceans rising 20 feet in less than 40 years, and polar bears drowning because of melting Arctic ice, just to mention a few. And, as the East Anglia email scandal shows, any scientist who expresses even the slightest bit of doubt about this very volatile issue can expect some very shabby treatment, indeed, from having their research suppressed to being accused as someone who should be tried and jailed for their beliefs.

To illustrate the extent to which Gore will go, one need look no further than an interview he gave to Ezra Klein of *The Washington Post* on August 22, 2013. In it, he likened the skeptics of man-made climate change to "those who have an alcoholic father who flies into a rage every time a subject is mentioned." [34] Not content to stop there, he also unloaded on his critics, likening them to racists, apartheid supporters, and opponents of abolition, which is curious indeed, since his father, who was also a Senator from Tennessee and a Democrat, voted against passage of *both* the 1964 Civil Rights Act and the Voting Rights Act of 1965.

Such *ad hominum* attacks are part and parcel of the political Left not only in this country, but in many others, as well. Anyone who dares question the prevailing orthodoxy in which it indulges can look forward to being marginalized at the least and destroyed at the worst. Because of the views he has expressed not only in *An Inconvenient Truth* but *Earth In the Balance,* as well, Gore has shown himself to be anything but the "tolerant," "compassionate," "open-minded" person he portrays himself to be, and just another bigoted, close-minded, intolerant political hack who cannot debate an issue on any kind of objective basis. Not only is this the case with Mr. Gore, it is the case as well with those who seek to impose the oppressive and ultimately deadly program known as the United Nations' *Agenda 21* on an unsuspecting world.

Agenda 21 poses a grave threat to the freedom and liberty of billions around the world. Its environmental mandates will restrict economic growth and will condemn these people to continued poverty, misery, and hopelessness. And, most ominously, its attempts to control the world's population through forced sterilization and abortion will doom untold millions more to oblivion before they even draw their first breaths, take their first steps, or utter their first words.

Americans believe, as our founding document, the *Declaration of Independence,* states, that "all men are created equal; that they are endowed by their Creator with certain unalienable rights; that among these are life, liberty and the pursuit of happiness." Think about that for a moment. There are two key words that we must all bear in mind. The first is "*created*," not "born." There is a crucial difference between the two, which is that while people are born into all sorts of unequal circumstances, they all come into existence in the same way, that is, at the moment of conception. This is a fact, and it is not open to interpretation. Therefore, their unalienable rights as human beings must be jealously respected by their fellow human beings.

The second key word in the *Declaration* deals with our unalienable, or God-given, rights, and the Founders knew exactly what they were doing when they listed "*life*" as first among the unalienable rights bestowed upon us by God. It was not by accident. They realized that without this most precious gift and, therefore, this most precious of all our rights, there can be no other rights, no freedom, no liberty, no private property, no pursuit of happiness, no nothing. That is why we have a government, to secure these rights. This is something a great many of us have forgotten, and it is something we continue to forget at our great peril, both as a people and as a nation.

It is the forfeiture of our sovereignty as a people and a nation under the provisions of *Agenda 21* that should frighten all of us, but worse is the fact that there are those among us, people like Al Gore, Paul Erlich, Bill and Hillary Clinton, and thousands of others, who care not a whit for anything that has to do with freedom, liberty, and individual rights. They champion what they call the "right of a woman to choose," yet, they care nothing for the rights of the most defenseless, the unborn. Even when many of them identified themselves as champions of the unborn at one time (like Gore and Bill Clinton once did), they soon changed their stripes for money, political power, or because they really believed deep down that it was permissible, even desirable, to kill children in their mothers' wombs. Where some were concerned, it was a case of "all of the above."

And, it is these individuals, the Al Gores, the Bill and Hillary Clintons, the John C. Holdrens, the Paul Erlichs, the Phil Joneses, the Barack Obamas and many more, who will be the vanguard of the new order of things. They will usher in a brave new world, a Green utopia that will see retarded economic growth, increased loss of freedom and individual autonomy, and a much lower population due to sterilization and abortion, especially among the great unwashed in the developing world. We would do well, indeed, to heed the warning signs, for they are all there in plain view for all to see. All we need do is take a good hard look at what is happening.

Agenda 21 and its nightmarish implications must be halted before it is too late. To be sure, there are groups like the American Policy Center in Herndon, Virginia, that have been on top of the whole *Agenda 21* program almost from the very beginning. The APC, which is directed by Tom De Weese, is the leading group that has sounded the alarm and exposed *Agenda 21* for the power grab that it is. Freedomworks, founded by former Rep. Dick Armey (R-TX) is another. There are more, including radio personalities Glenn Beck, Andrew Wilkow, and Michael Savage, as well as conservative activist Phyllis Schlaffly, and they are all dedicated to one thing, the restoration of freedom and liberty in the greatest nation on earth.

Others besides Freedomworks and the American Policy Center are engaging the international bureaucrats on the East River. All across the country, citizens from West Chester, New York to San Francisco, California, are filing suit against the U.N. scheme, and they are winning. Surprising as it may seem, not all who oppose *Agenda 21* are conservative or Republican. Many Democrats, especially in San Francisco, are filing suit to prevent the U.N. from dictating to them what they will do with their lives and property. Bravo!

In the end, this is our country, our world, and the last thing we need as individual human beings possessed of the unalienable rights that come from our Creator is any more power or control over our lives. *Agenda 21* represents perhaps the greatest threat we will face during the twenty-first century, especially to generations yet unborn. Man was not meant to live under the conditions it seeks to usher in and we must do everything we can to assure that this never takes place. As Ronald Reagan stated in his speech *A Time for Choosing,* which he delivered on October 27, 1964, "If we lose freedom in America, we have nowhere else to escape to. This is our last stand."

Mr. Reagan was right. *Agenda 21* poses precisely the kind of threat to freedom of which he spoke so eloquently, especially to those the elitists deem unworthy of life. We have seen this movie before, and we have heard the same justifications at other times in history, particularly in the twentieth century from people named Lenin, Stalin, Mussolini, Hitler, and Mao. They all yearned for a "new order," and we looked in horror at how it was very nearly brought about. The goal is no different where *Agenda 21* is concerned.

Those of us who value freedom and liberty the world over must stand as one and battle as we have never battled before. If we are ever to defeat the greatest threat to our liberties and individual rights that we have ever known, the time to act is now. As Mr. Reagan told his audience on that October evening over 50 years ago, we are faced with this choice: whether to stand for freedom both here and abroad while we are still able, or we will take "that last step into a thousand years of darkness."

It is time to heed Mr. Reagan's warning and resist the U.N.'s insane attempts to micromanage every aspect of our lives, and that includes deciding who will see the light of day and who will not before they ever leave the safety of their mothers' wombs. If we do not, we will sentence all of humanity, including the unborn, to that dark age about which we were first warned half a century ago, one into which we must never descend. And, if that happens, may God have mercy upon us, because there is no telling when (or even if) we will ever emerge.

Then what do we tell our descendants? Do we tell them how we rolled over and capitulated because we were duped and defrauded by a group of people who engaged in the greatest power grab in human history and who did so by perpetrating the greatest fraud Mankind has ever seen? Or, will we tell them that we had the courage to act while there was still time to turn back from the abyss? Not only will their judgment of us not be kind if we choose the former, but so, too, will that of history. However, the judgment we should fear the most is not that of Man or of history, but of He who gave us the most precious gifts we could possess—-the unalienable rights of life and liberty, and especially that of life. And, in the end, who in their right mind is willing to risk that?

The world is waiting for our answer.

NOTES

1. Earthpress, c. 1993. *Agenda 21: The Earth Summit Strategy to Save Our Planet.*
2. International Council for Local Environmental Initiatives, *The Local Agenda 21 Planning Guide*, 1996.
3. Ibid.
4. *Thomas Malthus' views on population*, www.uwmc.uwc.edu.
5. Ibid.
6. Malthus, Thomas, *An Essay on the Principle of Population*, 1798.
7. Baruch, Bernard. Introduction to *Road to Survival* by William Vogt, c. 1948.
8. Ibid.

9. Baruch, Bernard. Introduction to *Road to Survival* by William Vogt, c. 1948.
10. Vogt, William., *Road to Survival*, c. 1948.
11. Ibid.
12. Ray, Dixie Lee, and Guzzo, Lou, T*rashing the Planet: How Science Can Help Us Deal with Acid Rain, Depletion of the Ozone, and Nuclear Waste* (Among Other Things), c. 1990, Regnery Publishing, p.170.
13. Ray, Dixie Lee and Guzzo, Lou, *Environmental Overkill: Whatever Happened to Common Sense?* c. 1993, Regnery Publishing, p. 77.
14. Erlich, Paul, *The Population Bomb*, c. 1968.
15. Erlich, Paul, *The Population Bomb*, c. 1968, p. 135
16. Ibid, p. 138.
17. Erlich, Paul, *The Population Bomb*, c. 1968.
18. Ibid.
19. Erlich, Paul, *The Population Bomb*, c. 1968, p. 198.
20. Ray, Dixie Lee, *Trashing the Planet: How Science Can Help Us Deal with Acid Rain Depletion of the Ozone and Nuclear Waste (among Other Things)*, c. 1990, p.44.
21. Ibid.
22. Gore, Al, *Earth in the Balance*, c. 1992, p.39.
23. Gore, Al, *Earth in the Balance: Ecology and The Human Spirit*, c. 1992, p.144.
24. Gore, Al, Earth in the Balance: Ecology and the Human Spirit, c. 1992, p.314.
25. Ibid, p. 315.
26. Gore, Al, *Earth in the Balance: Ecology and the Human Spirit*, c. 1992 p. 315.
27. St. Mary Valley Bloom, *Pro-Life Al Gore?*
28. What Really Happened, *Al Gore's letter on Abortion*, July 1, 1984. www.geocities.com.
29. www.Garago.com/lifequotes.html.
30. Whatreallyhappened.com/WRHARTICLES. Geocities.com
31. Monckton, Christopher, *35 Inconvenient Truths: The Errors in Al Gore's Movie*. Science & Public Policy Institute, October 18, 2007.
32. Booker, Christopher, *Climate Change: This is the Worst Scientific Scandal of Our Generation. The London Daily Telegraph*, November 28, 2009.
33. Ibid.
34. Gore, Al, *The Washington Post*, August 22, 2013.

Chapter 8:

Profiles in Courage - Warriors against Abortion, Eugenics and Euthanasia—Heroes of the Pro-Life Movement

"Civil rights doesn't mean a thing without a right to life."
—Reverend Johnny L. Hunter, Columbus Day, 1999

In Chapter 1 of this work we examined the life of Margaret Sanger, the founder of Planned Parenthood. Chapter 2 took us inside the eugenics movement that blossomed in the United States in the first half of the twentieth century. Chapter 3 built on that theme by showing how American eugenicists inspired their counterparts in Hitler's Germany to commit the vilest and most disgusting atrocities imaginable against their fellow citizens in the name of *rassenhygiene,* or "race purity." In Chapter 4, we took a look at some of those who, by virtue of their status as black leaders, either wittingly or not, aided and abetted Sanger and her cohorts in imposing their racist program on people of color.

Chapter 5 examined the agenda of Planned Parenthood and warned that if it were allowed to continue, all of us would pay a huge price in the loss of life and more to the point, the loss of conscience of an entire nation and society. Chapter 6 sounded an urgent alarm that unless the pro-death movement of the American Left was stopped once and for all, we would witness nothing less than an extinction level event in this country, in general, and the minority black community, in particular. And, in Chapter 7, we saw how population control, brought about by sterilization, selective breeding, euthanasia, and abortion, is part and parcel of the United Nations' *Agenda 21* power grab that has dire consequences for all of humanity if it is ever brought into full implementation.

Now it is time to turn to some of those who are committed to turning us away from the road to national perdition, decline, and ultimately oblivion. We are going to highlight a few of the many tireless and dedicated individuals who value the sanctity of life in the womb, who see all such life as a gift from our Creator, one which by its very condition of helplessness and dependency of necessity must be protected so that it can take its rightful place in this world. We are going to focus particularly on some of these courageous individuals who happen to be Americans of color, and we are going to do it for one very simple reason: it is because they have seen firsthand how devastatingly sterilization and abortion have ravaged their community, far more than the evil and disgusting practice of slavery could ever have done.

Some of them have been mentioned briefly in passing in other parts of this book. Some were themselves taken in by the abortionists' claims that the life growing inside them was somehow not human, simply because it had not, yet, been fully born into this world. By the grace of God, these same individuals eventually saw the light because they took the time to think things out, to use the intelligence and the brains that He gave them to conclude that abortion is wrong, that it is an offense of monstrous proportions against God and Man, and they are using these elements of what makes us human to speak out against this evil and barbaric practice. Let us now look some of the heroes of the pro-life movement and the efforts they have mounted, often at risk to their freedom and personal safety, to stand up for the rights of the unborn. We owe each a tremendous debt of gratitude.

One such hero is the Reverend Jesse Lee Peterson, the founder and President of BOND, the Brotherhood Organization of a New Direction in Los Angeles, California. Reverend Peterson established BOND in 1990 to address the crisis facing black Americans in nearly every facet of daily life, from education to housing, to the breakup of the black nuclear family, and tragically, abortion. In addition to his work with BOND, he is a frequent guest on *The Bill Cunningham Show* and *The Sean Hannity Show,* and is the host of the highly-rated nationally-syndicated *Jesse Lee Peterson Show* in Los Angeles. He has appeared on such national cable news networks as CNN, MSNBC, and the Fox News Channel to offer the conservative, pro-life alternative to the current liberal black "leadership" in America. From the very beginning, the mission of BOND has been "rebuilding the family by rebuilding the man."

Reverend Peterson is the author, along with Brad Stetson, of the book *From Rage to Redemption,* which examines the death of common sense and critical thinking that has plagued so many black Americans over the years. He also has written *SCAM: How the Black Leadership Exploits Black America,* in which he shows how far too many of those who are trusted by their own people to lead them responsibly, are actually doing what they do for nothing more than purely personal gain. Reverend Peterson is also the author of *The Seven Steps to Spiritual, Family and Financial Success,* an indispensable guide for black Americans to escape the bonds of secularism, family breakup, and poverty.

A powerful and much sought-after public speaker, he is a forceful and articulate advocate for the unborn who regularly ministers to young women in front of abortion mills in Los Angeles, and his experiences have had a profound impact on him over the last 24 years. Reverend Peterson vividly recalls when and how he first heard of the Negro Project and what his reaction was to what he learned. "When I started BOND," he says, "I started getting these phone calls and people coming into my office talking about how bad abortion was in the black community." After he began investigating how Planned Parenthood places most of its clinics in the black inner city, he says, "I was shocked," but what really astounded him was how many women under the age of 25 were having these procedures and just how many of them they were having before they reached that age.

In fact, Reverend Peterson said many of these women had up to five abortions from the age of 13 until they were 25. "Not only are you killing that many children in your own body," he observes, "there is a lot of guilt and emotional destruction, and they will never, ever, recover from that, so it is emotionally destructive as well." [1] Peterson recalls finding out about the Negro Project "when I first got involved and how all this started happening." He was so appalled by what he found that his group began to hold rallies in front of Planned Parenthood facilities in Los Angeles. He recalls one instance in which he tried to counsel a young girl to forgo her abortion and keep her baby instead. "There was one young black girl who I think was thirteen and was around six months pregnant, on a Saturday morning coming in for her abortion," Reverend Peterson says. He told her she did not have to go that route and if she brought her baby to term, his group would adopt it out to a loving home, but she replied that it was already too late for that.

"She had already gone to Planned Parenthood," Reverend Peterson says of the young lady, "and had what seemed to be saline solution injected into her womb. They told her that it wasn't going to hurt, that it wasn't really a baby, but for three days the baby was kicking, grasping, fighting for its life." [2] What this young lady underwent in the wake of her encounter with the nation's largest abortion provider is almost too heart-wrenching to contemplate because, Reverend Peterson tells us, "she is emotionally and mentally scarred" by her experience.

His encounter with the young teenager, the reverend says, "broke my heart. It took me a long time to get over that, and especially now when I counsel her, she's an adult woman now and she can hardly function in life." His anguish is clear and unmistakable as he recalls his counseling sessions with her, trying to help her cope with the gravity of her situation. "I tell her that God is not holding this against her," he says, "but it's really hard for her to overcome it." It is clear from Reverend Peterson's remarks regarding what this young lady was told by Planned Parenthood that the "pro-choice" movement will stop at nothing, including any amount of deception, falsehoods, and outright lies to women about what abortion really involves, in order to further its deadly, blood-stained agenda.

Reverend Peterson is mystified by the failure of so many influential black Americans to express even the slightest amount of outrage at the number of abortions that are being performed every year upon members of their own demographic group, in particular the NAACP, and he makes no bones about it. In fact, he is quite blunt about the fact that the nation's largest civil rights organization has "no official policy" regarding Planned Parenthood, and he expresses his disgust at the country's highest elected black lawmakers for their unwillingness to voice even the slightest amount of criticism of either abortion, in general, or Planned Parenthood, in particular.

However, he is especially incensed at how and why so many of the nation's black ministers are so strangely silent about the holocaust that is taking place right before their very eyes and, yet, are doing next to nothing to stop it.

Taking note of the fact that so many black clergy belong to the NAACP and, therefore, are part of the group's refusal to take a stand on Planned Parenthood, Reverend Peterson charges that these "black preachers are in it for personal gain." He points out that BOND has led a boycott of the NAACP for the last 20 years, and charges that the group is "a political pawn of the liberal, elite Democrat Party and not about the people." [3] He warns, "As long as black people are having abortions, relying on the government, looking for someone else to lead them, the NAACP and others will continue to use them, and that's why they want to keep black Americans brainwashed, dumbed down, and demoralized. You can't control a moral people. You have to demoralize them in order to control them."

The NAACP and the Congressional Black Caucus, he charges, "are getting money from Planned Parenthood, the Democrat Party, and others for themselves, and the money outweighs what is right. They don't care about black folks, at all, because if they did, they would not support abortion. They claim that racism is a problem for black Americans, and, yet, Margaret Sanger was a racist and Planned Parenthood is carrying out the wishes of Margaret Sanger, and instead of standing against it, they are standing for it."

"The NAACP and the current black leadership," Reverend Peterson reiterates, "don't care about black folks, *at all.*" He also believes that the anger and resentment that is harbored by so many blacks against white Americans is a direct result of having been lied to by their own leaders over the years, to the extent that "they can't even see what's really going on. They don't see that the people they trust the most are using them for their own personal gain. That is why," he says, "we have been trying to help them overcome their anger, so that they can really see what's going on." [4]

Yet, as maddening as the situation is, Reverend Peterson is heartened by a number of recent developments that suggest a change in mind on the part of younger Americans. One is the fact that more of them now identify themselves as at least "leaning" toward the pro-life position, a clear departure from years past when most of those who were surveyed identified themselves as being "pro-choice." Another is that more than 80 abortion mills closed their doors for good in 2013. He also is encouraged by the success of such medical advances as sonograms and ultrasounds that show the mother that the life growing inside her body is, indeed, a human life that is, therefore, deserving of protection.

Reverend Peterson is "very happy that fewer people are supporting abortion than before, especially among the young people. If we can get them to turn back to what is right," he says, "then we can start saving the lives of these unborn children." Further, he credits the use of sonograms and ultrasounds in convincing more women to turn away from abortion. These advances, he says, "have had a great impact because you can see that it really is a child, and a lot of young people have been convinced that a baby is not a baby until it is born; they do not see it as a child in the womb. I think that along with that and serious education, to educate these folks about abortion has had a major impact." [5] "Once they see the child developing in the womb," Reverend Peterson says, "I think it's hard just okaying taking the life of a human being."

Regarding eugenicists like Peter Singer and his belief that it is permissible for parents to kill their children up to the age of two, Reverend Peterson has one word to describe such a thought process: evil. "That's what evil does," he says. "Once you let evil have its way, it doesn't stop. It just goes on and on and on and on to destruction. It doesn't stop at one thing, at all." He also takes those to task who have failed to arm themselves with the proper facts about abortion and eugenics. "It's happening," he says, "because people are uninformed. They are deceived, and once you deceive the people, you can easily destroy them. That is one of the reasons up to now that it has been easy to do this."

Alerting and informing the general public, a public that has been asleep at the switch for decades or even generations on this critically important issue is one of the big reasons Reverend Jesse Lee Peterson is doing what he has been doing with BOND for nearly 25 years. "I believe that if we can bring back God's order," he says, "and that order is God in Christ, Christ in Man, man over woman, and woman over children and family, because it's a spiritual order, if we can bring that order back, a lot of these women would not be having these abortions because they would have their husbands there to feel safe with." Reverend Peterson adds, "I hear a lot of young girls who say that they don't have a man and they don't feel like they can raise a child on their own. That's why they don't feel good and that's why," he believes, "they are having their unborn babies aborted."

Strong family ties are extremely important to Reverend Peterson. "I grew up on a plantation in Alabama under the Jim Crow laws," he recalls. "There were places where we could live, but we had the family, and growing up I had never heard of an abortion, because women were married for the most part, and when they had children the father was there to care for them and to help with the kids and to be responsible." [6] Remarking on how the black family began to disintegrate after government social policy changed in the 1960s, he says, "I noticed that was the first thing that they did, they broke up the family and made the woman vulnerable to the world." Reverend Peterson believes that it is absolutely imperative to, in his words, "restore the family, which is God's order. And then, we can end abortion by bringing the man back into the home." However, Reverend Peterson warns that other demographic groups are not immune to the attack on the family. "It's already happening to the white family," he says. "They call the white man a racist, they say he hates women, that he wants to control this and that. If they can turn his family away from him, they can do to the white family what they have done to the black family."

"They can't do it if the men are there," Reverend Peterson continues, "because the men will protect their families. They will protect their wives and children. The family feels safe with the man there." But if he is not," adds the reverend, "he can't (protect them) and the woman feels vulnerable to the world." Reverend Peterson firmly believes that the popular culture is one of the leading causes of belittling the traditional role of the father because "he represents Christ on earth. He is the spiritual head of his family. Evil," the reverend says, "understands that, and that's why it goes after the man first, to get him out of the picture." Reverend Peterson and BOND are working tirelessly to reverse this trend and return the man to his rightful place at the head of the traditional family unit and to end the scourge of abortion, not just among blacks, but among all Americans. He knows that the taking of unborn human life is an abomination and completely unworthy of the greatest nation on earth. God willing, it will not take BOND and other groups another 25 years to revive the traditional family, and that it will not take another 40-plus years until America awakens from its abortion-induced stupor and realizes just what it has done. To learn more about Reverend Peterson and BOND, visit the group at www.bondinfo.org.

• • •

One of the highest-profile and most outspoken members of the pro-life movement is Dr. Alveda C. King. Born in Atlanta, GA, on January 22, 1951, she is the first of five children of the Reverend A.D. King, and a niece of the Reverend Martin Luther King, Jr. Dr. King is a graduate of Central Michigan University, and she holds an M.A. degree from that institution. She briefly ventured into the political arena, serving for two terms (1979-1981) in Georgia's State House, representing the citizens of that state's 28th District. Recently Dr. King, whom we met earlier in this book, has been a Pastoral Associate and Director of African-American Outreach with Priests for Life, a pro-life organization based in Staten Island, New York, and Gospel of Life Ministries. [7]

Dr. King's extensive resume also includes authorship of several books such as *How Can the Dream Survive if We Murder the Children?* and *I Don't Want Your Man, I Want My Own*. Dr. King is also the founder of King for America, Inc. She is the winner of several awards, among them the Life Prize Award, the Legatus Organization's Cardinal John J. O'Connor Pro-Life Hall of Fame Award, and the Civil Rights Award from the Congress of Racial

Equality (CORE), all of which were bestowed in 2011. She holds an honorary Doctorate of Laws Degree from St. Anselm College and serves on the boards of several organizations such as Heartbeat International, Georgia Right to Life, the MLK Center, Bible Curriculum in Public Schools, and Abortion Recovery International. [8]

As a young girl growing up in the Jim Crow South, Dr. King literally lived every day with the threat of not only being deprived of her civil rights, as happened when she was jailed for her part in the open housing movement, but of having her very life taken from her. This threat became quite real when her family home in Birmingham was gutted by a fire set by southern racists, who also destroyed her father's church office in Louisville, Kentucky. To put it mildly, Dr. King has seen and been through a lot in her time on this earth. Her courage and intestinal fortitude have served her well over the years, and have stood her in good stead as she campaigns for an end to the cruelest deprivation of a person's basic right to exist, that of abortion.

Having been on both sides of the abortion question, she knows whereof she speaks because she herself underwent two abortions earlier in her life. She is well-aware of what abortion really involves, the lies and deceit the "pro-choice" movement employs to further its agenda, and the disastrous effect America's current group of black "leaders" has had on its followers by guiding too many trusting individuals down a suicidal path. And, she knows how disastrous the Negro Project was for her fellow Americans of color. She found out about Margaret Sanger's scheme "several years ago, I would say, around the late 1990s." During that time, Dr. King says, she met the true twentieth-century civil rights leaders "who were against oppression of any kind, including genocide and eugenics, Dr. Johnny Hunter, for example, and others, and as they began to tell me about eugenics and genocide, and the Negro Project, and that Margaret Sanger had targeted black women for sterilization, when she was telling them they were a credit to their race, I was shocked."

But, Dr. King says, this "didn't throw me for a loop because I know oppression, things that had happened during slavery, segregation, and Jim Crow, and so I just began to realize that people would go to every length to eliminate or decrease the numbers of the African-American population, but also the poor. It isn't limited," she adds, "to a skin color situation." [8]

Dr. King believes that "the poor, the oppressed, Latino, and African-Americans, of course" are also prime targets for elimination. "So I know pretty well now, more than many people know, because even in the underground, the human trafficking and what they do with experimentation, taking organs from people and all of that." Dr. King cites Kermit Gosnell, the Philadelphia partial-birth abortionist who went to jail after being convicted in 2013 in the deaths of several children who survived his attempts to kill them, and a female patient on his operating table as a prime example of what she means.

"Gosnell," Dr. King reveals, "kept the feet and hands, but especially the feet, of babies after he aborted them, and some of them were born alive, so that leads you to wonder what he did with the organs and things of the babies. So there's a lot of experimentation, there's a lot of racism, and Margaret Sanger was at the heart of that." Dr. King believes strongly that the supporters of eugenics, sterilization, and abortion have much for which to answer in unleashing their nightmarish agenda not just on people who are poor or who are of a different skin color, but on all Americans.

When asked what the circumstances were behind her uncle being chosen for Planned Parenthood's first Margaret Sanger Award in 1966 and the implication that he would have, therefore, supported abortion, she replied, "It was accepted in his name. He did not attend the ceremony, he did not write the speech." Referencing his famous Christmas 1967 speech, she reminds us that "basically, he said that we need to learn to respect the human personality, and when we love people we won't kill anybody. Injustice anywhere," she echoes the civil rights icon, "is a threat to justice everywhere. He would not," she adds, "have supported fertility blockers, this carcinogenic birth control, he would not have supported sterilization, he would not have supported abortion." [9]

Dr. King is hopeful that the change in attitude among younger Americans regarding abortion will continue, and she says, "I know that even ten years ago, when I went to work for Priests for Life, where I work now, you had more abortion clinics than pregnancy care centers. Now there are two pregnancy care centers for each abortion killing center. That's a good indicator the pro-life message is resonating." When asked if the emphasis should be put more on reaching younger people rather than their parents and grandparents, she replies, "That is happening now, and what we are very grateful for is that young people, if you go to the March for Life in Washington, there are thousands, hundreds of thousands, of young people, and their rallies are just packed out. Young people are being reached with the message, and more and more of them are pro-life." [10]

Dr. King credits such groups as the National Black Pro-Life Coalition, of which she is a member, with educating black Americans about abortion and says, "we have a very influential voice in the African-American community as far as life is concerned." She mentions two documentaries the group has produced, *Maafa 21,* in which she plays a central role, and *Blood Money,* in which she serves as narrator, with making a dramatic impact on the nation's black community regarding the life issue. "America's leaders," she says, "need to learn the difference between serving the public and killing the public."

Alveda King is a tireless advocate for the rights of the most defenseless among us. Her dedication and passion for the unborn are apparent to all who come into contact with her, and the alarm she sounds about abortion in the black community is one to which all true Americans, regardless of skin color, must pay strict heed if we are to remain faithful to our founding principles, which include the most important unalienable right we have, the right to life. Nowhere is that alarm clearer than in the powerful testimony that she has given, titled *How Can the Dream Survive if We Murder the Children?*

Dr. King writes: "We have been fueled by the fire of 'women's rights' for so long that we have become deaf to the outcry of the real victims whose rights are being trampled upon, the babies and the mothers." She acknowledges, "Of course a woman has the right to decide what to do with her body. Thank God for the Constitution." But, at the same time, she reminds us that a woman "also has a right to know the serious consequences and repercussions of making a decision to abort her child. Then, too," Dr. King writes, "what about the rights of each baby who is artificially breached before coming to term in his or her mother's womb, only to have her skull punctured, and feel, yes agonizingly feel, the life run out of her before taking her first breath of freedom? What about the rights of these women who have been called to pioneer the new frontiers of the new millennium only to have their lives snuffed out before the calendar even turns?" [11]

"Oh, God," Dr. King wonders, "what would Martin Luther King, Jr., who dreamed of having his children judged by the content of their characters, do if he'd lived to see the contents of thousands of children's skulls emptied into the bottomless caverns of the abortionists' pits?"

She calls for the United States "to lead the world in repentance, and in restoration of life! If only," she muses, "we can carry the freedom of repentance to its fullest potential. If only America can repent and turn away from the sins of our nation." Dr. King reminds us that "partial birth abortion stands at the forefront of our destruction," and she should know. "My mother tried to abort me in 1950," she reveals, yet her life was spared and she went from having two abortions to raising six children and becoming one of the most passionate and articulate defenders of the rights of the unborn in the nation.

Regarding these procedures, Dr. King says, "In the 1970s, I suffered one involuntary and one voluntary abortion. My involuntary abortion was performed just prior to *Roe vs. Wade* by my private physician without my consent. I had gone to my doctor to ask why my cycle had not resumed after the birth of my son. I did not," she states, "ask for and did not want an abortion." What came next was both tragic and gut-wrenching. "The doctor said, "You don't need to be pregnant,'" she writes. "He proceeded to perform a painful examination which resulted in a gush of blood and tissue emanating from my womb." He explained that he had performed a 'local D and C.'" One cannot help but wonder, is this what pro-choice advocates mean when they call abortion a "safe" procedure? However, more physical and psychological pain awaited Dr. King when she became pregnant for, yet, a second time.

"Soon after the *Roe vs. Wade,* decision," Dr. King writes, "I became pregnant again. There was adverse pressure and the threat of violence from the baby's father. The ease and convenience provided through *Roe vs. Wade* made it too easy for me to make the fateful and fatal decision to abort our baby." Dr. King then addresses one of the shopworn arguments used by the "pro-choice" movement to ease the guilt experienced by so many women who are torn between killing their unborn child and deciding to bring that baby into the world. "I went to a doctor and was advised that the procedure would hurt no more than 'having a tooth removed,'" she says. [12] But, as she would learn shortly thereafter, this was far from the case.

"As soon as I woke up I knew something was very wrong," Dr. King reveals. "I felt very ill and very empty. I tried to talk to the doctor and nurses about it. They assured me that 'it will all go away in a few days. You will be fine.'" But nothing was "fine," nor, as it turned out, did it "go away in a few days," despite what the confused, conflicted young mother had been told by the medical professionals she had trusted so completely. In fact, as Dr. King testifies, the situation became increasingly worse as time went on.

"Over the next few years," she states, "I experienced medical problems. I had trouble bonding with my son and his five siblings who were born after the abortions. I began to suffer from eating disorders, depression, nightmares, sexual dysfunctions, and a whole host of other issues related to the abortion that I chose to have. I felt angry about both abortions and very guilty about the abortion I chose to have. The guilt I felt," Dr. King tells us, "made me very ill." Again, is this what "pro-choice" advocates mean when they call abortion a "safe" procedure?

Again, that was not all. The pain and heartache of Dr. King's choices did not stop with her, but came to adversely impact those around her, including the six children whom she brought into the world. "My children," she testifies, "have all suffered from knowing that they have a brother or sister that their mother chose to abort. Often they ask if I had ever thought about aborting them and have said 'you killed our baby.' This is very painful for all of us." And, as she reveals, the ripple effect of her choice was felt by other members of Dr. King's family, as well.

"Also," she says, "my mother and grandparents were very sad to know about the loss of the baby. The aborted child's father," she adds, "also regrets the abortion. If it had not been for *Roe vs. Wade,*" Dr. King concludes, "I would not have had that abortion." [13]

"My grandfather, Dr. Martin Luther King, Sr., once said, 'No one is going to kill a child of mine,'" Dr. King tells us. "His son once said, 'The negro cannot win if he is willing to sacrifice the lives of his children for comfort and safety.' How can the 'Dream' survive if we murder the children?" she asks. "Every aborted baby," she says, "is like a slave in the womb of his or her mother. The mother decides his or her fate." [14] It is because she experienced first-hand the physical, emotional, and psychological devastation of abortion and has seen the disastrous impact it has had on so many of her fellow black Americans that Dr. Alveda King has become such a staunch, unwavering advocate for the rights of the unborn. And, just as important, it is why she is sounding the alarm about the coming extinction of her people if they continue to proceed down the road they are currently traveling. It is also because of her experiences that Dr. King is a member of Silent No More, a nationwide network of women who have had at least one abortion and who have had to cope with many of the same things that she herself has undergone. For years and even decades, these women have been reluctant to share the guilt and shame that came with exercising their "reproductive rights," but have since decided to come forth and tell the world what it is with which they deal each and every day. Because of people like Alveda King and actress Jennifer O'Neil, they now know that they are not alone and that someone actually cares about them and their plight.

"I join the voices of thousands across America who are SILENT NO MORE," Dr. King writes. "We can no longer sit idly by and allow this horrible spirit of murder to cut down, yes cut out and cut away our unborn, and destroy the lives of mothers." And, as would be expected of a descendant of one of the greatest religious leaders of the twentieth century, she continues, "I feel very grateful to God for the Spirit of Repentance that is sweeping our land. In repentance," she reminds us, "there is healing. In the name of Jesus, we must humble ourselves and pray, and turn from our wicked ways, then God will hear us from Heaven and heal our land." [15]

King appeals to those in authority to turn our nation back from the brink in this powerful passage of her testimony by saying, "I can only beseech the powers-that-be to hearken to the voice of our Lord and remember that human life is sacred. By taking the lives of our young and wounding the wombs and lives of their mothers, we are flying in the face of God. We cannot play God." She warns, "if we continue down this path of destruction, we will be met at the gates of our own doom." Reminding us that she was born on January 22, she tells us that this day is especially painful and infamous for her, for "each year this is marred by the fact that it is the anniversary of *Roe vs. Wade,* and the anniversary of death for millions of babies."

"We must end the pain of post-abortion trauma," Dr. King pleads. "If the dream of Dr. Martin Luther King, Jr. is to live, our babies must live. Our mothers must choose life. If we refuse to answer the cry of mercy from the unborn and ignore the suffering of the mothers, we are signing our own death warrants." In closing her testimony, Dr. Alveda King sounds a cautionary note of hope. It is a note that is firmly rooted in the religious convictions instilled in her by her family, a family that includes the most famous icon of the civil rights movement, the Reverend Dr. Martin Luther King, Jr. "I, too, like Martin Luther King, Jr., have a dream," she says. "I have a dream that the men and women, the boys and girls of America, will come to our senses, and humble ourselves before God Almighty and pray for His mercy, and receive His healing grace. I pray, that this is the day, the hour of our deliverance. May God," she prays, "have mercy on us all." [16]

• • •

Reverend Walter B. Hoye served as the Executive Elder of the Progressive Missionary Baptist Chruch in Berkley, California, a suburb of Oakland, from 1991-2010, and is now, along with his wife, Lori, a full-time pro-life advocate for the Issues 4Life Foundation. In his nearly 20 years at the helm of his congregation, Reverend Hoye became deeply involved in ministering to the good people of his community. A 1980 graduate of Michigan State University,

Reverend Hoye earned a Master's degree during his time at that institution. Three years later, he earned a second degree, in Business Administration from the U.S. International University (now Alliant University). Reverend Hoye serves in a number of capacities with several organizations such as Issues for Life Foundation, which he established and now serves as its President; the Frederick Douglass Foundation of California; the National Black Pro-Life Coalition, and the Morning Center, which provides free, full-service maternity care to women in urban and underserved areas. [17]

Reverend Hoye is the recipient of a number of citations, including the 2014 Students for Life of America's West Coast Conference Defender Award, the 2011 "Hero at Heart" Award from Life Issues Institute, the Family Research Council's 2009 "John Wise" Award, and, along with his wife, Lori, the 4th Annual Walk for Life West Coast's St. Gianna Molar Award for "Courage under Fire," among others. With all this activity, Reverend Hoye has also authored a book, *Leadership from the Inside Out,* and is a much sought-after speaker on pro-life issues and the impact abortion has had on the black community, including the economic devastation it has visited on that particular group of Americans. For example, he was invited in 2012 by former Congressman Allan West (R-FL) to address lawmakers on Capitol Hill on the "economic impact of abortion." [18]

In his time as Pastor at Progressive Missionary Baptist Church, Reverend Hoye has seen many things that have negatively impacted both his congregation and the citizens of his community. Crime, poverty, drug abuse, illiteracy, and the astronomically high rate of abortions have placed a heavy burden on Reverend Hoye over the years, especially the latter. He is a firm believer that life begins at conception, and that to eradicate that life is an abomination against God, who he believes used his experience with the premature birth of his son (six months, 2.1 pounds) to teach him that the fetus is indeed a person, a living, breathing, human being. [19]

His courage, integrity, and commitment to the preservation of unborn life have earned him enormous respect among his peers, including Dr. Alveda King, one of his associates with the National Black Pro-Life Coalition, Dr. Levon R. Yuille, Director of the National Black Pro-Life Congress, and many others. Reverend Hoye also has given selflessly of his time to attend pro-life rallies across the country. He is a true pro-life hero who stands in stark contrast to self-proclaimed black "leaders" like Jesse Jackson and Al Sharpton, who were at one time fierce opponents of abortion, but elected to turn their backs on the unborn in return for the money and political influence that the "pro-choice" movement offered them.

Like Reverend Peterson and Dr. King, Reverend Hoye was extremely appalled and shocked to discover what Margaret Sanger, the founder of Planned Parenthood, and her cohorts in the eugenics movement had devised when they embarked on the Negro Project in 1939. "I first got involved with this in my church," he recalls. "I was frustrated with us not talking about issues that matter." To that end, he says, "A few years ago I took the time to literally put together a conference called 'Issues that Matter.'" The event drew a number of people, including conservative writer and political activist Star Parker, and they discussed a range of topics that were not being addressed from the pulpit. It was through that conference, Reverend Hoye says, "that the numbers just started becoming clearer and clearer, and it was quite obvious at this point that we needed to do more on this subject." His reaction to Sanger's scheme, Reverend Hoye recalls, "was one of outrage. It was very difficult for me to understand how this could have gone virtually undetected in our community." [20]

"I began to do more research on it," Reverend Hoye says of the Negro Project, "and the more and more research I did, it became quite evident that we've got to somehow communicate this truth." There is no doubt," he says, "that when you become aware that Planned Parenthood's founder, Margaret Sanger, launched her Negro Project in 1939, after which, of course, her organization changed its name from the American Birth Control League to the Birth Control Federation of America, you realize over the years that black Americans have become victims of genocide, their own genocide by their own hands." [21] So it is vitally important, he believes, "that we communicate this message, that people understand this history, and that once we begin talking about it, we'll know what to do."

To show just how dire the situation that confronts black America is, Reverend Hoye urges us to look at the data, not from "pro-choice" groups like Planned Parenthood, but from government agencies like the Centers for Disease Control and Prevention in Atlanta, Georgia.

You've got to look at the numbers," he says, "and the current data, such as the CDC's 2010 report, which is just out, reveals that black Americans are responsible for 35% of all abortions in the United States. Given that we're 14 % at best of the population, we're looking at that 14% being responsible for 35% of all abortions." [22] And, since half the black population is female, Reverend Hoye points out, "you're looking at really 6 or 7% being responsible for that 35%."

He breaks things down even more, stressing that since all these abortions are being performed on women of child-bearing age, "you're now looking at 3%" of these women "being responsible for 35% of all abortions in the country. I am very concerned," Reverend Hoye adds, "that if we don't do something about this soon, we (his fellow black Americans) are going to face the very real possibility of being extinct."

When asked if he agreed with the analogy of a canary in a coal mine as it applies to abortion in the black community, Reverend Hoye replied, "Yes, I would. We're talking about an endangered species, and I figure that it's very clear that this is happening all around us. And, we're still staying in the coal mine in the dark, but the light's got to come on. We've got to get to the point where we can start talking about this, that we can start talking about strategies that work, specifically in communities of color, and I'm hoping that this pays off." But this, he believes, will require different tactics to be employed to reach those outside the "mainstream" elements of life in the black community.

An indispensable part of Reverend Hoye's work with the Progressive Missionary Baptist Church is ministering to pregnant women who are about to enter abortion clinics in Oakland. And, while many of the women he encounters follow through with their decisions to terminate the lives of their unborn children, Reverend Hoye and those who stand with him are successful in getting at least a few of these women to change their minds and bring their babies to term. It has not been easy, and he has, unfortunately, run afoul of the law, at times. One such instance occurred on May 13, 2008, in front of the Family Planning Specialists Medical Group abortion mill in Oakland. Reverend Hoye was there, as he had been previously for more than two years, urging women who were contemplating abortion to change their minds and keep their babies.

Armed with nothing more than a black baseball cap, a sign reading, "JESUS LOVES YOU AND YOUR BABY. LET US HELP," and genuine love for his fellow man, Reverend Hoye was simply attempting to show these women that they did not have to take the lives of their unborn children and that there was indeed another road down which they could travel, but this apparently was too much for the staff at the clinic to tolerate. And, they certainly could not have him asking their clients inflammatory questions like, "Could I talk to you about alternatives to the clinic?" [23]

They demanded that he be arrested for harassing their patients, and wanted him jailed for violating the city's so-called "Mother, May I?" ordinance, which was passed on December 18, 2007. Under the ordinance, which was enacted in direct response to Reverend Hoye's activities outside the clinic, it was against the law to "approach within eight feet of any person seeking to enter a 'reproductive health care' facility in order to offer literature; display a sign; or engage in oral protest, education or counseling without that person's consent." [24]

Reverend Hoye was arrested and charged with violating the Oakland law. At the trial which followed, his accusers could not provide any evidence that he had harassed any woman entering the abortion facility. For instance, a number of "escorts" hired by the clinic to guide clients past the reverend testified that they had felt "intimidated" by him as he stood quietly on the sidewalk holding his sign, but were completely discredited when a videotape was presented that showed that the clinic director *herself* was harassing him, not the other way around. Nevertheless, he was convicted and was sentenced on January 15, 2009 to thirty days in jail and fined $1,130 by Judge Stuart Hing, who had wanted to take him into custody immediately, but was persuaded not to by the reverend's defense attorneys, who had promised that he would stay at least 100 yards away from the abortion clinic while awaiting sentencing. While agreeing to observe the ordinance as passed by the City Council, he stated that obeying the stay-away order was a violation of his free speech rights. This led to the fine and jail time, which Reverend Hoye eventually served after two more months of legal wrangling. He finally was taken into custody on March 20, 2009, and was released on April 7.

If the people at the Family Planning Specialists Medical Group had any illusions that Reverend Hoye had "learned his lesson" and was no longer a force with which to be reckoned, they were sadly mistaken On April 8, the *Contra Costa Times* reported, "Hoye went free Tuesday with a wider network of anti-abortion supporters than before he went to trial." [25] The *Times* reported, "Now, his backers said, the city's year-old 'bubble law' has backfired." Pastor Dion Evans of Alameda's Chosen Vessels Christian Church was quoted as saying of Reverend Hoye's adversaries, "They would have been in a better position if they had left him alone. They picked on one man on one street, one day a week trying to reach one woman at a time with one sign for one hour. [26] Now," he said, "a mobilization has come together because they've created an unjust law. People like me who have been cheerleading are not on the sidelines anymore. Now we're in the game."

Of his arrest, Reverend Hoye says, "The police came at the request of the abortion clinic. The police found nothing wrong with a man on a public sidewalk with a sign that says 'GOD LOVES YOU.'" He also points out that despite the best efforts of the "escorts" that were hired by the clinic, the women he was attempting to reach "really wanted to talk. They were looking for help." But, although many young women are seeking alternatives to aborting their babies and more younger Americans identify themselves as at least leaning in the pro-life direction, both positive signs to be sure, Reverend Hoye says that he cannot include the young people of his own community among them, at least not yet.

"The numbers regarding abortion in my community," he laments, "are not decreasing like the numbers in the larger community." He does believe that the use of sonograms and ultrasounds are helping to turn the tide, and he calls them "highly effective." But, he adds, "the numbers" of women who still choose abortion are "still very high." In terms of those percentages, he says, "I'm still looking at 35%. Alan Guttmacher (Planned Parenthood's information-gathering arm) says it's at 30%, the CDC says 37%, and the CDC report does not reflect California, which had over 200,000 abortions all by itself. It is the leading abortion state in the union. [27] Their numbers are not included, and they still get 35%."

"The point," Reverend Hoye says, "is that the numbers in the minority community are just higher. So, while you can look at things that are effective, that have been turning it around, I applaud all that, but the truth of the matter is that it is still a real problem in my community." And, while the situation in California is dire and desperate, indeed, the reverend points out that it is far worse in some other parts of the U.S. "That's very well illustrated in New York," he says. "For every 1,000 live black births in my community, there are over 2,600 abortions. And, hard as it may be to wrap one's brain around these figures," he adds "that has *increased*. So when we look at the numbers and we look at the strategy, we've got to come to grips with the fact that we've got to employ different tactics and different strategies to reach these communities.

"We've got to understand," Reverend Hoye believes, "that in communities of color, our strategies that are common in the pro-life movement aren't really 'moving the dial' in my community. For instance, you're not going to get a conversation started with the black ministers talking about 'let's remove the President,' or 'let's repeal Obamacare,' or 'let's reverse *Roe.'*

These strategies are just not effective in my community. But," he adds, "there are some other strategies that are effective in my community, and I hope we can come together and realize that on different battlefields you're going to have to use different types of tactics and strategies to get the job done."

Sidewalk counseling is one tactic that, while not successful all of the time, can be very effective in reaching women who believe that abortion is the only way out of their often desperate situations. Reverend Hoye calls such counseling "near and dear to my heart. This ministry represents the very last stand that you can take. You're literally right in front of an abortion clinic and you only have seconds to communicate God's love. And there's a risk in doing that, as my case in Oakland points out. But, as a movement, we've got to come to grips with the fact that we're going to have to take a look at different ways of communicating the message."

"The bottom line," Reverend Hoye says, "is that message plus messenger equals motivation. We're going to have to realize that you're going to have to get the right message communicated by the right messenger that can motivate the people. Then you're starting to get on the right track." Getting black Americans to realize what has been happening to them for nearly 80 years and to do something about it is no small task, and it will take incredible drive, determination, and love to bring an end to this insanity, but Reverend Walter Hoye has shown that he embodies all of these qualities. And, with God's help, his efforts on behalf of the unborn will not have gone for naught. He is a true pro-life hero, and we are, indeed, fortunate to have him in our midst.

• • •

As the founder of the Life, Education and Resource Network (LEARN), Reverend Johnny L. Hunter has been involved in the life issue for decades. Reverend Hunter, whom we met earlier in these pages, has seen firsthand the economic and social devastation of the black community in America that has resulted directly from the failed policies of the last fifty years, including the most destructive policy of all, the legalization of abortion on demand in 1973. He knows that because of the staggering number of black children that are being butchered in their mothers' wombs every day, this particular demographic group now finds itself in dire peril unless something is done, and done quickly, to reverse this suicidal trend. This is primarily why Reverend Hunter established LEARN.

Based in Fayetteville, North Carolina, LEARN was created to "ensure the survival of people color and to encourage Judeo-Christian family values when addressing bio-ethical decisions." [28] To further its work, the organization relies on the expertise of "the most valuable resources of all, human beings with experience." LEARN offers help to a wide range of individuals in need, including the poor, the sick, victims of crime, and those who require prenatal and parental training. And, it makes clear the inspiration for its existence: "We have a Savior who is willing to forgive. His name is Jesus. We have a Lord who is willing to rein in our lives. His name is Jesus. We have victory, and it is in the name of Jesus."

Reverend Hunter has seen the red flags, he has heeded the warning alarms about what abortion is doing to his community, and he knows that the situation cannot continue without an enormously disastrous conclusion. "Those working with LEARN," Reverend Hunter says, "have an opportunity to save the minority community, which is on the verge of extinction. Data taken in 2004 set off the alarm; the birth of African-Americans has dropped below replacement level. In order for a people to sustain themselves, they must have 2.1 children per couple. African-Americans have 1.9 children per couple. This level is silently annihilating our communities." [29] And, as we have seen thus far, this crisis has both deepened and widened over the following ten years, as the replacement rate among black Americans has plummeted to 0.7 live births per female. "As a person who values human life," Reverend Hunter says, "I feel very troubled that the youngest of our race is not guaranteed the opportunity to have our day in the sun."

"We do not," he continues, "want our people to perish because of ignorance. Ignorance and apathy have hindered the proper response to the main destroyer of our future and the child. The single biggest threat to the survival of children, especially children of color, is imposed death by induced abortion." [30] Reverend Hunter calls on "all women of our nation to become like the mothers and midwives of ancient Egypt. Do not obey the death order." He urges the religious leaders of the black community, far too many of whom are so silent in the face of so much needless death, to take a firm stand against the self-imposed genocide confronting his people by appealing to "evangelists to step off the well-furnished pulpits and go into the streets to call the nation to repentance. It is time, for pastors to make use of the shepherd's staff and boldly face the wolves," he says. "Pastors must chase them out of the pastures so that God's lambs can grow safely and be nurtured."

Reverend Hunter calls America's black churchgoers to action, as well: "Congregations need to escape from those pastors who invite the wolves into the sanctuary lest on the final day of reckoning they realize that they were robbed of their souls." And, he issues a plea to those in positions of responsibility to display compassion, courage, fortitude, and backbone: "It is time for leaders nationwide to become outraged. It is time to insist that the killing stop. It is time to refuse to be ignored!" [31] To achieve what is needed, Reverend Hunter reminds us, "We must emulate the acts of the apostles and the civil rights movement in America. As people of faith and action, we must speak up for justice. Let our voices," he says, "be silent only in death prior to our resurrection. Let us not go silently into the night. Make noise! Wake up our brethren and our sisters who are in a deep slumber lest they too be slaughtered." Reverend Hunter calls for the nation to "join us as we implement new strategies, recruit the compassionate, and educate our people to avoid the various disguises of death. In every local city where we are invited," he vows, "we will help local Christians combat this evil through fervent prayer, skillful praise, the acquiring of knowledge, and above all, charity."

Strong words, passionately held and expressed, from a man who has been at the forefront of the battle to save an entire race of people before it is too late. But, it was not always this way with Reverend Hunter. He recalls that he became active in the pro-life movement first as the director of a crisis pregnancy center, and then as the result of an incident involving his wife, Pat, in Lock Port, New York, some years back. At the time, he was employed in the natural gas industry and served as director of development for Port Centers, an administrative position that provided a rather lucrative income. During that time he was a director at his local church, the Faith Tabernacle, and he also oversaw its Bible studies program. Reverend Hunter recounts what led him to take action. "It was about two days before Christmas," he recalls, "and some folks at our church got disturbed because they found out than an abortion clinic was going to be opening that weekend. And, my wife was very hurt, and the church secretary, the nice quiet ladies, usually." [32]

The good ladies of his church "wanted to do more than just pray," Reverend Hunter recalls. "Pat asked for permission," which the reverend gave, knowing that "they were going to do more than just pray." Shortly thereafter, he says, "I got a phone call from her later on, saying, "Honey, I might not be home for Christmas.'" He asked her what had happened, "and she said, 'we've been arrested, and God told me to go all the way.' So they didn't just go down there and pray, they actually prayed in front of the abortion clinic and wouldn't move when the police came. She said that the police were mad at them because 'they had to stop a party for children to come and arrest us, a judge came off his holiday recess, and he's going to tell us we have to pay bail, and we ain't payin' no bail.' So she was just radical," he recalls, adding that she told him, "No child should die two days before Christmas."

Reverend Hunter recalls the reaction of the faith community when they learned what had taken place: "The people from other churches, when they heard where the police were holding Pat and the others, they came out and surrounded the building with prayer." The husband of one of Mrs. Hunter's fellow participants "was disturbed that his wife had ever gotten arrested. "She was so nice and quiet" the reverend says. "He even called the Governor and the Attorney General. I mean, he was *upset!*" But as so often seems to be the case, when one door closes, another opens in its place because, as Reverend Hunter tells us, "I got another call that day, one from the Holy Spirit." [33] It was a call that would spur him on to become the pro-life hero that he is today.

The call, he says, prompted him to ask himself, with whom is God most pleased. "Is God most pleased," he asks, "with the police who were always having a little Christmas something for children, is he more pleased with ministers like me who do Christmas cantatas and all those things, preached the sermon about the wives, saved the babies, you know? Or is he more pleased with those few people from our church that said 'no child should die two days before Christmas?' In the true spirit," Reverend Hunter asks, "with whom is God most pleased?" [34]

Not long afterward, Mrs. Hunter again sought her husband's permission to return to the clinic, but this time it would not be she who was taking the risk, but Reverend Hunter himself. "No," he told her, "you're not doing any more of this. From now on, I'm going to do it."

"That's when we got involved," he continues, "and the first time we went out, we went to a march between Canada and the United States. And, it disturbed us because we didn't see that many blacks at the march. And, it disturbed me because when I looked at abortion, this is women, this is the worst thing that could ever happen."

The reverend cites his time as a campus radical at Hampton Institute in North Carolina for his later activism on behalf of the unborn. "We were so radical that they mailed us our degrees," he recalls. "They sent us home four months before college was over. That was in 1971. Things were in turmoil at colleges all around the country. Everything we were doing," he says, "we were not doing for ourselves, but for our negro brothers and sisters." Because of this, he holds many current black "leaders" who once were pro-life, but who now favor abortion, in very low regard. To him, it is quite simple... money and prestige.

"A lot of the time," Reverend Hunter is convinced, "what people are doing is going for the prestige, going for the respect, and the power, and the fame, rather than what the true calling is." He also agrees that this was a prime motivating factor that led so many black leaders of Margaret Sanger's day to buy into her program of eugenics and her Negro Project in 1939. "When you look at the Bible," he says, "there are only three sins, lust of eyes, lust of flesh, and pride of life. Pride of life is the most dangerous of all." Further, speaking to the financial aspects behind the black ministers' acquiescence in the abortion issue, he states "The Bible says that the love of money is the root of all evil, so I'm sure they've put some money behind it, as well. He reminds us that "Where there's real commitment, you can't be bought off."

As evidence of whereof he speaks, he cites a visit that former heavyweight boxing champion Muhammad Ali paid to Hampton Institute. "Ali," says the reverend, "was going to be a Gold Glove boxer. He was going to be a world champion, that was his dream. And, even when he reached his dream and they wanted him to come into the military, he felt that was against his religious beliefs. He put his religious beliefs over the greatest thing he wanted to achieve. So, his commitment was really rich, and we had the greatest respect for him, because in the prime of his life, he was knocked out of boxing altogether because he stood by a certain set of principles." Reverend Hunter urges the leaders of the civil rights movement to show the same commitment to core principles that Muhammad Ali displayed in his boxing career when it comes to the abortion crisis in the nation's black community.

Reverend Hunter vividly recalls that first march after his wife and her associates were arrested for praying in front of the Lock Port abortion clinic: "When I went out to that march and saw just a few blacks out there, I wondered, '*what in the world is going on?*' Because when I went to the abortion clinic, I saw something else, and it wasn't good. There were a whole lot of blacks going in." But what was even more stunning, he says, was the reactions of women following their abortions. Speaking of the clinics, he tells us, "In our work in pro-life, we've actually had people who went inside and worked there briefly before they got fired. I remember one thing one lady told me while she was in there. She only heard girls do one of two things when they woke up" from the procedure. "Either they said, 'I'm hungry,' which means they've already denied it, or they woke up crying, 'I've killed my baby, I've killed my baby! Oh, my baby!'" Those, Reverend Hunter says, were "the only two things" the woman told him that she ever heard. [35]

"The thing that got me," he says, "was seeing blacks so fooled and duped, and I realized something: Oh, my goodness, everything we ever worked for in the civil rights movement is being taken away from us, simply by a child being aborted. That's why I say what good is love, what good is educational opportunity for a dead black child? What good are voting rights for a dead black child? What good is equal job opportunity for a dead black child?" When a black baby is aborted, Reverend Hunter reminds us, "you have destroyed every single right that child would have ever had. The only difference between that and what the Klan did," he points out, "is that at least the Klan waited until you were born to lynch you."

"The reason I'm so upset," Reverend Hunter says," is that Margaret Sanger is dead and gone, and, yet, from beyond her grave, her hand, through Planned Parenthood, is strangling the black community." [36] This, Reverend Peterson tells us, is a primary reason why he founded LEARN. "We started in 1993," he recalls, "and one of the things we wanted to do when we first got started, because there were twelve of us, and there were many people out there, we were crying, hollering, and shouting. We had never met each other before, and everybody was in their own place, thinking that they were the only blacks that were concerned. We were going to honor Erma Clardy Craven (a pro-life advocate who worked against abortion in New York State prior to the legalization of abortion on demand by the Supreme Court and who put together a pamphlet titled *Abortion, Poverty and Genocide* in 1970)." Unfortunately, Mrs. Craven was unable to attend the ceremony honoring her, but she sent the people at LEARN a message.

According to the reverend, she told a representative of the group that "she had lived to see what she wanted to see. Tell them," Craven said, "that you blacks are going to be just fine. It's going to be hard, but just keep fighting. "Just to see you was enough," Mrs. Craven knew, to realize that the tide was eventually going to turn. Sadly, she died not long after her message to LEARN.

"It was gut-wrenching," Reverend Hunter says of her passing, "but it made us understand the seriousness of the fight, to really stay with it. So we looked at groups like Planned Parenthood and I noticed something. The next year," he recalls proudly, "when we did that march across the Canada Bridge, I made sure I had black folks out. Black folks from the church, their friends, family, we *packed* the place!" But as encouraging as that was to the reverend, there was one problem: the media.

"However," he says of the coverage of the event, "the media, which started in Canada and came across to the other side, they did the piping, the bagpipe blowers, they did the Nurses for Life, and they got to the blacks, and *they cut the cameras off!* they cut to the next group that they saw and they filmed them. But, he adds, "it's not so much what the news reports sometimes, it's what the news does *not* report. What isn't it writing about? What is it they're not saying?"

Reverend Hunter gives great credit to his wife for making him an activist for the unborn, and he says, "This whole abortion thing could easily be over now except for one thing: Christians who are not involved. You know, there are people who give a lot of good lip service, but they're not doing the action behind it that needs to be done. And, no matter what it is, something that is evil always comes back to haunt you." He also warns of the coming economic crisis that is accompanying the looming demographic disaster that abortion in the black community portends. "It (the economy) will collapse because we have lost over 50 million people, but we've not only lost over 50 million folks, we've lost the descendants of those 50 million also." [37] And, Reverend Hunter goes farther than just the economic loss that abortion represents. He is deeply troubled by the staggering loss of intellectual capital caused by abortion. "What is also missing from society," he says ruefully, "is we don't know what *ideas* we've lost."

"We don't know what new inventions we've lost," he points out. "And abortion," he adds, "is haunting us (the black community) real good because blacks are now the minority of the minority." Reverend Hunter recalls hearing about the demographic and economic aspects of abortion for the first time from the late Mike Schwartz, chief of staff to Senator and Dr. Tom Coburn (R-OK). "Years ago," he says, "I went into his office and he had a book he wanted me to see, and that's when I did the statistical analysis." One of the things Reverend Hunter learned from the census data contained in Schwartz's book was that the numbers of black Americans had declined to the point that Hispanics were now the largest minority in the United States. And, he cautions, while this may be the case at present, "The same folks that went after the blacks are now coming after them." This warning poses an interesting bit of speculation: will the day come when there are so few black Americans because of abortion that we begin to see Planned Parenthood put the majority of their abortion mills into Hispanic neighborhoods?

Reverend Hunter agrees wholeheartedly with Reverend Hoye in comparing blacks to a "canary in the coal mine," and adds, "You have to understand something, and that's that Margaret Sanger and the eugenicists knew that whites were going to get more abortions. They had reached a point where things were so bad, that there was a critical need, and that there was just going to be too much collateral damage. That's the way they looked at it. You'd think that Planned Parenthood would be ashamed of Margaret

Sanger," he says, "but they're not. I remember when they used to have (former Planned Parenthood President) Faye Wattleton and all that group out there; she was Margaret Sanger's dream child. And, even today, the reverend adds, "They're still recruiting young blacks out of high school."

Reverend Hunter recounts what happened when a friend encountered a young black lady who was attempting to tell him about the good that Planned Parenthood was doing in her community, and a black gentleman from a Planned Parenthood clinic. Needless to say, before he was finished, they had both received quite an education. In the first case, Reverend Hunter's friend asked the young lady if she knew about either Margaret Sanger or the Negro Project. "He began to explain it to this girl and he saw this girl's mouth drop," the reverend recalls. "She looked so ashamed that she wouldn't even look him in the eye afterwards. And she went off and he never saw her again." As for the man from the clinic, he was handing out abortion literature when the reverend's friend informed him about what PPFA was really doing. "I told the fellow," Reverend Hunter's friend said, "and he was going, '*What?? No!*' And, he didn't even know about Margaret Sanger!'"

It is just this type of ignorance on the part of so many black Americans that the "pro-choice" movement must preserve if it is to survive. It is this kind of ignorance that Reverend Johnny Hunter and his associates at LEARN are fighting every day. "I hope the country will get it right," he says. "My goal is to end abortion this year." While this may seem unrealistic, he says there is a reason for it. "When slavery was going, they actually had an opportunity to undo it. When the *Dred Scott* decision was made by the Supreme Court, that was a 7-2 Supreme Court split and it went the wrong way. In other words, this fellow was not protected by the U.S. Constitution. That was their opportunity to get it right, and they missed it."

Reverend Hunter fervently hopes that this nation can avoid the kind of division over abortion that tore it apart over slavery, a division which resulted directly from the disastrous *Dred Scott* decision. He looks at *Roe vs. Wade* as equally catastrophic, and in many ways even worse. During the Civil War, he relates, Abraham Lincoln took note of how each side would pray to God to help it win. "Whose prayer was God going to hear?" Reverend Hunter asked. But Lincoln "made a speculation," he says. "Perhaps the War itself is a curse for the blood and sweat of slaves." Lincoln understood, he adds, "that God can end something, but you don't want to see God end it." While the Civil War at last put an end to the vile, disgusting institution of slavery, Reverend Hunter points out that war was the worst possible way to bring that result about. And he says, "If this nation ended up split over slavery, and our nation as a whole went to war with each other, right now we are living in a country that is so completely divided (over abortion), it's just like the North versus the South." And, he adds, "I tell people that if we think the radical Muslims are barbaric for cutting off peoples' heads, think how barbaric we are to cut off the head of a baby in its mother's womb." [38]

If, as Reverend Hunter says, "blacks are unwilling to stand up for the civil rights of a little innocent baby, if we now have become so gullible, because the mother especially is the first protection that child has, the most *adamant* protection that child has, and Planned Parenthood uses all the nice terms it has, to get her to actually drop her defenses to save her baby, we're all in trouble." He stresses also that "there are men out there who have no problem laying down with a woman, but don't want to be responsible when she gets pregnant." The black community, he points out, "has suffered a major blow. This thing (abortion) is destroying us. It is doing to us what the Klan could not have dreamed of doing." [39] He also reminds us that, due to abortion, more black deaths occur in one week than all the lynchings that took place in the South from 1870 to 1950. "That," he says, "is scary."

He also reminds us that black "leaders" like Jesse Jackson, by taking money from Planned Parenthood, have been silent on this issue. "The main civil rights group out there is just sitting on its laurels of things of the past, and they are not the people of the future. I only spoke to the NAACP at its convention in Atlanta once," Reverend Hunter recalls, "and I told them then that if they don't lift their fingers to stop this killing of these little innocent babies who are going down, and they stand before God on the Day of Judgment, they are not going to make it in (to Heaven)." Reverend Hunter believes that every person is put on Earth for a reason, "and I know what my calling is. I'm going to save as many lives as I can before I leave here. But, at the same time, there are people that belong to the NAACP who have been called to do the same thing, but for them it's a matter of prestige and pride, and that pride has destroyed them. It has made them ineffectual. And Planned Parenthood is winning. Margaret Sanger is dead in her grave and she is beating the living daylights out of the NAACP. She is winning, not them." Strong words, indeed, words that the black community sorely needs to hear. May this tireless, selfless, dedicated pro-life hero and his associates at LEARN succeed in this mission before it is too late.

• • •

One of the longest-serving and most beloved members of the pro-life movement is the Reverend Levon R. Yuille, Pastor at the Bible Church in Ypsilanti, Michigan, and Director of the National Black Pro-Life Congress. As the leader of the NBPLC, Pastor Yuille has dedicated his life to protecting the rights of the unborn. His work with this organization has earned him effusive praise from his peers in the pro-life movement, and his reputation for honesty, decency, and compassion for all has spread far beyond the confines of his small Ypsilanti church. National leaders in the movement consider him to be among their nearest and dearest friends, not to mention their closest ally on behalf of the unborn. Reverend Johnny L. Hunter calls him "my hero." Reverend Walter Hoye calls him "a great friend and a patriarch of the black pro-life movement." High praise, indeed, from two of the most visible and outspoken defenders of the rights of the unborn.

"Brother Lee," as he is affectionately known to tens of thousands of loyal listeners to *Johsua's Trail,* a weekly talk show airing Saturday mornings from 8 a.m. until 10 a.m. on WDTK-AM, a Salem Broadcasting affiliate in Detroit, Michigan, was born in Atlantic City, New Jersey, in 1940. He received his ministerial training at the Avery Church and Bible School in Chicago and came to the Bible Church in 1978. During that time, he has been quite active in a number of organizations, including the NBPLC; the Ypsilanti, Ann Arbor and Vicinity Ministerial Alliance, where he served as president for six years; the Neighborhood Health Clinic, which assists those who cannot afford health insurance; Parents Together, a grass-roots drug-prevention agency, of which he was not only a member, but its Chairman as well; Leaders in Prevention; the Hope Clinic Pastoral Advisory Board, and as the Chairman of the Michigan Black Republican Council. [40]

With all these responsibilities, one would think that there would be very little time for anything else. Yet, Pastor Yuille, along with his wife, confidante, traveling secretary, and soul mate Sally, has found time to go to Africa on three separate occasions, visiting Uganda, Kenya, and Tanzania to speak to the good people of that continent about the life issue. The Yuilles have also traveled to Canada, Mexico, and England, and have visited all 50 states. His travels have brought him in close proximity to such leading conservative lights as Illinois Representative Henry Hyde, author of the Hyde Amendment, writer and activist Star Parker, and U.S. Supreme Court Justice Clarence Thomas. The Yuilles are also the proud parents of eight beautiful children. [41]

Pastor Yuille is the organizer of the annual "Stand for Life" Rally each spring across from Detroit's Cobo Center. This event coincides with the NAACP's yearly "Fight for Freedom" dinner at the convention hall, drawing dozens of pro-life supporters from all around the Detroit area and across the country to demand an answer as to just why the nation's largest civil rights group refuses to take an official stand on Planned Parenthood. Past attendees have included two pro-life heroes profiled in this chapter, Dr. Alveda King and the Reverend Walter Hoye. This event has become a critical tool in bringing to the public's attention the genocidal aspects of so many abortions in the black community.

As a production of the NBPLC, the *Joshua's Trail* radio show brings abortion and a host of other critical issues that face the black community into clear, sharp focus. Pastor Yuille and the other members of the "abolitionist roundtable" (Milt Harris, Ron Edwards, Charles McCollough, and Dr. Ellis Washington) have been providing this crucial service to the metropolitan Detroit area every Saturday morning since the program debuted in October of 2004. One of only a handful of programs hosted by black conservatives, its title of "a talk show like no other" is well-earned. *Joshua's Trail* takes its inspiration from the Biblical story of Joshua, who was hugely successful in battle until he suffered a defeat which made him look inward for the reasons for his having done so. It is in this spirit of introspection that Pastor Yuille and his co-hosts hold forth from the broadcast booth each Saturday morning.

Pastor Yuille is adamant in reminding his audience that "a people cannot separate its plight from its politics," and he strongly believes that many of the problems that face the black community stem from its almost monolithic support of the Democrat Party. He goes to great lengths to point out the racist past of the Democrats, and wonders why so many blacks are so willing to forgive the party that enslaved them and which supports the wholesale slaughter of black children in the womb (the Democrats), yet, refuse to support the party that abolished slavery and was instrumental in passing of civil rights legislation, as well as opposing the annihilation that abortion represents (the Republicans).

To show the level of Pastor Yuille's commitment, his passion, and his dedication to preserving the lives of the unborn, Reverend Hunter tells this story about an incident that occurred in 1989: "He (Pastor Yuille) and another minister led the first all-black rescue in the country. In 1989, in East Lansing, Michigan, he and his folks went inside an abortion clinic, and some of them literally chained themselves in. They did a sit-in at an abortion clinic and the media made sure it did not cover that story. I found out about it and I said, 'Oh, my goodness.' It was people like Levon Yuille out there doing it even when the media would not recognize the work he was doing. If there were more pastors out there like him, this thing would have been over years ago."

Testimonies such as this from his peers show why Pastor Yuille is held in such high esteem. A life-long supporter of the civil-rights movement, he considers abortion to be precisely that—-a civil-rights issue. This was how, he says, he first learned of Margaret Sanger and the Negro Project. "The pro-life issue," he states, "is certainly a civil-rights issue, and in studying that and coming across friends who had done research on Margaret Sanger, I was made aware of who she was. And, like so many others, upon discovering her, I did quite a bit of research. I have a parishoner who's done volumes of research, and who presented me with a large amount of information on Margaret Sanger, and she had a very difficult life." [42] The Pastor elaborates further: "She was very embittered toward the Church, and she adopted a very hostile attitude concerning anyone who did not have a 'right' perspective about the quality of life and the human being. There were categories that she put human beings in. And all human beings were not equal in Margaret Sanger's eyes. She became," Pastor Yuille states, "quite an advocate for the eugenics movement, who would be fittest for survival, the thoroughbred of the human race, etc."

"As we read that," he recalls, "and that most chilling letter to Mr. Clarence Gamble in 1939 that 'we want to exterminate the Negro and we don't want him to know it, all of that certainly gave me cause to not only want to know about her, but to publicize who this woman was." And he adds, "It is one of the great tragedies, because the educational system is so acquiescent to political correctness, it has overlooked the dark side of this lady and only projects a really false image of who this lady was." To illustrate this whitewashing of one of the twentieth century's most infamous figures, Pastor Yuille takes note of the current narrative of the Planned Parenthood founder as "simply this great feminist, etc., when she had a very dark side and a very dark agenda, and specifically about abortion."

He also reminds us that Sanger had "a philosophical relationship with" Adolph Hitler, and that "they agreed on many issues" revolving around the eugenic movement in both the United States and in Germany. "That's why," he says, "now we're facing, relative to Margaret Sanger's organization, Planned Parenthood, that it should be told, this dark side of the story should be told. And," he adds, "I think it is criminal that five hundred million dollars of our tax money go to these folks, and they are the product and the offspring of somebody like Margaret Sanger." [43]

Pastor Yuille deplores the rise of infanticide in the United States as advocated by Peter Singer and his followers. It troubles him deeply that "one of the towering intellects of the day is promoting infanticide up to the age of two. This is frightening," he says, "and hopefully more folks will continue to sound the alarm and let America know what kind of insidious forces we're dealing with here." Pastor Yuille places the blame for the lack of awareness of the damage that abortion is doing in places like Oakland, California on "a great failure of the Church in these communities and the ministers not appropriately approaching this subject and speaking to it in a very profound and strong way."

It is critical, he believes, that these religious institutions "educate their young people that it (abortion) is a dimensional issue; it's dealing with the physical and the spiritual, and the natural side of life. And while the physical and natural sides can most certainly be synonymous, the spiritual side where the Scriptures have spoken so strongly about the destroying of innocent life, and nothing is more innocent than an unborn child who is being killed in the womb."

Pastor Yuille then examines the physical ramifications of abortion "that have been documented by numerous studies of the tragic end results of having an abortion. And the high rate of breast cancer in the black community can be *directly* tied to the too great a prevalence of abortion in the community. So," Pastor Yuille says, "I see the Church has miserably failed, then our political entities, the elected black officials both locally and nationally, and the civic organizations like the NAACP and others, who have aligned themselves with the 'pro-choice' mantra. This is regrettable," he continues, "but there is a light at the end of the tunnel, and it's not a locomotive coming this way." After being in the pro-life movement since the late 1970s, Pastor Yuille says, "I have seen movement toward understanding the issue," an understanding that has come about in no small part because of such documentaries as *Maafa 21,* which exposes the genocidal agenda of both Margaret Sanger and her acolytes in the eugenic movement to the harsh light of truth.

"Just a few weeks ago," Pastor Yuille says, "I shared this great DVD. And when even black folks are properly educated, there can be a sea change in their perspective of the way they look at this issue. I wish more of them would be profoundly touched from a religious perspective," he adds, "but regrettably, if you don't come from the culturally promoted racial aspect of it, then it's hard to get the attention of so many of our young people. But, the *Maafa* tape that shows the intent, the racist intent, of abortion, has been a positive instrument, and it has been changing hearts and minds." [44]

In addition to documentaries like *Maafa 21* and the advances in medical technology that have come about in recent years, Pastor Yuille has an especially warm place in his heart for the efforts of sidewalk counselors around the country who, in some cases, spend all of their time trying to convince women to forgo ending the lives of their unborn babies in abortion mills. "We can't ignore the sexual revolution that has most certainly been a very instrumental part of this destruction of human life, like sex without consequences, teaching young folks that abstinence is an impossible mountain to climb," he says.

But the Pastor begs to differ, and he differs quite strongly. "It is not an impossible mountain to climb," he believes, "and if young people would hear more about it, they would be more inclined to practice abstinence." But, he cautions, "We have the forces on the Left that don't even want the subject brought up. I think that it should be, and we should give our kids alternatives and educate them about the value of their bodies. The sacredness that is involved in the sex act, etc." Pastor Yuillle strongly believes that "there should be a strong emphasis from the Judeo-Christian perspective relative to sexuality." In reference to how that act has been portrayed in the popular culture over the years, he adds, "We've given it to television and the movies and we need to take it back." [45]

The Pastor decries the loss of traditional values in America over the past 50 years, a loss that he believes has resulted in the mind-numbing number of abortions that have taken place since 1973: "They want to celebrate it (abortion)," he points out, "and even in the Church, the statistics show that 80% of church-going kids are sexually active. When I came in," he recalls, "we didn't share the same experience. The worst thing that could happen was an illegitimate child, a girl becoming pregnant. And back then, the girl would disappear. Someone would," for example, "send them down South. But now," he says, "it's celebrated. That's a tragedy. It's not that we should condemn people and put them down, but we should not elevate having a child outside of marriage as being the same as having a child in the confines of marriage."

Pastor Yuille applauds one minister in Detroit, the Reverend Marvin Wynans, for having two ceremonies, one for the birth of a child within marriage, and another for one born outside of it. "He'll dedicate them both a certain way, but he makes a distinction so that he can elevate the marital situation, and I think we need to get back to that type of thinking." And he agrees wholeheartedly that those who graduate from high school, go to work, and defer having children until after getting married are far likelier to avoid the pitfalls of poverty and societal ruin. "It's off the charts," he says. "Traditional, eternal, Judeo-Christian principles are beneficial to humanity and society."

"The quality of life that we have experienced in America," he points out, "from the founding principles that guided this nation that were steeped in the Judeo-Christian faith, it shows you that when you apply these values, you're successful. When you reject them or discard them as we're doing in America, you see the consequences. And one of the great tragedies of this type of abandoning of our traditions," Pastor Yuille maintains, "is not just the individual, but all of society which, in some way or another, pays for the shift with which we're now dealing. It's detrimental to all of us."

To illustrate just exactly where this shift will lead unless society pulls back from the abyss, Pastor Yuille refers to "our own Kermit Gosnell in Washtenaw County," which lies directly west of the Detroit metropolitan area. "There were a number of us pro-lifers who stayed on the case for years until finally that 'gentleman' closed down his business," the Pastor recalls. "And one of the most gratifying moments I've had in the pro-life movement," he adds, "is that I joined with this group as we would be out with our graphic pictures showing a dismembered child's body." And he fondly remembers what took place as a result of those protests.

"A couple walked in with a beautiful baby," he recalls. "They didn't go to our church, but they said, 'Pastor, this baby lives because you were standing out on that corner that day. When we passed and saw you standing by that sign, we said, "We cannot kill our baby." We were going to kill our baby, but we saw you. And, because of you standing there, this child lives today.'" Small wonder, then, that Pastor Yuille calls this "one of the most gratifying moments and one of the most encouraging moments," in all his time in the pro-life movement.

At the same time, while stories like this warm his heart, Pastor Yuille reminds us that there is still much work to be done before the scourge of abortion is lifted from this nation. There are still far too many men and women who choose such a destructive path. "When people are desperate and when their value system has been so eroded, as we've seen in the last thirty to forty years, and because in our society we put such low value on human life, to hear very little pro-life conversation over the general media, until mothers and grandmothers and grandfathers feel like, in this desperate situation, they've got to do what they've got to do. Which, again, speaks back to the failure of the organizations, the Church, etc., which should be teaching people the value of life. And so, regrettably," he concludes, "this is too common." For example, Pastor Yuille says, "I've lost track of the number of people who were intimidated by a mother or a grandmother" into having an abortion. "And, the grandmother part even astounds me more than the mother, because I believe that there should have been enough history there in the mind of the individual to know that this is a dastardly thing to do."

"But we have so cheapened life in America," Pastor Yuille points out, "that we are literally at a point where a woman, who we always see as epitomizing the love for a child and baby, to think that a mother would do this is terribly disheartening." Equally sad and tragic, Pastor Yuille says, is the prevailing attitude of many civil rights leaders and black politicians on the abortion issue. The NAACP and the Congressional Black Caucus "are the primary defenders of genocide" in the black community. "You cannot promote the genocide of your own race," he states emphatically, "and they know what they're doing."

"Most of these people," Pastor Yuille observes, "are college-educated black people, who know about human life, but because it is profitable and politically and socially expedient, and the circles they run in promote the genocide of their own people, they do it. But I join with Jesse Peterson in abhorring the fact that we have so-called black 'leaders' that promote the genocide of their own race. This is not an act of love," Pastor Yuille says, "this is a total, selfish, Godless, *heartless* act." Like all of the many pro-life heroes whom we have examined thus far, Pastor Levon Yuille realizes that the road that lies ahead remains a long one. Many hearts and minds yet remain to be changed. Many obstacles still lie in the way, and there are still many hurdles that need to be cleared. But it is a challenge that he and the National Black Pro-Life Congress firmly embrace because it is the right thing to do. And with God's help, it is one that they will not only continue to meet head on, it is a battle from which they will ultimately emerge victorious.

• • •

Another passionate defender of the rights of the unborn is Ron Edwards. A nationally-syndicated commentator and the host of *The Edwards Notebook,*

Ron is a monthly co-host of the *Joshua's Trail* radio talk show along with Pastor Yuille in Detroit. Born in Cleveland, Ohio, Ron came to the Detroit area in the early 1990s, but he has also called Sedona, Arizona, home, as well. He is a fierce defender of the unalienable rights laid down and set forth in the *Declaration of Independence*, especially the most important right of all, the right to life. His *Edwards Notebook* commentaries can be heard in more than a dozen markets around the country, and he frequently fills in for such conservative black talk show hosts as Star Parker. Ron's artful commentaries pull no punches when it come to exposing the multitude of crises that face this nation, and the abortion issue is right at the top of his list. A frequent speaker at conservative events around the country, Ron has established a reputation for honesty, integrity, and commitment to God. He is a staunch defender of the values that made the United States the exceptional nation it is, and he is a powerful voice against the constant onslaught against our freedoms, rights, and liberties that is currently underway by an out-of-control federal government. Ron is a dedicated family man and a proud defender of time-honored American ideals like faith, patriotism, individual responsibility, traditional marriage, and family. He, his wife, Denise, and their son Ronnie currently reside in Huntington Woods, Michigan.

Ron's insights on the issues of abortion and eugenics are both timely and compelling, and like his radio commentaries, they pull no punches, either. And, he is not one to shy away from sharing those thoughts. "The first way I found out about this (the Negro Project) was from my own father," Ron recalls. "He was the first person to tell me that Margaret Sanger was an avowed racist who was hell-bent on wiping out the Negro population. And, she was able to persuade the NAACP and these fabulous preachers who had charming personalities, or as she called them, 'engaging personalities,' to persuade their flocks to go against the word of God, and to persuade them to kill or murder their innocent babies. So he was the first. I had never," Ron adds, "learned about this in school, these government schools. And I thought I had gone to some pretty good schools." As he got older, Ron recalls, he began to find out more, and he was almost dumbfounded at what he soon discovered.

"Later," he says, "after I had gone to college, in doing research into eugenics, into Germany, and the German eugenics movement, that's where I found out more, because Sanger had linked up with them. And," he adds, "this is what's mind-blowing: how they were able, the very organization that was hell-bent in this country to keep black Americans oppressed, depressed, could at the same time keep them *impressed* with them to the point where to this day, after all that they've done and perpetrated against the black American community, this goes all the way back to the eugenics movement. They have," he says," been hell-bent on dumbing down not just black Americans, but Americans, in general. Because people don't understand that the move against black Americans," he explains, "was part of a greater movement to destroy the United States from within. They knew they could never do it militarily; they knew they could never do it even on a large scale through the mind. But, if they could focus on what at that time was perceived as the 'victims' of this country, they could zero in on them and say, 'We're sorry about how America has treated you, you're victims, they hate you. Let us come beside you and help you.' 'When they said that, that was the first element they used to weaken the black man."

Anyone who has studied the life of Frederick Douglass," Ron says, "and would remember some of his great quotes, one of his greatest quotes was when he begged the federal government and even some of his fellow abortionists not to coddle the black man, and not to oppress them, either. Allow him to rise or fall, just like anyone else, on his own efforts. And, he said that through the natural process, blacks would perform as well as or better than anyone else." [46] As Ron sees it, the spirit of self-reliance and personal responsibility on the part of many black Americans has been replaced with an attitude of entitlement, victimization, and dependency on government, and it pains him greatly.

"Case in point," Ron continues, "Frederick Douglass, thirty years before Abraham Lincoln said, 'I'm going to free the slaves,' this man decided himself that he was free, and he freed himself. Not only physically but monetarily, and every other way you can imagine, he was freer than most black Americans in this country today. He was so free that he acquired an economic base for himself through his own private sector efforts that when he died, he left three hundred thousand dollars in the bank, which is close to seven million dollars today.

This man forgave almost all of his former slave masters, and he didn't walk around with bitterness and allow that to keep him down. He actually *loaned* two of his former slave masters money and became their friends." [47] This is why, Ron maintains, the story of Frederick Douglass is no "If black, white, or any other Americans would learn the life of Frederick Douglass and look at that," Ron believes, "what he was able to overcome even before the end of slavery in this country, everyone would look in the mirror and say, 'What excuse do I have for not being able to make it today?'" Ron is greatly saddened by the failure of so many to look to the example of this great man and use it as a guidepost in conducting their own lives. And, he is especially angered by what has become known over the last fifty years, at least attitudinally on the part of so many of his fellow black Americans, as the "plantation mentality." One of the heartbreaking aspects of this development, he says, "is something I had to come to the realization of, and then gain the intestinal fortitude to say this publicly: many people who have been wallowing in this mentality have been so brainwashed that they prefer living the way that they do, even if it means the downfall of America."

"You can see the evidence," Ron says, referring to those "who would rather go down to hell as long as America falls. When you hear people going around saying, 'The white man has kept me out of opportunities, they don't allow us this, they don't allow us that,' that is a pack of lies. That is a big lie because how can you say that the white man is keeping you from doing something, how can you say that the white man is killing you off, when it has been only black people who are killing each other today, when it is only black people who for the most part are oppressing each other, and even keeping each other out of opportunities?"

This mindless, horrifying development extends as well to the number one killer by far of black Americans—-abortion on demand. Ron has particular contempt for abortionists like Kermit Gosnell, and he holds nothing back in voicing his revulsion at what this so-called "doctor" perpetrated for so many decades. "This idiot, this moron, this evildoer, he would be one of the first ones to talk about the white man being the oppressor of black Americans." Are these people talking, Ron asks, about "white men, or in the case of white women like Dr. Monica Miller (the director of Citizens for a Pro-Life Society and another defender of the rights of the unborn), as an oppressor because she stands tall against the murder of innocent life?"

"They don't talk about people like that," Ron points out, "who are heroes on behalf of black Americans, to save their lives." Dr. Miller, he points out, "has buried 5,000 aborted victims, most of whom were black." If this were a racist nation, Ron posits, "would you have the majority of pro-lifers being white, who are full of the knowledge that the majority of the abortions percentage-wise are blacks? If this were such a racist nation, would they be wasting their time fighting to save black lives in this endeavor?"

Ron decries the "double-pronged racism" of Sanger, Stoddard, Laughlin *et al,* and he adds that "to justify their motive to wipe black people off the face of the earth, they say, 'We cannot allow the likes of Frederick Douglass to get out as far as people knowing about them.' They say, 'We cannot allow them to rise economically and intellectually; so what we have to do is use the system to stupefy them, to put them into a position of lesser than.' So in their minds, what they're saying is, 'Look at those people. They need to be wiped out, they need to be marginalized. So, if we can't wipe them out physically, we can wipe them out economically, mentally, and spiritually, and keep them marginalized in their ghettos to the point where, as they did, they retired the Ku Klux Klan."

And, Ron continues, "Instead of the Ku Klux Klan hanging seven thousand blacks in its entire history, now, seven thousand-plus black babies are killed every *week*. So, here you have blacks doing the dirty work themselves at a greater clip than the eugenicists had ever thought about. Even they did not imagine the numbers and the damage. They didn't even think, as much as they hated black people, because they knew in their heart of hearts that black people weren't stupid; they just didn't like them, and they wanted them off the earth. They, in their own evil thinking, did not believe that black people could be dummied down to the point to be so stupid as to do to themselves what they're doing on a daily and weekly basis."

To Ron, Margaret Sanger's strategy of having black ministers invite her and her cohorts into their own churches to promote sterilization of their parishoners under the guise of "women's health," "child spacing," and all the euphemisms the eugenicists employed in their campaign to rid the world of "human weeds" is abominable. "That is so inherently evil," he says. "Things like that come to mind whenever the Negro thought police of today come to the likes of myself and call me an 'Uncle Tom' or a 'traitor to my race,' as people write me in emails when they hear the *Edwards Notebook* commentary, once they find out that I'm a black guy. And, the ones that I feel like responding to, I find out what they support, and everything they support is to the destruction of not only the black race, but to the American nation."

Moreover, Ron finds it necessary to respond to the accusations against him and set the record straight. "So, I have to write back to these people when they call me an 'Uncle Tom.' I must respond in kind and call them an 'Uncle Joe,' or an 'Uncle Marx,' or an 'Aunt Sanger' to the females. Because these people," he says, "after one, two, three, four, five, or six decades of total destruction, and it really came *en masse* in the 1960s," when Detroit, for example, went from a Republican mayor to a Democrat, in 1962. "How did that happen?" For Ron, it is quite simple. More than fifty years of failed liberal social policies that were enacted under a succession of Democrat mayors have virtually destroyed a once-great American city.

"The infusion of socialist thought, coupled with Sangerism stirred in with a good supply of communism, socialism, bitterness, anti-Christian thought, all of those things into this poisonous soup that permeated the minds of people in five years to the point that they were willing to burn down their own town. Now," Ron says, "tell me if life was worse for black people after they burned down their own town, burned out the businesses that hired them and all of that, than it was before they decided to torch their own town."

Ron believes that abortion is, first of all, a moral issue. "It is a right and wrong issue, a 'love yourself' issue. Black Americans have been so battered down," he says, "not by white oppression, but by self-inflicted wounds of making one feel bad about one's self. I have seen it first-hand in the black community and experienced it in the black community and it's like a self-perpetuating mental disorder that just rolls throughout the black community. On the one hand," he says, "they run around talking about how they hate the white man, they hate this country, and I'll go on the record: most blacks hate America as much as they hate the Ku Klux Klan or anything of that nature. They're not able to discriminate the crucial differences, pick the good, and build on that good. They're more concerned with how to destroy the country." As Ron sees it, nothing short of a "radical spiritual, mental, and moral turnaround" can save the black community at this point.

To illustrate what he means, he looks once more to the example of the great Frederick Douglass, "who," he says, "labored under just ominous, direct oppression and, yet, had the wherewithal not to hate the United States of America, and who did not even hate his oppressors. He did not learn to hate himself, he refused to allow others to come upon and overtake himself and his actions toward himself or others. He chose to look at America objectively. When he first looked at the 'three-fifths' clause in the U.S. Constitution, he believed what they said, that it just meant that blacks were supposedly three-fifths of a human being. But," Ron points out, "when he took the time to read the Constitution, the Bill of Rights, and the Federalist Papers, he found out that it had nothing to do with that. It had to do with voting numbers so that the South would not just overtake the legislative branch in Washington. When he read that, he said, 'Well, that makes sense.' And there were many other things. When he decided to read for himself, that instilled a love for this country in his heart. He said, 'Wow.'"

As a result, Douglas was able to "differentiate between the real Christians and the fake 'Christians' who enslaved him. He had *common* sense. Today, there is a blindness that envelops the minds of most black Americans." Ron is not shy about citing an actual figure of those who have been brainwashed: "Ninety-four percent of them," he says, "because that's how many voted for this present (Obama) administration, and which continues to follow that philosophy despite the fact that unemployment among black Americans is much worse today than it was the day before the first time Barack Obama took office."

But to Ron, there is more to the crisis than just high unemployment. It involves failure on a massive scale, from that of our education system to properly teach students and prepare them for life outside of the classroom to the refusal of our government to adequately protect us from internal and external threats to the almost cavalier attitude toward the taking of unborn human life that is displayed by so many of his fellow black citizens. "Let's say they (the federal government) had done the right thing," he posits. "Let's say that they sealed our borders and stopped aborting black American babies. Let's say if they were born and went to pro-American schools and they were truly educated in the way they should be and they were more in the mindset of Frederick Douglass instead of, say, Adam Clayton Powell or Al Sharpton. Let's say that these things had occurred."

"What would have taken place," Ron firmly believes, "is a very productive society. You would have a very strong, cohesive United States of America. So, what do you do? You destroy the country mentally from within." Then Ron says, "While you cut the native population, you have an influx of enemies flood in and infiltrate your country." To make his point, Ron cites an incident which occurred near San Jose, California, on April 16, 2013, in which 17 electrical transformers were attacked and heavily damaged by sniper fire. [48] He believes that it was clearly a terrorist attack mounted by people who had come across the border with Mexico, and he says, "They did all this destruction, and we have not heard one peep out of the White House over this event. It caused hardship. Now, Al Sharpton and Jesse Jackson and all these other individuals are always running around talking about 'oppression' and 'hardship.'"

"I have not," Ron says, "heard one of these individuals, from the 'White House to the outhouse,' as Jesse Jackson likes to say, talk about the cruelty and oppression on our soil as a terrorist act to destroy transformers and interrupt electricity to hospitals and homes. So, they're happy that these kinds of things are happening. I believe it, I know it, and can prove it. It doesn't take a rocket scientist to know this." Ron sees a "clear interconnectedness" between what happened in California and the abortion issue in the American community. "I know we're talking about primarily the black community and abortion," he says, "but these events affect all Americans. We're Americans."

What keeps drawing back to America "at large," Ron says, is this: "I was brought up by my father as an American, and he did not say, 'You're a black American.' He didn't say, 'You're an 'African-American.' In fact, he never heard that word. But he did say that I'm an *American* and that I should be proud of my country, that I should love my country. He told me this as a black American who was reasonably successful in this country and who went through certain racist incidents, but he did not apply that to America as a *whole*. He always focused on individuals, and he lived that way."

"He lived that way first of all," Ron recalls, "by the way he raised me and my two older sisters. Second of all, by the people he associated with, by the many Jews who would come to our house at Christmastime to celebrate Christmas. How about that? To the many Jehovah Witnesses who would stop by our house and have coffee and tea with my dad as he would present Jesus Christ to them, and Christianity. And," Ron adds with the pride and satisfaction that only a loving son could have for his father, "they loved him anyway." He also praises his father for introducing him to "the many Americans from all walks of life that I met because of my dad. Black, white, Asian, Jews, Italians. That's how he lived his life. He didn't walk around telling everyone, 'I'm a black guy, who loves you,' it's just the way he was. He had many friends because he *made* himself friendly to others."

"He did not carry a bitter patch on his sleeve for everyone to see what the white man did to him," Ron says of his father. He challenges all Americans, not just blacks, "If their sincere desire is to build a better life not only for themselves but for their children and their children's children, to change their focus from bitterness to better; from toil to tending; from tyranny to triumph over evil. From hate of America to love and respect for America." Ron reminds us that the Constitution and the Bill of Rights were "inspired by the Word of God, and if you have a modicum of respect and love for our God and our Creator, you cannot help but love and respect the Founding Fathers for having the *cojones* to put such words to paper, such ink, to paper." But Ron fears that "because we have focused on the 'majors and the minors' in this country, we are losing our property rights, our rights to protect ourselves, and in many instances we're losing the right to speak out against tyranny" as it is represented by a huge and overbearing government apparatus. This loss of essential freedoms includes the black community, as well, which he warns will "suffer the same amount of oppression" that the majority population will experience. Even so, Ron can say, "I still love this country," not only because of what his father taught him, but because "God shed his grace upon America."

"It's in our song," he reminds us. Many Americans, he believes, are doing the right things to persevere in the face of great adversity, and he adds, "I have personal reason to believe, because of my faith in our Father through his son Jesus Christ that it is not over for this country. God is a God of mercy. He hears our cries. He says, 'If my people will humble themselves and pray and ask for mercy,' He will hear from them and He will honor their prayers. He will hear from Heaven, and will heal our land." And God is giving signs, Ron believes, "that He wants to redeem this country back to its rightful place as being the light of the world. Because this country was built not so we can be fat and happy. This country was built so that we could be a light to the world, to show the rest of the world that there is a better way."

Where the black community is concerned, that better way, Ron says, involves the following: first, "learning how to love the one who gave them life;" second, "learning to appreciate the country that, at least on paper, recognizes their right to exist;" and third, to "love themselves and their families." Women must learn to respect their men, and the men, in turn, to love their wives, "and women in general, because it's a two-way street." Fourth, Ron advises parents to "love their children enough to raise them in the correct manner so that they will be in a position to build for themselves a better life, which builds a better country. And the better you do," he says, "the better I'm going to do, even if you never give me a dime. If everyone prospers and everyone is working, you're going to be too busy to hate."

That, he concludes, is the key to breaking the vicious cycle of poverty, death, and social breakdown, and not just among black Americans. Ron Edwards is a pro-life hero to be sure, but he is something more. He is a great American patriot who cares deeply and passionately about the future not only of his particular demographic group, but that of the United States, its people, and its way of life.

• • •

When it comes to the pro-life message, it would be difficult to find a more articulate voice than that of Dr. Ellis Washington. Since 1982, Dr. Washington has been a tireless defender of the most important of our unalienable rights, the right to life, and he has used his love of freedom, his deep personal sense of history, and his powers of logic and reason to deliver a strong and urgent message to the black community. That message is this: black America today finds itself in crisis mode that has resulted because of its fealty to the failed liberal/Progressive policies of one political party, the Democrats, and those "leaders" who have promoted them. His *Washington Report* essays, which can be found at www.elliswashingtonreport.com, together with his website www.elliswashington.com, are an absolute must for anyone, regardless of race or skin color, who wishes to know the real truth about the demographic nightmare that faces the black community today. Both are a desperately-needed antidote to the "victim" mentality and sense of entitlement displayed by so many black Americans today. Dr. Washington is a former Staff Editor of the *Michigan Law Review.* He has also served as a law clerk at Sixty-Plus Elder Law Clinic and the Rutherford Institute. A 1983 graduate of DePauw University, he then attended and graduated from the University of Michigan (1986), and John Marshall University Law School, as well (1994).

In addition, Dr. Washington did post-graduate studies in History and Law at Harvard GSAS, Harvard Law School, and at Michigan State University. He currently serves as an adjunct Professor at the National Paralegal College, where he teaches Constitutional Law, Legal Ethics, Administrative Law, Contracts, and Advanced Legal Research and Writing. An extremely gifted and productive writer in his own right, Dr. Washington is the author of over two dozen law review articles and seven books, the most recent of which is titled *The Progressive Revolution: Liberal Fascism Through the Ages, Volume 2,* and is "a comprehensive collection of 230 essays and Socratic dialogues." [49] A loving husband and dedicated father, he and his family currently live in Grosse Pointe Farms, Michigan.

A keen student of history, Dr. Washington has looked extensively into the activities of Margaret Sanger and eugenics movement, their connections to the murderous regime of Hitler and the Nazis, and the complicity of Sanger's organization, Planned Parenthood, in the wholesale slaughter of tens of millions of unborn black children since abortion on demand became legal in the United States in 1973. "I've been familiar with the infamous work of Margaret Sanger for about thirty years," he says, "and there are some informative websites about Sanger's genocide against blacks through the organization she founded, Planned Parenthood," for example, www.margaret sanger.blogspot.com. Another site he recommends is national-association-for- the-abortion-of-colored-people, which displays various articles from Life Site News about the NAACP's support of abortion, despite its protestations that it has 'no official position' regarding Planned Parenthood.

Yet, these articles, which go back at least as far July of 2004, clearly show that the NAACP, far from remaining neutral in the matter, actually *approves* of the practice. In fact, it approves of it so enthusiastically that it not only voted in February of that year to sanction abortion for the first time in its history, it also adopted a resolution in support of a planned pro-abortion march on April 25, an event which was co-sponsored by Planned Parenthood, NARAL, and the National Organization for Women (NOW). [50] But, despite this, the event was poorly attended, with fewer than 25% of those who were expected to come actually showing up. Now, given that a large majority of the NAACP's leaders are members of the clergy, why would these people support a group that was founded by a notorious racist who was not only a eugenicist, but was openly *hostile* to any kind of organized religion? And, why would any of them support the slaughter of more than one-third of their unborn children? For Dr. Washington, the answer is simple.

These people belong to what he calls "the cult of acceptance," a phenomenon about which he wrote in an article for *World Net Daily* on May 10, 2013. He uses the term to show that it is far easier for people to cast aside their values in favor of that which is expedient or lightly obtained. In the ministers' case, this involved the abandonment of their Biblical principles in favor of money, influence, and political power, [51] and it has caused too many of them to guide their flocks down a dead-end road, a road which has led to dependency, despair, and the deaths of tens of millions of unborn black children.

Dr. Washington has been involved in the pro-life movement "since my college days at DePauw University 30 years ago, which was the same time I became a conservative," around December of 1982. "My first published essays," he says, "were written in January and February of 1983 at www.renewamerica.com." His decision not only to become a conservative but to stand for the rights of the unborn, has not been without cost. About abortion, he says, "I only have a sister who is a typical black Democrat who believes in all of their genocidal propaganda without either questioning or critical thinking. It has really been a divide in my family," he laments, "which has fostered great resentment between her, my mother, who is also an unrepentant Democrat, and myself, so I keep my distance. Ironically," he adds, "it was my mom who, as a single mother 45 years ago, first took me to the public library, the C.J. Walker Branch on Mack and Montclair" in Detroit.. These weekly Saturday trips," he reminisces, led me to read and to fall in love with the written word." [52]

Through his online articles and essays, Dr. Washington draws numerous parallels between days of slavery and contemporary times, and finds the situation facing black America today to be remarkably similar to what it was prior to the outbreak of the Civil War, most notably when it comes to abortion. "Abortion," he says, "is the epitome of arrogance, ignorance and hatred, all rolled up into one." He points out how, under the slave masters of the 1850s, blacks were subjected to all forms of physical terror and abuse to keep them in line, and how thousands were actually killed at the hands of their masters. He also points out how, even after the slaves had gained their freedom, they were still intimidated, threatened, and even murdered by many of their former masters who now belonged to the paramilitary arm of the Democrat Party, the Ku Klux Klan.

And, it is this same Democrat Party, Dr. Washington maintains, that has been so complicit in returning black Americans to the "new plantation." But, what is so stunning to him is that so many blacks willingly place themselves in this situation without ever questioning or thinking about what they are doing. Whereas the slaves were forced into dependency in the cotton fields of the Old South, their descendants have put *themselves* into positions of depending on government for their existence. In one particular column for *World Net Daily*, titled *KKK or KKK (Kwame "Klan" Kilpatrick)?*, Dr. Washington uses a debate hosted by the Greek philosopher Socrates and attended by the Grand Dragon of the Klan and former Detroit Mayor Kwame Kilpatrick, who is now serving multiple sentences for corruption and other crimes he committed while in office, to make his point. In the debate, the mayor attempts to show how much better things are today in the black community because of its almost monolithic allegiance to a single political party for the past half-century. However, Socrates shows that blacks are worse off now than they were before the full effects of the so-called "Great Society" came into play. The Grand Dragon chimes in, as well, at one point in the discussion, pointing out that "what black leadership has done to their own people over the last forty years has surpassed even the wildest dreams of the KKK. You abort over one-third of your babies, killing them by the millions to this day," he tells the mayor. [53]

Moreover, he goes on, "The KKK killed only a few thousand black people, and that was over a one hundred-year period. Most ironic is that in election after election, you vote for a political party whose major platforms are all directly against the vested interests of your own people. At the height of our power in 1925," the Grand Dragon reminds him, "the KKK had over four million members. We proudly marched forty thousand strong down Pennsylvania Avenue in front of the White House, yet, our demonic hatred of the blacks, Jews, Catholics, and immigrants has no comparison with the pathology, despair, ignorance, and black-on-black crime affecting the state of black America today—-terrorist tactics done by their own people with big-city black mayors, the public schools, the Congressional Black Caucus, and the Democrat Party." At this point, the Grand Dragon asks rhetorically, "Yet, the *KKK* is a racist organization?" [54]

It is the craven capitulation to the cult of acceptance by the current black leadership that Dr. Washington believes rests at the heart of the black community's moral and spiritual crisis.

And, while many younger people whose parents and grandparents bought into the abortionists' agenda now consider themselves to be pro-life, he sees little hope that their elders can be reached. "There is always hope," he says of the older generations, "but as with anything, God is only so patient, although His patience with us is very long-suffering and enduring. But there is a tipping point, a time where God literally says, 'Enough!' I'm pulling back and will allow Man his evil deed and evil intent against the most helpless members of society to suffer the consequences for their deeds."

As Dr. Washington sees it, America can turn away from the path of abortion and move things back in the right direction. However, he maintains that the country is in need of a "third Great Awakening" that will jar a lethargic, apathetic Church and conservative political apparatus from their collective slumber and make them come to convince the nation that the butchering of the young in the womb can only lead to disaster and national suicide in the long run. Absent such a spiritual renewal, he says, "I don't really see how the hearts of men can ever be soft enough to hear the pitiable cries of our precious pre-born babies. Yet, I remain hopeful and prayerful that God sends in the Holy Spirit to convict the hearts and minds of Mankind to repent and save these little babies from this modern-day Holocaust."

Just as with the other pro-life heroes who have been featured in this chapter, he applauds the medical advances that have come about in recent years that clearly show how an unborn child is exactly that—-a child and not a "clump of cells" or a "non-viable" tissue mass, as the abortionists claim. Dr. Washington says, "These new technologies (ultrasounds and sonograms) are helping some young mothers considering abortion to repent and save their babies, and I'm hearing from Dr. Yuille that pro-life groups all over America, including the Knights of Columbus, are offering free X-rays to the mothers so that they can actually see that the life in their womb is NOT just a formless blob, but a living baby that God loves just as much as anyone else." But, that is not all, as he is quick to point out. Equally crucial to changing the public perception of abortion, as he sees it, are the efforts of sidewalk counselors and crisis pregnancy centers. In fact, they are very near and dear to his heart.

As a co-host on the *Joshua's Trail* radio broadcast, Dr. Washington praises sidewalk counselors and the selfless people who work at crisis pregnancy centers as those whose efforts "are recorded down to the smallest detail in Heaven," and who comprise "the last line of defense in the epic battle between the forces of evil (the Democrat Socialist Party) and the forces of good (those people who actively promote Judeo-Christian traditions in the Bible)." He believes that these efforts will be even more successful "if God pours out His grace on humanity at such a time as this." As an object lesson about what is truly at stake, Dr. Washington offers this cautionary tale of the tyrant Haman, who laid siege to the Israelites in the time of Esther: "We know how that story turned out. Haman and his ten sons were all hanged on the same scaffolds that they unjustly erected to hang every Jew in the world because Mordecai the Jew and the King refused to bow down to this egomaniac." We would do well to heed this lesson as a nation and a people. Dr. Ellis Washington fervently hopes that we will do so, because if we continue to disrespect our Creator, He who gave us life, He who reminds us that "before I formed ye in the womb, I knew ye," we will continue to risk the loss of His holy grace. And, that is not a prospect any of us should take lightly.

• • •

There are tens of thousands of pro-life heroes all across America, from people in positions of great power and influence to simple, everyday folk who fight the good fight in their own small way. However, all are driven to do what they do by a single purpose, whether it involves passing laws protecting unborn life, raising public awareness of what abortion truly involves, attending pro-life rallies, joining pro-life groups, ministering to women who are contemplating taking their unborn children's lives, or donating money to a crisis pregnancy center. That purpose is based on the firm, unshakable belief that all life is a gift from God, that unborn life is by its very nature the most defenseless and, therefore, most in need of protection, and that it is unspeakably unjust and barbaric to end such life in such a fashion as that which abortion entails. They have truly suffered much in this endeavor, from the loss of their personal freedom, ridicule, libel, and slander from their adversaries, and even the alienation of some members of their own families.

Through it all, they have persevered magnificently because they believe deeply that their cause is right and just. They know that no child, regardless of the way it which it was conceived, should ever be denied that most precious of all our rights as human beings—-the right to life. They know that no child should be denied its place in this world because it is "unwanted," unplanned," or "inconvenient." We owe each and every one of these individuals our thanks and support as they seek to put an end to the cruel, inhuman, and barbaric practice of abortion. Their cause, after all, is our cause.

For God our Heavenly Father does not consider the lives of unborn children to be any less important than those He has already brought into this world. Neither should we, and with His grace, His love, and His help, that message will one day be heard and taken to heart by the vast majority of Americans. Abortion will come to an end, once and for all. And, when it does, it will be thanks in large part to the tireless work of people such as those who have been profiled here, as well as those who are far too numerous to mention in these pages.

May God continue to look with favor on and bless the efforts of Reverend Jesse Lee Peterson and the BOND organization, Dr. Alveda King, Reverend Walter B. Hoye and Priests for Life, Reverend Johnny L. Hunter and the Life, Education and Resources Network, and Pastor Levon R. Yuille and the National Black Pro-Life Congress. And, may He bless as well Ron Edwards, Dr. Ellis Washington, Dr. Monica Miller and the Citizens for a Pro-Life Society, and all the pro-life heroes who do His work with such selflessness, passion, commitment, dedication, love, and compassion for their fellow men and women. May their great works bear fruit not only for this generation, but for all of those who follow.

The Bible speaks of those who are the "salt of the earth" and the "light of the world." Every day these individuals are shining examples of that axiom. And, with God's help, His grace, and above all else, His enduring love, all of these great Americans, and many, many more, will continue to prove that they are exactly that, the salt of the earth and the light of the world. We are, indeed, fortunate to number them among us, but far more than this, so are they who are yet to come into this world. May God bless these extraordinary individuals and keep them as they seek to make sure that entrance is a successful one.

NOTES

1. Interview with the author, January 30, 2014.
2. Ibid.
3. Interview with the author, January 30, 2014.
4. Ibid.
5. Interview with the author, January 30, 2014.
6. Interview with the author, January 30, 2014.
7. Priests for Life African-American Outreach webpage.
8. Interview with the author, February 6, 2014.
9. Interview with the author, February 6, 2014.
10. Interview with the author, February 17, 2014.
11. King, Alveda, *How Can the Dream Survive if We Murder the Children?*
12. King, Alveda, *How Can the Dream Survive if We Murder the Children?*
13. King, Alveda, *How Can the Dream Survive if We Murder the Children?* www.silentnomoreawareness.org.
14. Ibid.
15. King, Alveda, *How Can the Dream Survive if We Murder the Children?* www.silentnomoreawareness.org.
16. King, Alveda, *How Can the Dream Survive if We Murder the Children?*
17. www.issues4life.org/founder.
18. Ibid.
19. Ibid.
20. Interview with the author, February 7, 2014
21. Interview with the author, February 7, 2014.
22. Ibid.
23. Wilson, Colette, *The Persecution of Rev. Walter Hoye, Celebrate Life Magazine*, July-August 2009.
24. Ibid.
25. *Contra Costa (CA) Times*, April 8, 2009.
26. Ibid.
27. Interview with the author, February 7, 2014.
28. LEARN Mission Statement.
29. LEARN Mission Statement.
30. www.learninc.org, *What's going on with LEARN?*
31. www.learninc.org, *What's going on with LEARN?*
32. Interview with the author, February 14, 2014.
33. Interview with the author, February 14, 2014.
34. Ibid.
35. Interview with the author, February 14, 2014.
36. Interview with the author, February 14, 2014.

37. Interview with the author, February 14, 2014.
38. Interview with the author, February 14, 2014.
39. Interview with the author, February 14, 2014.
40. www.joshuastrail.org, About Pastor Yuille.
41. Ibid.
42. Interview with the author, February 8, 2014.
43. Interview with the author, February 8, 2014.
44. Interview with the author, February 8, 2014.
45. Ibid.
46. Interview with the author, February 8, 2014.
47. Ibid.
48. Smith, Rebecca, *Assault on California Power Station Raises Alarm on Potential for Terrorism. The Wall Street Journal,* February 5, 2014.
49. www.elliswashington.com, About Ellis Washington.
50. Ertelt, Steven, *NAACP Criticized for Blocking Pro-Life Efforts to Overturn Abortion Policy.* www.life news.com, July 12, 2004.
51. Washington, Ellis, *Symposium: Cult of Acceptance,* www.worldnetdaily.com, May 5, 2013.
52. Interview with the author, March 2, 2014.
53. Washington, Ellis, *KKK or KKK (Kwame "Klan" Kilpatrick), World Net Daily,* March 5, 2008.
54. Washington, Ellis, *KKK or KKK (Kwame "Klan" Kilpatrick)? World Net Daily,* March 5, 2008.

Chapter 9:

Fighting Back: Learning and Acting Upon the Lessons of the Negro Project

"All that is necessary for the triumph of evil is for good men do nothing."

—Edmund Burke

Evil: Adjective meaning 1) morally bad or wrong, wicked; 2) harmful or injurious; or 3) unlucky or disastrous; or, Noun meaning 1) wickedness or sin; or 2) anything that causes harm, pain, etc."

—*Webster's New World Compact Desk Dictionary and Style Guide*, 2nd Edition, c. 2002. p. 169

As stated in the introduction, the purpose of this volume is to "tell a story in many ways lost to American history that affects the lives of a specific racial demographic, namely Americans of black descent. It is a story of evil, a story of ugly prejudice, and one that examines the unholy alliance forged between the American eugenicist Margaret Sanger and a handful of duplicitous black Americans from all walks of life, but particularly those ministers who became unwitting dupes in one of the most monstrous plots ever conceived."

We have covered much ground in the preceding two hundred-plus pages. We have taken a look at the Negro Project, and have met a number of those who were most responsible for the havoc and destruction it unleashed, even down to the present day. We learned that black Americans, in particular, were deliberately targeted for extinction by Margaret Sanger and those who bought into her warped utopian vision of creating a race of "perfect" people through the discredited practice of eugenics, first through sterilization (which was itself enough of an abomination), and later on through the cruel and barbaric act of abortion.

And, while the failed attempt by nations and men to create such a "super" race of beings through sterilization has been largely confined to the ash-heap of history, one cannot say the same where abortion is concerned. Can anyone not, after reading what is contained herein and who refers to the definitions given above, conclude that the whole business of eugenics and abortion is, in fact, exactly that, evil? There is an old adage which states that simply because one has the ability to do something, it is not necessarily so that one *should* do it. This axiom is one that applies to all aspects of the eugenics and abortion movements.

In Chapter 2 of this work, it was stated that because of the success of geneticists like Gregor Mendel and his experiments in cross-breeding plants, and because it was feasible to successfully create hybrids of some animals, those who became involved in eugenics believed that it was possible to achieve the same results where human beings were concerned. It was also stated that people are not plants, nor are they animals. As bitter experience has shown us, the road down which Margaret Sanger, Lothrop Stoddard, Harry Laughlin, and others sought to lead us was not only a dead-end street, it very nearly resulted in the annihilation of an entire race of people in the middle of the last century.

Pick any definition. Choose any description...."morally wrong," "wicked," "harmful or injurious," "disastrous," "sin," "anything that causes pain or harm." When it comes to any and all aspects of eugenics (sterilization, either forced or voluntary, euthanasia, abortion), they all fit exactly what a reasonable person would describe as evil. Any way one views it, if one has a soul, a conscience, or even a shred of basic human decency, one cannot come to any other conclusion than that what was imposed on mankind beginning in the late nineteenth century and which continues down to the present day, is pure insanity, pure malevolence, pure inhumanity... pure *evil.*

Yet, even though we know what happened both here and in other countries as a result of the eugenic movement during that time; even though the historical record is clear, stark, and unmistakable; even though we have been warned by history not to repeat the mistakes of the past, we continue, in this day and age, to ignore the signs. We have, for example, respected leaders in this country and overseas who still buy into the notion that we can "improve" the human race and condition by actually having *fewer* people, not more.

We have academics and politicians in this country (Peter Singer and Wendy Davis) who believe that people should be able to kill their own children if their "quality of life" is such that it imposes a "hardship" based on a certain set of arbitrary criteria. We have judges who seriously believe that the simple act of giving food and water to a helpless woman who is in a permanent vegetative state (Terri Schiavo) poses some kind of a perceived "threat." And, now, we see legislative bodies in other nations that have actually voted to revive the same barbarism the Nazis imposed on their own people that was so rightly and justly condemned by the rest of the world when it finally came to light. In February of 2014, the Belgian Parliament voted 86-44 to allow parents to euthanize disabled children of all ages. [1]

What is going on here? Have we learned nothing from history? Have we become so blind to the horrors and atrocities that were conducted in the name of "human progress" in the last century that we have lost all perspective? Has life been so cheapened by the increasing secularization of society both here and around the world that it no longer has any meaning for anyone? Are hundreds of millions of deaths in pursuit of a utopian dream not enough for the culture of death that has arisen over the past few decades? If so, something is wrong here, very wrong, and we had better begin to back away from the moral abyss into which we are staring before it is too late.

As we have seen by the comments of some of America's true civil rights leaders in the previous chapter, the black demographic is in dire peril at this very moment. It finds itself in this predicament because it has, either through its own ignorance or willful blindness, bought into the eugenic program of one of the most notorious racists in the history of this nation, Margaret Sanger. As we have also seen, the evidence is in full view for all of us to examine, if only we take the time. But, as Ellis Washington has so eloquently stated, far too many black Americans either cannot or will not question this orthodoxy because they simply do not think critically about this issue. That is frightening. Even more than that, it is suicidal, and it is time to take action. It is time to *fight back*.

It is time we begin to seize the initiative and proudly stand for the sanctity of unborn human life. We must face this issue squarely and proclaim that what has been taking place for far too long is wrong, but it is more than that. What is happening before our very eyes must be referred to by its proper name—-genocide. It is time for America to experience what Dr. Washington referred to in the previous chapter as the "Third Great Awakening," an event in which this nation realizes that it is on the wrong track and begins to repent of the sin of eugenics in all its forms, including sterilization, euthanasia, and abortion. It is by no means a stretch to say that America finds itself today in the midst of a spiritual and moral crisis, a crisis that traces its roots to the warped, racist vision of a handful of individuals led by one woman, Margaret Sanger, who believed that certain members of the human race were not worthy of the same right to life that they enjoyed, simply because they thought such people "unfit," "inferior" or "a drain on society."

It is time that we reject out-of-hand the notion that a child should not be allowed to be brought into this world because it is "inconvenient," "unwanted," or would have an "inferior" quality of life. Or, because it happens to be the wrong color. Beyond reading about the disastrous results to which it led in Germany under Hitler and the Nazis, far too many Americans are unaware of the dark, terrible history of the eugenics movement in their *own country*. They are blissfully unaware of its underlying basis, the philosophy behind it, and the fact that it is even now experiencing a resurgence of sorts on some college and university campuses. Americans must be made cognizant of the fact that eugenics never really died, but has merely been dormant for several decades, awaiting the time when it would regain its former appeal.

The American people must come to realize that abortion is a key component of the whole eugenics movement. It always has been, and it always will be that way until the day comes when this nation decides that far too much innocent blood has been shed and far too many innocent lives have been extinguished in the name of "a woman's right to choose." The road, as has been stated before, will be long and arduous. Many hurdles need to be cleared. Many obstacles remain to be removed. Many roadblocks are still in our path. We have our work cut out for us, to say the least. We will be called "anti-choice" and "misogynistic" by our opponents. We will be accused of waging a "war on women" and of yearning for a return to the days when women were forced into dangerous "back alley" abortions. But, we must ask ourselves, haven't we seen enough of how things are when abortions take place on the operating tables of people like George Tiller and Kermit Gosnell, just to name a few? Just ask the survivors of these procedures how "safe" abortion was for them!

Yes, the road ahead will not be easy. It is no easy task to end something as monstrous as the wanton slaughter of tens of millions of unborn children. To any rational person the issue would be a no-brainer: unborn life is the most defenseless and, thus, needs the most protection. Abortion is wrong. Sadly, it seems that there are a lot of irrational people who must be reached, and that is the challenge. We must not only change hearts, but minds, as well. However, with God's help, we can accomplish miracles. We can realize the goal of people like Alveda King, Walter Hoye, Jesse Lee Peterson, Johnny L. Hunter, Levon R. Yuille, Ron Edwards, Ellis Washington, and so many others. And, we can do it in our lifetime. We can win this fight. So let us now examine the ways in which we can accomplish this goal.

In order to be successful, it is important that any endeavor involve a plan of action, a strategy that will persuade others to follow along. The case is no different where this issue is concerned. To win this battle, it will be necessary to develop a strategy that includes the following: 1) educating the public about the different facets of eugenics, in particular, its most visible and controversial aspect, abortion; 2) the urgent need for individual citizens to become more active in stopping this horrible scourge on our society. This is critically important where the black community is concerned, as it has been so deliberately and cynically targeted for extinction by the eugenicists of the past; 3) legislation that will protect the innocent unborn from the tender mercies of the abortionists' scalpels, surgical scissors, and suction devices, and 4) the simple act of prayer. Let us start with the first part of our strategy: education.

As we have seen from our examination of the eugenics movement in Chapter 2, the proponents of "selective breeding" used many ways to communicate their ideas to the general public. Since there were no forms of mass communication available at the dawn of the movement, the most common way in which the message was disseminated was through the printed word, such as books, magazines, journals, and periodicals. Margaret Sanger's *Birth Control Review* is a good example of spreading the eugenic message by means of the written word. Madison Grant's *The Passing of the Great Race* is another. While *Mein Kampf* is universally viewed and condemned by the vast majority of people as an obscene work of hatred directed at an entire group of people (the Jews), it is also notorious for its author's views on the eugenic issue. And, things would only get worse as new forms of communication were introduced in the early part of the twentieth century.

The motion picture was an especially useful tool for the eugenicists, who made wide use of the new medium to get their message out to greater and greater numbers of people. As we saw in Chapter 3, things took a particularly insane and deadly turn in Germany as Nazi Propaganda Minister Joseph Goebbels would use documentaries and feature films to promote and win public support for the practice of eugenics. This, we know all too well, was not confined merely to "selective breeding," but extended to euthanasia and abortion, as well. But books, magazines, periodicals, documentaries, and feature films were only a part, albeit an important one, of a much bigger picture.

As we also saw in Chapter 2, the appeal of eugenics was so seductive that it was actually promoted as a legitimate science in hundreds of college and university courses in America by the end of the 1920s. In college classrooms all over the country, this new "science" taught that it was not only possible but indeed desirable to create, if you will, a race of "new and improved" human beings who would be free of many of the defects that had plagued Mankind since he first appeared on the scene thousands of years ago (or millions, depending on one's point of view). Eugenics promised people a longer life, fewer diseases, and a better overall quality of life than had been possible before. For centuries, people could only dream of creating a utopia, or a "heaven on earth," but it had remained just that, a dream. Now, with the new "science" of eugenics, that dream was finally on the verge of realization. Defective traits and characteristics could, for the first time, be bred out of a person's genetic makeup. Healthier children could now be born, and a stronger society would be the end result.

History, of course, proved eugenics to be a pipe dream, and it is amazing that so many people of great intelligence and common sense practically fell all over themselves to embrace the new "science" without seemingly ever questioning whether or not it was a good idea or, more importantly, where it would lead if it were ever allowed to reach its logical conclusion. But, far more than that, and far worse than that, is that some people had no qualms about combining eugenics and their personal prejudices to eliminate those whom they believed were somehow not "worthy" of living, in their estimation. Thus, we have had to deal with the havoc that was wreaked by people like Margaret Sanger, Lothrop Stoddard, Madison Grant, Adolf Hitler, and Heinrich Himmler, people who believed that life was only worth living if one happened to be a member of some genetically-superior "chosen people."

As it was with eugenics in their time, so it is today with abortion, the deadliest component of the overall eugenic issue. We have been told so often for more than 40 years now that children should only be "planned" and that an "unwanted" pregnancy is one of life's greatest hardships, that we just casually accept this premise without even so much as questioning its validity. To accept this notion would mean that if all children who were not "planned" by their parents were never born, the world would have a lot fewer people around, to say the least. How many of our great leaders were "unplanned?" How many doctors, lawyers, athletes, entertainers, scientists, businessmen and women?

And, for that matter, how much of life itself is "planned?" How often do things in our daily lives go as planned? Humans are imperfect beings who have to deal with life as it comes. While it is true that we can reckon with certain factors in our lives which enable us to make educated guesses, the vast majority of us are not possessed of some kind of "second sight" or "sixth sense." We do not have a crystal ball. We cannot see the future and what it may hold for us and our offspring. To say that a child who is conceived under anything less than ideal circumstances should not be allowed to come into the world is not only arbitrary, it shows tremendous arrogance and even cruelty on the part of the parents who conceived that child.

Moreover, there are, as we know, more excuses masquerading as reasons for abortion, and they all illustrate an amazing selfishness on the part of the "pro-choice" movement that utters them. A baby is "inconvenient;" it will not have a "decent quality of life;" "it's my body and my choice;" "I made a mistake;" and on and on. While abortion in the case of rape or incest may sound compelling and even compassionate on the surface, we must ask if we are now going to assign a value to a human life based on how it is conceived. Is that not just as bad as arguing that a child should be aborted simply because it may be of the "wrong" race or ethnicity? Who in their right mind wants *that* kind of responsibility?

Remember what Margaret Sanger wrote about "human weeds" in *The Pivot of Civilization* in 1922: " reckless breeders spawning human beings who should never have been born." Recall, as well, that Madison Grant, in *The Passing of the Great Race,* called interracial marriages "a crime against nature" that should be punishable by death. And finally, bear in mind that Adolf Hitler, history's most notorious racist and one of its worse mass murderers, looked to both Sanger and Grant for inspiration, and even referred to Grant's book as his "bible."

This is why it is so important to educate people as to the true nature of the eugenics movement, in general, and abortion, in particular. The whole story is not being told, the whole truth is not getting out, and anyone who dares to question the motives of either the eugenicists of the past or the abortionists of today risks incurring the wrath of the Left and its allies in the media, the political arena, and the halls of modern academe. This wrath is often too much for most people to handle, so they remain silent on the issue and keep their true thoughts to themselves. It is far too easy to say, for example, that "I personally am against abortion, but I would not impose my beliefs on others." What does that say about us? Do we truly value innocent unborn life as we say, or do we only value it under certain circumstances?

By saying that one does not want to "impose" one's values on others, does that mean that while one personally opposes lying, cheating, stealing, and even murder, does that person then not want to "impose" those values on someone else? A normal person would in all likelihood find such a statement to be patently absurd, and for good reason. Such activities are wrong not only because they go against societal norms that have existed for many thousands of years, but they are in *direct* violation of the Word and teachings of God. Without strong sanctions against them, chaos and anarchy would reign supreme. The concepts of ordered liberty and the rule of law are essential to the proper functioning of any free society. So is a healthy respect for human life, particularly unborn human life, and it is this respect, this basic tenet of simple human decency, which must be imparted over and over again, from one generation to the next, so that we can truly remain free.

There are many ways, many means, by which the general public can be properly and fully informed about eugenics and abortion. A number of books and publications have been cited in this volume, all good sources of knowledge about this dark time, not only in the last one hundred years, but all the way up to the present day. Documentaries like *Maafa 21* are also an excellent way to get a clearer view of the eugenics movement and its most notorious component, the Negro Project. Produced in 2009, *Maafa 21* tells the story of Margaret Sanger's insane scheme to eventually exterminate the black race in America. It shows the Planned Parenthood founder as she really was—a monstrous racist who, along with her disciples, used the eugenics movement to achieve her goals. And, as Reverend Johnny L. Hunter points out, she may be dead, but her hand is reaching out from beyond the grave to "strangle the black community."

At two hours, thirty-three minutes, *Maafa 21* covers a great deal, but there is a great deal to tell. The truth is often that way. While the documentary is available through the mail, it can also be viewed online. Either way, it is well worth the time if one really wants to know the true story of not only the "patron saint" of abortion herself, Margaret Sanger, but those who aided and abetted her monstrous scheme, a scheme that remains in full effect even in our own day and age. Another way in which the public can access the truth about eugenics and abortion is through organizations like LEARN, Priests for Life, the BOND organization and the National Black Pro-Life Congress, which publishes *The 25 Historically Significant Black Experiences in America,* an invaluable resource that exposes the leftist orthodoxy about race relations in America. It is available through the NBPLC and can be obtained by calling Pastor Yuille's Bible Church at (734) 487-5678.

In addition to this, the internet holds a wealth of valuable information on the subject of eugenics. With the mere touch of a button, one can access all kinds of online articles and videos which cut through the smokescreen of propaganda and obfuscation that has surrounded the eugenics and abortion movements over the years. For example, one can log on to www.blackgenocide.org to learn more about the Negro Project. One can also go to Concerned Women for America's website to discover the extent to which abortion has so damaged the social fabric of this country for the last 40-plus years. By typing in key words on a search engine, one can also learn more about such critical aspects of this issue as the Comstock Act, Harry Laughlin's Model Eugenical Sterilization Law, or the U.S. Supreme Court's infamous ruling in *Buck vs. Bell* in 1927.

By entering Margaret Sanger's name on a search engine, one can find a vast amount of information on the woman herself from numerous articles and archival footage of interviews that she gave before her death in 1966. Her *Birth Control Review* can also be found online, complete with a month-by-month listing of the articles which it featured, including those by prominent blacks who bought into her Negro Project. Online synopses and reviews of books like *The Pivot of Civilization, The Passing of the Great Race,* and *The Rising Tide of Color Against White World Supremacy* can be viewed, as well. Though the material contained in each is disturbing, one owes it to one's self to be as completely informed about this issue as possible.

We must be sure of our facts if we are to make a credible and persuasive argument that the time has come to end the madness and restore our nation to its rightful place as a force for good. We cannot voice our indignation at the human rights abuses that occur all over the world while at the same time we turn a blind eye to what is happening to more than a million unborn children a year right here in our own country. We cannot complain about genocide in Somalia while we ignore the genocide that takes place twenty thousand times a week in the name of "choice." And, as much as we abhor the mass murder of the Armenians in World War I and the Holocaust of World War II, as much as we vow that this will never happen again, we cannot, if we are truly a moral people, sit back and do nothing about the *American* holocaust that began on January 22, 1973.

This is why we must educate ourselves about the eugenics movement and all of its components: sterilization, euthanasia, and abortion. It is also why we must impart this information to others so that they, too, have the facts they need to make an intelligent decision. And, it is obvious that we must take this route because the truth has been hidden from the American people by the mainstream media for far too long. As proof of this, one need look no further than the Gosnell case in Philadelphia and the print and electronic media's refusal to bring his activities to the public's attention. It is a damning indictment, indeed, when groups like Live Action must do the job the established media has refused to do in exposing the criminal activities of organizations like Planned Parenthood. As the old saying goes, "When you want something done right, do it yourself." If we are not getting the truth, we must seek it out for ourselves. The truth shall set you free. Knowledge is power. Let us use the knowledge and power that is found in the truth to educate our fellow citizens so that together we may set the unborn free and end the plague, the scourge, the sin of abortion, once and for all.

Once we are educated, that is, once we have the information we need, we are now ready to pursue the second part of our strategy: becoming active in the battle. This can be accomplished in two ways, either on the front lines of this fight, or behind the scenes. A good example of the first instance would be to attend a pro-life rally at the local level or, if one is able, an event like the annual March for Life which is held each January 22 on the National Mall in Washington, D.C. In fact, there is seldom a week which goes by in which some kind of rally or march is not held, either locally, statewide, or nationally. A number of pro-life organizations post these events on their websites, so keeping informed about when and where each is being held is rather easy.

Another example of getting involved on the front lines is by taking an active interest in and supporting a local crisis pregnancy center. The selfless, compassionate individuals who staff these facilities perform a badly-needed service to the community by showing young girls and women that viable alternatives exist to aborting their unborn children. But, they don't stop there. Once the baby is born, arrangements can be made to help either with adopting the child to a loving home, or, if the mother decides to keep her baby, to provide all the help she needs as a new mother. There is a crying need for volunteers to help at these facilities, but it is important to remember that a certain level of training is involved in counseling women at a crisis pregnancy center. It would, therefore, be wise first to contact a local center before proceeding any further, More importantly, since many of these places are underfunded and in need of virtually all kinds of things to help these young mothers and their children, one might also consider providing financial and material support, as well (money, baby items, maternity clothing, etc.).

A third way of getting involved on the front lines entails some risk, but the rewards of seeing a young woman change her mind and forgo abortion are so profound that mere words cannot describe them. We are talking, of course, about those who minister to young women in front of abortion clinics. These sidewalk counselors can be seen every day in big cities and small towns all over the country armed with little else than a rosary and, in some cases, a Bible. They do not engage in heavy-handed tactics when talking to those whose minds they are attempting to change, but silently pray that these women will show mercy and compassion to the children growing within them.

Sidewalk counselors are rare individuals, indeed. They literally are, as Dr. Ellis Washington observes, "the last line of defense" in the fight to preserve unborn human life. They not only risk exposure to the elements by being out in all kinds of weather, but hostility from clinic workers and some clients, and even the loss of their own personal freedom, as well, as we saw in the case of Reverend Hoye, who was arrested and jailed for wanting nothing more than to end the genocide of abortion one person at a time. They draw no pay for the work they do, and they desire none. That is not why they do what they do. All that matters is to change the mind and heart of the woman so that she will at least consider keeping her unborn child. Unfortunately, their rate of success is not very high; indeed, most of the time the woman does not change her mind or open her heart to what is being said, and the abortion takes place. They are all well aware of this and are fully prepared to deal with rejection. However, when that one woman who does listen decides to turn away from abortion and keep her child, well, that makes all the difference.

Thanks to abortion, it seems that sidewalk counselors will always have another opportunity to change a heart, to change a mind, and to save a life. However, until it ends, they will be there to try to assure that the unborn at least have half a chance to enjoy the same right to life that we all enjoy. Since no formal training exists to be a sidewalk counselor, it is important to remember that some individuals may not feel comfortable in approaching a stranger and talking to them about such a sensitive and deeply personal subject. That is why it is so necessary to show sympathy, love, and compassion for these women and their situations. We must remember that they often are completely unaware that there are viable options to killing their unborn children. Often they have been told so many times that abortion is the only means they have of dealing with their problems, that they think there simply are no other options. It is the job of the sidewalk counselors to listen to them and to point them onto the right path, the path of life. And, even though they are successful only a small fraction of the time, the work they do, the hearts and minds they change, and the lives they save give them a very special place in the eyes of God. That is what makes their efforts so necessary, so worthwhile, and so very, very, rewarding.

The third part of our strategy involves persuading our elected officials to sponsor legislation aimed at ending abortion once and for all, or at least restricting it as often as is possible. Elsewhere in these pages we examined the efforts of those courageous State representatives in Texas, Illinois, and Florida who authored various laws to protect the unborn, as well as the reactions they received from radical pro-abortion activists. We saw how in Illinois the legislature debated a state version of the federal Born Alive Infant Protection Act, and how a future President of the United States was the only state senator to oppose it. We saw how a lobbyist from Planned Parenthood endorsed infanticide when she stated her group's opposition to a similar measure in Florida. We also saw the hysterical reaction from pro-abortion members of the Texas legislature when a measure was introduced that would require an abortion clinic to have admitting privileges at a local hospital in case the procedure was not successful.

It is important to know that each measure passed with flying colors, despite the efforts of the pro-death lobby in Texas to have the law overturned. We should rightly be heartened and encouraged by these developments, because not only do they show that a convincing case can be made that life does, indeed, begin at conception, they give us hope that we can one day see the end of a practice that has tainted our reputation as the one nation that was founded on the concept that our rights, including our right to life, come from God. But probably more important, we know that there are still lawmakers and jurists who are willing to act on the courage of their convictions and stand for what is right. We can also take heart from a recent court decision in Kansas in which the U.S. Tenth Circuit Court upheld a state law banning the use of taxpayer money to fund Planned Parenthood. [2] The three-judge panel ruled 2-1 that the state was within its rights under the Constitution to withhold federal family planning funds from the nation's largest abortion provider. Who knows? Maybe there is hope for some of our judges, after all.

We can follow Kansas' example and deny funding to pro-abortion groups simply by refusing to deal with the businesses, large and small, that donate to organizations like Planned Parenthood. Many people who are horrified at the thought of killing a baby before it is born would be shocked to know that some of the companies with which they do business regularly give at least a small fraction of their revenues to the largest abortion provider in the United States. Perhaps they are too busy to look into this by themselves. Maybe they just aren't aware of this fact. And, it could be that they know all about it and simply do not care. This would be more than tragic; it would show in no uncertain terms just how many ordinary folks have become so brainwashed over the past 40 years that they cannot bring themselves to admit what is so obvious to any rational, thinking human being: that life does begin at conception, and no one has the right to play God and destroy it, despite their assertions that it is their "right" to do so.

The group Life Decisions International lists literally dozens of major corporations and charities that lend financial aid to Planned Parenthood, like Darden Restaurants (the parent company of Olive Garden and Red Lobster), the American Association of Retired Persons (AARP), the American Cancer Society, Bank of America, the Muscular Dystrophy Association, Chevron, Nationwide Insurance, Midas (the automotive service chain), and even the Girl Scouts. [3] These companies and charities are blatantly complicit in the slaughter of more than one million unborn children per year, one-third of them black, and the devastation that has occurred as a result. LDI has exposed that complicity with its Corporate Funding Project and Boycott List, which has seen 281 companies end their support of Margaret Sanger's genocidal organization to the tune of more than forty million dollars, according to Kenneth Garvey, Director of Communications for LDI.

While the LDI boycott is encouraging, we must also recognize that the legislative process is equally as important, if not more so. The job of government at every level is to secure our unalienable rights, including the right to life. It is also to protect the people, all of us. That also includes the unborn, and we must constantly remind our lawmakers of this fact. It is critical that we continue to lend support to our elected officials when they sponsor pro-life legislation. Call them, write to them, email them, visit their offices. Contribute to their campaigns at election time.

When the going gets tough and they receive threats from the pro-death cult, we must let them know that we "have their backs" and will do whatever it takes to make sure that they succeed. If our elected officials do not support the rights of the unborn, it is our job, our responsibility to support candidates who will. However, if no one will step forward, it must also be our job to step up, to step in, and to run for that office instead. Moreover, we cannot be concerned with those who call standing for the protection of unborn life a "single issue." It is not a single issue, it is the *only* issue, when all is said and done. Think about that for a moment. As Reverend Hunter reminds us, if in the end there is no right to life, nothing else matters. There is no right to free speech or press; no right to property; no right to either freedom of religion, association, or self-defense. No right to vote, no right to due process or trial by jury. In short, *no rights at all!*

This is why we must stand firm against the culture of acceptance and the culture of death, and those who write our laws must be made to understand that. More than that, they must be encouraged to *act* on it, and act decisively at every opportunity. As citizens of this great Republic, it is our duty to stay informed about the laws that are being proposed and debated in our city councils, our state houses, and our nation's capital. Unfortunately, we have not always held up our end of things as a people. We tend to let things go and are not always as involved as we need to be in the affairs of state. We sometimes fall asleep at the switch and can only look on in surprise and astonishment when something slips by us. No more. Time is too precious to waste. The lives of tens of millions yet unborn are at stake. The unborn cannot speak for themselves, and if the "pro-choice" movement has its way, their voices will never be heard.

This is why we must support legislators at every level—-local, statewide, or nationally—-who believe in and are willing to defend unborn life and the laws they write to protect that life against those who would put an end to it in the most brutal and barbaric way. And it is vitally important to remember that, since so many judges are directly elected by the voters, we must support those like-minded jurists, as well. When a candidate runs for president, it is critical to pay close attention to that person's views on the life issue because the Chief Executive is responsible for filling vacancies on the U.S. Supreme Court. Since the "Supremes" ruled in 1973 that abortion on demand is a fundamental Constitutional right, the pro-life movement has prayed fervently for the day when the High Court would revisit and ultimately overturn *Roe vs. Wade.* That day has not yet come, but that is not to say that it will never come. Do not forget that the Supreme Court once ruled that one man, Dred Scott, was the property of another, and we know what happened only a few short years hence: a bloody Civil War lasting four years, pitting state against state, father against son, brother against brother, and costing the lives of more than 600,000 Americans.

Given that, can it not be reasonably argued that the war unleashed against the unborn, who have no defense against their attackers, has been far longer, far bloodier, and has set at least as many Americans against each other as the war to end slavery? As Reverend Hunter has observed, "God can end something, but you don't want to see God end it." And, that brings us to the fourth and final element of our strategy, prayer.

Throughout history, Man's deep and abiding faith in his Creator has guided him through many dark and troubled times. It has provided him hope and given him strength to persevere and prevail against some of the most monstrous forms of oppression one can imagine. In Biblical times, Moses was able to lead his people to throw off the shackles of Pharaoh's tyranny and guide them to the gates of the Promised Land because of his firm and unshakable faith in God. So, too, David's faith in God enabled him to defeat the giant Goliath.

In more recent times, the faith of the Pilgrims led them to cross three thousand miles of open ocean and establish what would become the greatest nation in the history of the world, the United States of America. Additionally, their faith and the prayers that they offered saw them through that first harsh, brutal winter in the Plymouth colony. Our Founding Fathers believed so deeply in the existence of God that it was not by accident that they placed their "firm reliance on the protection of Divine Providence" when they undertook this nation's war of independence from Great Britain

Sometimes, faith and prayer are all a people have to see them through. Such was the case during the time of slavery in the Deep South. For nearly three hundred years, blacks in many parts of the United States were held in unspeakable bondage. We may never know, for example, exactly how many were abused, maimed, tortured, and murdered by their masters. Likewise, we may never know exactly how many female slaves were abused and raped by their overseers. Yet, in their dark time of trial and tribulation, it was the faith of so many slaves which led them to believe that a better day would eventually dawn for them, that God would hear their cries and deliver them from their plight.

For nearly 80 years during the twentieth century, tens of millions of people in Russia and Eastern Europe fell under the iron boot of communist oppression. Following the end of the Second World War, governments from Poland to East Germany, Hungary, Bulgaria, Czechoslovakia, Latvia, Lithuania, Estonia, and many others abolished religion in all its forms. Churches were closed and those who openly expressed their faith in God and prayed to Him for deliverance were arrested and placed in "re-education" camps or "psychiatric hospitals" to force them to conform to the new state religion of atheism. However, the official state bans on religious expression did not keep people from worshipping when and where they could.

Churches were closed, but *more* people were actually worshipping, albeit in secret, under the new system than they were before the communist takeover of Eastern Europe. When the Iron Curtain fell in 1989, it was due largely to the efforts of four great leaders who were also proud Christians, Pope John Paul II, Solidarity President Lech Walesa, British Prime Minister Margaret Thatcher, and Ronald Reagan, President of the United States. Thanks to their faith in and prayers to God, tens of millions of people became free for the first time in more than three-quarters of a century. Despite the denials of the secularists and the atheists who ridicule the existence of God, all of these examples show clearly and unmistakably that faith can indeed move mountains. It can soften the hearts of men, and it can literally change the face of the world.

We in the pro-life movement can take heart and learn from this truth. As our forbears sought God's help in winning and securing our unalienable rights, as they looked time and again to our Heavenly Father to protect them against evil, so, too, must we seek His guidance through the power of prayer to put an end, once and for all, to the genocide that eugenics represents. Our faith in and reliance on His love and mercy were critical in facing down our foes in time of war. Now we find ourselves in another fight with an even deadlier enemy. That enemy represents an evil that is embodied in a social movement that was spawned over a century ago and whose fiercest and most visible champion, Margaret Sanger, left a legacy of race hatred, blood, ruined lives, and the butchered, dismembered bodies of tens of millions of innocent

The lessons of Margaret Sanger's Negro Project must no longer be lost to history. We must make sure that future generations see it for what it was, a cold, calculated, brutal, and systematic attempt to eradicate an entire race of human beings based solely on the color of their skin, all the while disguised as an attempt to "help" them improve their lives. We owe it to our children and their children to tell the truth about eugenics and the evil, the misery, and the destruction it came to represent. We must make sure that they know the role that so many well-known black Americans played in this tragic episode in American history.

The Spanish philosopher George Santayana cautions us that any people that forgets its history is doomed to repeat it. After all we have seen in these pages, after all the warnings we have received from the courageous individuals who stand at the forefront in the battle against abortion and the larger issue of eugenics, after all the ruined lives, the rivers of blood, and butchered bodies of the pre-born that have resulted over the past forty years, we dare not forget any longer. Time is short, not just for our black brothers and sisters who have been so victimized, so brutalized, and so traumatized, but for all Americans. The Reverend Martin Luther King, Jr. once eloquently observed that the true measure of any society lies in how it treats the weakest and most defenseless of its people.

How right he was. Those children who are waiting to take their place on the world stage *are* the weakest, the most vulnerable, the most defenseless of us all. The act of destroying them in their mothers' wombs is a crime, not only against them, but against all of us. Just as the laws mandating sterilization of the supposedly "unfit" robbed them of any hope of bringing children into the world, the act of aborting an unborn human being is just as evil, just as appalling, and just as intolerable.

This must stop. It must stop, sooner rather than later, and with God's help, His love, and His grace, it will stop sooner. However, until that time is upon us, we who are here, at this time and place, must serve as His holy vessels, the conduit through which His will is to be done. His will is that we end this slaughter masquerading as "choice." Every life, no matter how it is conceived, is precious. All children, no matter the circumstances of their entry into this world, must be respected, cherished, valued.

We cannot play God, particularly where the lives of innocent humans who have yet to be born into this world are concerned. They are our future. God willing, many of them will become our leaders, our innovators, our teachers. They will grow up to explore all sorts of new frontiers in medicine, science, mathematics, and so many other fields of human endeavor. Or, they may simply grow into decent, hard-working, law-abiding, God-fearing citizens, the kind of people on whose shoulders great republics are built.

The eugenics movement was a utopian's dream. It offered a "scientific" remedy to all of the world's ills. Because of what it promised, people heeded its siren call. After all, who could possibly be against improving the world's genetic stock? However, the proponents of this promise of "Heaven on earth" forgot one thing: in order to have a perfect society, one must have perfect *people.* As we have seen throughout this volume, those who so loudly and vociferously trumpeted this idea were very far, indeed, from perfect.

Because so many listened to and followed the likes of Darwin, Galton, Sanger, Stoddard, Hitler, and Grant, the world became not a utopia, not a Heaven on earth, but descended into a savagery not seen in nearly two thousand years. Tragically, because so many people today listen to and follow the likes of Vogt, Erlich, Singer, and Holdren, we find ourselves once more at a precipice, a tipping point of ominous proportions. The world got a reprieve the first time, when in the aftermath of World War II the unspeakable atrocities of Hitler and the Nazis were laid bare for all to see. Eugenics fell out of favor, discredited almost completely as a legitimate scientific discipline. We got a second chance. We tried our best to make things right. We vowed, "Never again." This time around, we may not be so fortunate, for eugenics is rearing its ugly head, once again, in the twenty-first century.

We have seen it in the recent vote in the Belgian Parliament to permit the killing of unwanted children. We have seen it in the euthanasia laws in some American states. And incredibly, we see it in the twenty thousand abortions of unborn babies that take place every week all across this great land with barely a syllable of protest from the American public, save for those courageous individuals from every walk of life who stand for an end to the genocide.

When will the killing stop? When will the slaughter end? When will the blood stop flowing so needlessly? When will people awaken to the fact that entire bloodlines are being severed by this legally-sanctioned form of murder? We would never dream of doing to a pet, or to any animal for that matter, even so much as a fraction of the barbaric things we inflict on another human being in the name of "choice." Is human life that cheap? Have we become so callous and consumed with our own self-centeredness that we have lost all perspective, all reason, all compassion?

America, this is our wake-up call. It is time we abandoned the cultures of death and acceptance that eugenics in all its ugly forms, including abortion, represents. How much of a decline in the black population that is due exclusively to abortion are we prepared to tolerate? How many more lives are we prepared to see ended before they even begin? And, if we in other demographic groups think that this crisis is peculiar only to our black brothers and sisters, we are in for very rude awakening, indeed. This is *our* crisis, America. We must turn back before it is too late.

At the close of *Maafa 21*, the Reverend Johnny Hunter, after having laid out in clear, unmistakable terms just what is at stake, not only for the black community, but for all Americans, asks one simple, direct question: "Now that we know, what are we going to do about it?"

Yes, indeed, Reverend Hunter, what *are* we going to do about it?

NOTES

1. Baklinski, Peter, *Belgium Parliament Passes Law allowing Children to Be Euthanized.* From *Life Site News*, February 13, 2014.
2. Hegeman, Roxanna, *Appeals Court Rules Kansas Can Stop Funding Planned Parenthood.* The Associated Press, March 25, 2014.
3. Ertelt, Steven, *Pro-Life Group Lists Companies Backing Planned Parenthood.* From www.LifeNews.com, September 21, 2011.

Bibliography

Alinsky, Saul, *Rules for Radicals*, c. 1971

Burke, Theresa, *Forbidden Grief: The Unspoken Pain of Abortion*, c. 2000

Burleigh, Michael, *The Third Reich: A New History*, c. 2000

Coulter, Ann, *Godless: The Church of Liberalism*, c. 2006

Dorr, Gregory Michael, Ph D., *Fighting Fire with Fire: Black Americans and Hereditarian Thinking, 1900-1942*

Eakman, Beverly K., *Educating for the New World Order*, c. 1991

Erlich, Paul, *The Population Bomb*, c. 1968

Galton, Sir Francis, *Inquiries into Human Faculty and Its Development*, 1881

Golberg, Jonah, *Liberal Fascism: The Secret History of the American Left from Mussolini to the Politics of Meaning*, c. 2008

Gore, Al, *Earth in the Balance: Ecology and the Human Spirit*, c.1992, 1993

Grant, George, *Grand Illusions: The Legacy of Planned Parenthood*, c. 1992

Grant, Madison, *The Passing of the Great Race*, c. 1916

Handel, Karen, *Planned Bullyhood: The Truth about the Planned Parenthood Funding Battle with Susan G. Komen for the Cure*, c. 2012.

Hermann, *Trauma and Recovery*, c. 1992

Hitler, Adolf, *Mein Kampf*, 1925

Holdren, John C., and Erlich, Paul, *Ecoscience*, c. 1977

Jasonoff, Sheila, *Reframing Rights: Bioconstitutionalism in the Genetic Age*, c. 2011

Kessler, Ronald, *Inside the White House*, c. 1995, 1996

Last, Jonathan, *What to Expect When No One's Expecting*, c. 2013

Lifton, Robert J., *The Nazi Doctors: Medical Killing and the Psychology of Holocaust*, c. 1986

Malthus, Thomas, *An Essay on the Principle of Population,* 1798

Marshall, Robert G. and Donavan, Charles A., *Blessed Are the Barren,* c. 1991

Ray, Dixie Lee, and Guzzo, Lou, *Trashing the Planet: How Science Can Help Us Deal with Acid Rain, Depletion of the Ozone and Nuclear Waste (Among Other Things),* c. 1990

Ray, Dixie Lee, and Guzzo, Lou, *Environmental Overkill: Whatever Happened to Common Sense?* c. 1993

Sanger, Margaret, *An Autobiography,* 2nd Edition, c. 1938

Sanger, Margaret, *The Pivot of Civilization,* c.1922

Schulman, Ryan, and Schulman, Donna, *Racial Hygiene: Deaf People in Hitler's Germany.*

Sereny, Gitta, *Into That Darkness: An Examination of Conscience,* c. 1983

Shostak, Arthur, and McClouth, Gary, *Men and Abortion: Lessons, Losses and Love,* c. 1984

Stoddard, Lothrop, *Into That Darkness: Nazi Germany Today,* c. 1940

Stoddard, Lothrop, *The Rising Tide of Color Against White World Supremacy,* c. 1920

Vogt, William, *Road to Survival,* c. 1948

Zimmerman, Mary K., *Passage through Abortion,* c. 1977

CPSIA information can be obtained
at www.ICGtesting.com
Printed in the USA
BVHW042351170620
581544BV00005B/278

9 781480 918627